D0825550

Other McGraw-Hill Books of Interest

More C Tools for Scientists and Engineers

Louis Baker, Ph.D.

McGraw-Hill, Inc.

New York St. Louis San Francisco Auckland Bogotá
Caracas Hamburg Lisbon London Madrid
Mexico Milan Montreal New Delhi Paris
San Juan São Paulo Singapore
Sydney Tokyo Toronto

To Jennie

Library of Congress Cataloging-in-Publication Data

Baker, Louis.
    More C tools for scientists and engineers / Louis Baker.
      p.   cm.
    Includes bibliographical references and index.
    ISBN 0-07-003358-7
    1. C (Computer program language) 2. Algorithms. I. Title.
  QA76.73.C15B34   1991
  510'.285'5322—dc20   90-6491
                                          CIP

Copyright © 1991 by McGraw-Hill, Inc. All rights reserved. Printed in the United States of America. Except as permitted under the United States Copyright Act of 1976, no part of this publication may be reproduced or distributed in any form or by any means, or stored in a data base or retrieval system, without the prior written permission of the publisher.

1 2 3 4 5 6 7 8 9 0 DOC/DOC 9 5 4 3 2 1 0

ISBN 0-07-003358-7

The sponsoring editor for this book was Theron Shreve, the editing supervisor was Alfred J. Bernardi, and the production supervisor was Thomas G. Kowalczyk.

Printed and bound by R. R. Donnelley & Sons Company.

LIMITS OF LIABILITY AND DISCLAIMER OF WARRANTY

The author and publisher have exercised care in preparing this book and the programs contained in it. They make no representation, however, that the programs are error-free or suitable for every application to which a reader may attempt to apply them. The author and publisher make no warranty of any kind, expressed or implied, including the warranties of merchantability or fitness for a particular purpose, with regard to these programs or the documentation or theory contained in this book, all of which are provided "as is." The author and publisher shall not be liable for damages in an amount greater than the purchase price of this book, or in any event for incidental or consequential damages in connection with, or arising out of, the furnishing, performance, or use of these programs or the associated descriptions or discussions.

    Readers should test any program on their own systems and compare results with those presented in this book. They should then construct their own test programs to verify that they fully understand the requisite calling conventions and data formats for each of the programs. Then they should test the specific application thoroughly.

Subscription information to BYTE Magazine:
Call 1-800-257-9402 or write Circulation Dept.,
One Phoenix Mill Lane, Peterborough, NH 03458.

Contents

Preface

What's in It (This Book) for You

This book is intended to provide a collection of tested algorithms which may be immediately applied to real-world problems encountered by scientists (physical and social), engineers, and programmers. All codes have been tested and are supplied with "driver" programs that provide test cases to benchmark the codes on problems with known answers. The reader will easily become a user who does not have to reinvent the wheel.

This book is a response to the gratifying reception given its predecessor, *C Tools for Scientists and Engineers*. It builds on some of the results developed in that book. That book contained methods for solving linear systems, systems of stiff and nonstiff ordinary differential equations, determining eigenvalues and singular values, solving nonlinear systems and finding roots, among other things. See that book for a discussion of scientific and numerical programming in C. Here, we add a number of techniques of great interest, such as multigrid methods for partial differential equations and conjugate-gradient and block matrix methods for sparse systems.

The word "tools" in the title might wrongly suggest that only fragments of programs are provided, and that users must be experts to employ those building blocks in constructing their programming edifices. While many of the programs found here can serve with or within larger codes, many are complete programs. Others may require a minimal amount of scaffolding for specific problems.

All of the methods used are explained and documented. Users do not have to take the author's word that the method presented is valid; they will be given the information to use it intelligently and knowledgeably. Much of "computer science" is still an art. Therefore, it is desirable that readers understand what programs are doing in order to avoid any possible pitfalls. Users should not only run the test problems to convince themselves the programs are working as they should; users should also critically examine their working runs to be sure the results are reasonable.

How to Use This Book

There are a number of ways to use this book. One is to lift a program bodily, run the test case, and then apply it to the problem at hand. Most of the methods presented in this book could conceivably be used with little or no modification on common problems. I do encourage readers to read the discussion and understand the methods discussed. This will help to avoid embarrassments later. Another use for this book would be as a set of examples of working C code. Readers uncomfortable with pointer variables, for example, will see many applications of them and could learn how to use them from seeing them in action. The numerical methods used could be a useful supplement to texts on numerical analysis, and the non-numerical algorithms should be of interest to programmers. The statistical methods will be of interest to statisticians, social scientists, or students in such courses. Similarly, engineers and physical scientists, researchers, and students should all be able to find useful programs in this book.

C for Scientists and Engineers

This book is written in C for a number of reasons. This language is rapidly becoming the lingua franca of the computer world. It is on machines from microcomputers to supercomputers, PCs to Crays. It is a structured, high-level language. Algorithms written in C should be very portable, and easily converted with reasonable readiness into other high-level languages.

What This Book Contains

The algorithms are grouped by method rather than by application. The selection is intended to provide useful methods for a broad variety of disciplines. Possible applications are discussed.

Rarely is one algorithm better than all others for all cases. For this reason, alternative methods for the various cases that may appear are discussed where appropriate. While every effort has been expended to use methods that are "state-of-the-art," computer science changes at a rapid pace, and it is possible that improvements will be discovered. I would appreciate hearing from readers with improvements, corrections, better algorithms for some problems, etc.

It is my sincere hope that readers will save themselves much grief by being able to use the routines presented here with a minimum of effort. I also hope that students and others will take the opportunity to learn from the methods presented here. They are not perfect, but most derive from a long series of efforts by workers in the fields of programming and numerical analysis. Therefore, they represent the distilled effort of many people. I apologize to those workers whose contributions I fail to adequately cite, through ignorance or error. Readers of this book might justly feel that they are standing on the shoulders of many giants when they use some of the methods contained herein; they will almost certainly "see" further by doing so than by relying on only their own legs.

Acknowledgments

I'd like to thank many colleagues for help, especially B. S. Newberger for contributing FORTRAN programs they had written, and A. Giancola for much critical advice. K. McGuire drafted the figures. The book was typeset with Ventura publisher (excluding program listings), the figures scanned with a Princeton LS-300, and camera-ready copy was produced with a PS Jet +.

A Word to the Wise

While every effort has been made to test and ensure the correctness of the methods presented here, final responsibility rests with the user for assuring their results are correct. The programs presented here are without warranty, and no liability shall be incurred by the author or the publisher for any loss or damage caused directly or indirectly by the programs or algorithms described in this book. Please read the full disclaimer which precedes this Preface and please check all programs and results carefully. In addition to running the test problems contained in this book, generate your own to confirm that you fully understand the calling conventions and data formats. To paraphrase John Philpot Curran, the condition upon which freedom from errors depends is eternal vigilance.

Louis Baker

ABOUT THE SOURCE CODE

The source code for the programs contained herein is available on an IBM-PC-compatible double-sided diskette by mail order. Send $14.95 (New Mexico residents add applicable gross receipts tax, 5.5%) to:

Dagonet Software
2904 La Veta Dr. N.E.
Albuquerque, NM 87110

Write for information on other disk formats.

ABOUT THE AUTHOR

Louis Baker, Ph.D., is a senior researcher at Mission
Research Corporation in Albuquerque, New Mexico. Prior
to this, he held positions at Sandia National Laboratories
and the Naval Research Laboratory in Washington, D.C.
Dr. Baker has written numerous articles on
electromagnetic field propagation, computer interfacing,
artificial intelligence, and computer simulation.

Chapter 1

Sparse Systems: The Conjugate Gradient Method

Chapter Objectives

In this chapter we will present tools to:

– solve the linear system $\mathbf{Ax} = \mathbf{b}$ where $\mathbf{A}$ is a symmetric, positive-definite (SPD) matrix (the SPD matrix will be defined below)

– solve the linear system $\mathbf{Ax} = \mathbf{b}$ where $\mathbf{A}$ is a general matrix

The method used to solve the linear systems will be the method of conjugate gradients, which is particularly suited to solving sparse linear systems. Its application to optimization problems will also be discussed.

Introduction

The conjugate gradient method is an interative method, i.e., one which is repeated to generate succesively better approximate solutions to a problem. This chapter will develop the theory of "preconditioning" and "operator splitting" methods to accelerate the convergence of each iteration to the desired answer. Such methods have broad applicability beyond the congugate gradient method, and we will encounter them again in Chapter 3.

The Conjugate Gradient Method

The method of conjugate gradients, which will be discussed here, is not merely a potent method for solving linear systems in general and sparse linear systems in particular. It is actually a powerful family of methods that has applications to diverse branches of numerical analysis, including non-linear optimization problems and the solution of partial differential equations. These theoretical ideas will have a much broader applicability than the conjugate gradient method.

Sparse Systems

A sparse system is a linear system $\mathbf{Ax} = \mathbf{b}$ in which many, if not most, of the entries in the $\mathbf{A}$ matrix are zero. Banded matrices, which have the principal diagonal and its neighbors nonzero, e.g. the tridiagonal matrix:

$$\begin{pmatrix} a_{11}\, a_{12}\, 0 & 0 & 0 \\ a_{21}\, a_{22}\, a_{23} & 0 & 0 \\ \cdot \quad \cdot \quad \cdot & \cdots & \cdot \\ 0 \quad 0 \quad a_{n,n-2} & a_{n,n-1}\, a_{nn} \end{pmatrix}$$

are a common case of sparse matrices. There are special programs in the LINPACK collection for solving sytems with such matrices. Often, when solving the systems that arise out of finite-difference or finite-element representations, the matrices that arise are sparse but the sparsity pattern is not so simple. This is particularly true if the computational domain is not a simple rectangle but is a more complex region in the space of the independent variables. The computational domain will still be a "logical" rectangle in polar coordinates, for example, if the compuational domain is a sector of a circle in physical space.

The difficultly with applying the $\mathbf{LU}$ factorization or similar methods to such problems is that they do not generally maintain sparsity. The $\mathbf{L}$ and $\mathbf{U}$ factors of a banded matrix generally retain the banded pattern of the matrix they are the factors of, but the inverses of $\mathbf{L}$, $\mathbf{U}$ and hence $\mathbf{A}$ tend to be full, and this will cost us both in storage and in computing time. For this reason, special methods that preserve the sparsity of the problem are of great value. The conjugate gradient method does not modify the matrix $\mathbf{A}$ in the course of finding a solution. For large problems, only rows or columns of $\mathbf{A}$ or auxilliary vectors of length N need be "in core" at one time, with the remainder of the $\mathbf{A}$ matrix in auxilliary storage. Because $\mathbf{A}$ need not be modified, and intermediate results are a few vectors of length N rather than matrices of size N^2 , the conjugate gradient method is quite attractive for the solution of large, sparse linear systems.

Heuristic Derivation Of The Method

The following discussion will omit a few of the algebraic details necessary for a rigorous derivation of the method, but will instead be an heuristic derivation. We hope this will make the derivation more readable. Our aim is to make the basis of the method understandable. Rigorous proofs of the claims made here may be found in many books, including those by Scales,

Axelsson and Barker, and Golub and van Loan. Our discussion is a synthesis of the derivations to be found in these books.

Minimizing a quadratic form. Positive-Definite Matrices

The conjugate gradient method arose as a means for mininimizing the quadratic function of a vector x:

$$f = x^\wedge H x / 2 - x^\wedge b + c$$

where the matrix H is positive definite. A matrix is positive-definite if the (scalar) value $x^\wedge Hx$ is greater than zero for any vector x (unless of course x is the zero vector). The matrix H cannot be asymmetric, for example, but merely being a symmetric matrix is not sufficient. This seems like a very restrictive condition, and indeed it is, but we will show how it may be circumvented later. For the moment, accept that many problems of interest give rise to such matrices. For example, many variational developments of finite element methods, and finite difference methods involving Laplacians or biharmonic operators, give rise to such matrices. The solution to the linear system $Hx - b = 0$, i.e., $x = H^{-1} b$, may be found by minimizing the quadratic form given above. Therefore, we can solve linear systems by treating the minimization problem given above.

Because H is positive-definite, the contours of the values for the function f in any two-dimensional subspace are ellipses (the scalar c merely shifts the minimum value achieved, and the vector b merely shifts the center of the ellipse). The problem is to determine the center of the ellipse. Because we can be assured that it is a hyper-ellipse, we will have a true minimum and not a saddle point (as a hyperboloid of one sheet would give). Furthermore, you will recall, (I hope) from some discusssion in a mechanics class, that quadratic forms can be diagonalized, i.e. the axes rotated, so as to point along the principal axes of the ellipses. If you don't recall any of this, briefly refer to Chapter 4 of *C Tools*, for example, where this problem is discussed ("principal axes" are eigenvectors, for example). The transformed matrix is now diagonal, and the eigenvalues give the values assumed by each of the diagonal elements. The reciprical square roots of the eigenvalues give the lengths of the principal axes of the ellipse. Thus, if the quadratic form happens to be an n-dimensional hypersphere, each 2-d projection through the center is a circle of the same radius, and all the eigenvalues are the same. For a general hyper-ellipsoid, the ratio of the maximum and minimum eigenvalues gives a measure of how distorted or aspherical the matrix is, and is called the spectral condition number of the matrix H. If it is large, i. e. if the level surfaces are very elongated and nonspherical, the minimization problem can be difficult for some algorithms if the initial guess is unfortunate. We will illustrate this below.

Derivation Of The Method

Error Residuals

Consider the vector $r = Hx - b$. We have called it r because it is the error residual, as seen from the linear system whose solution is the same as that of the minimization problem. If x were the solution to either problem, r would be zero. The vector r can be given another interpretation, however. It is the gradient vector at the point x, as may be seen by differentiating the functional f with respect to the vector x. When we have reached a minimum, the gradient is zero, so these interpretations are consistent.

To minimize f, given an initial guess the vector x_0, we will consider an iteration of the form $x_{k+1} = x_k + t_k d_k$, where t_k is a scalar and d_k a vector search direction. The subscript keeps track of the iteration number. For the inital step, since r is the vector giving the direction in which f is most rapidly increasing, it makes sense to try minimizing f by going in the opposite direction: $d_0 = - r_0$. We still need to figure out the step size t_k and the subsequent search directions.

Exact Line Search

The step size may be determined by the requirement that we minimize $f(x_{k+1})$ for the chosen search direction d_k. (This method of determining t_k is called exact linear search in Scales' book). We can find that $f(x_{k+1})$ is

$$(x_k{}^\wedge Hx_k + t_k{}^2 d_k{}^\wedge Hd_k) / 2$$

$$+ t_k d_k{}^\wedge Hx_k - b^\wedge x_k - t_k b^\wedge d_k + c$$

In the above, we have exploited the symmetry of the dot product operation to rewrite $b_k{}^\wedge d_k$ as $d_k{}^\wedge b_k$ as well as the symmetry of H. To minimize, set the derivative with respect to tk equal to zero,

$$t_k d_k{}^\wedge Hd_k + d_k{}^\wedge Hx_k - b_k{}^\wedge d_k = 0$$

giving:

$$t_k = - d_k{}^\wedge (Hx_k - b)/(d_k{}^\wedge H_k)$$

We notice this can be rewritten as

$$t_k = - d_k r_k/(d_k{}^\wedge Hd_k)$$

Because **H** is positive-definite, the denominator will not vanish unless **d** is the zero vector. This can be shown not to occur unless the residual vector **r** vanishes, in which case we have found our optimum and need not continue.

Conjugacy and Exact Termination

We now have to determine our search directions d_k. A set of vectors **d** is termed mutually conjugate to the (positive-definite) matrix **H** if and only if

$$d_i{}^\wedge H d_j \ = \ 0$$

for all i and j unless i = j. We will choose our search directions to fulfill this criterion. Each search direction **d** will be conjugate with respect to **H** to all the previous **d**. This choice is motivated by the fact that, under this condition, the search directions will form a complete set that spans the space being searched. That is, they are linearly independent. If they were dependent, we could form a linear combination:

$$\sum_i c_i{}^\wedge d_i = 0$$

in which case, multiplying by **H** and then taking the dot product with $d_k{}^\wedge$:

$$\sum_i c_i d_i{}^\wedge H d_i = 0$$

By the conjugacy property, all terms except i = k vanish, and we have $d_k{}^\wedge H d_k = 0$, which contradicts the positive-definiteness of **H**. This linear independence means that any point, and in particular, the desired solution point x, in the n dimensional hyperspace must be reachable, i.e., in the span, of n search directions. From this it may be shown that, using the "exact linear search" procedure of the form shown above, we will in fact get to the desired solution point in at most n choices of search directions, i.e., after n iterations of the method. (This statement is strictly true only with exact arithmetic, and must be modified due to the presence of round-off errors). This is because with exact linear search, when $x_{k+1} = x_k + t_k d_k$, the gradient vector r_{k+1} at the point x_{k+1} will, by the condition whereby t_k was determined, be orthogonal to d_k. We can then show (see any of the references cited, although notation will vary somewhat among all of them and in this book as well), that $d_i{}^\wedge r_n = 0$ for all the n d_i. This can only happen if $r_n = 0$, as the d_i span the n-dimensional problem space.

The great value of this (theortical) finite termination is that simpler methods do not necessarily converge to the exact solution in a finite number of iterations, even with exact arithmetic. For example, if we set all the search directions $d_i = -r_i$ we have the search method called "steepest descent." Figure 1 shows what may happen when such a method is used on a matrix with a moderate-to-large spectral condition number. The search directions oscillate in sign and get smaller in magnitude, but they tend to remain approximately parallel. This, of course, gets worse as the spectral condition number increases. We have an "exact linear search" method, but

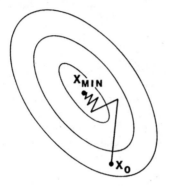

Figure 1.1. Steepest Descent Iteration Path

because the search directions lack the conjugacy property, they lact the finite termination property as well. The conjugacy condition in effect forces the searches to avoid wasting time cycling back and forth in approximately parallel directions, as can happen in the steepest descent method (see Fig. 1.1).

How do we determine the d_i so as to fulfill the conjugacy property? We will assume that, after $d_0 = -r_0$, we have in general $d_i = -r_i + s_i d_{i-1}$ where s_i is a scalar. It may be shown that, with proper choice of this scalar, the search direction d_i may be made conjugate to all previous d_i. By mathematical induction, we will then build up a set of d[i] all mutually conjugate. Hestenes and Stiefel found in 1952 that s_i could be found without exoribitant computational effort, and was given by:

$$s_i = (r_i - r_{i-1})^\wedge r_i / (r_i - r_{i-1})^\wedge d_{i-1}$$

Other workers found alternative expressions, such as:

$$(r_i - r_{i-1})^\wedge r_i / r_{i-1}^\wedge r_i$$

or

$$r_i^\wedge r_i / (r_{i-1}^\wedge r_{i-1})$$

which give equivalent results for s_i (with exact arithmetic). They may vary in computational and storage requirements, or when finite-precision arithmetic is used, or when the conjugate gradient method is applied to solve a problem other than minimizing a positive-definite quadratic form, which it sometimes is.

Roundoff error, i.e., finite precision arithmetic, creates problems because the conjugacy condition is no longer exactly fulfilled. Attempting to enforce it by something like a Graham-Schmidt orthogonalization process (see Chapter 4 of *C Tools* on eigenvalue problems) would be very costly. For this reason, the conjugate gradient method is not considered a direct method, i.e., one that reaches the "exact" (to computer precision) answer, but, rather an iterative method. Shortly after the introduction of the method in 1952 by its discoverers, the method fell into limbo when this problem was realized. It was resurrected in 1971 by Reid when he realized that, viewing it as an iterative method, the roundoff problems do NOT cause the solution to become garbage, but merely delay convergence. Therefore, one could still get a very acceptable approximate answer to a problem after a reasonable number of iterations. If the accuracy were sufficient for the application, the computational savings compared to a direct method could be considerable, depending upon the matrix. Reid showed how the method could be used with great advantage on sparse problems.

General Matrices

Let us turn to the general case, where the matrix of the linear system we want to solve is not symmetric positive-definite, e.g., $\mathbf{Ax} = \mathbf{b}$. Formally, all we need do is multiply through by the transpose of $\mathbf{A}$: $\mathbf{Hx} = \mathbf{b}'$, where $\mathbf{H} = \mathbf{A^\wedge A}$ and $\mathbf{b}' = \mathbf{A^\wedge b}$. It is easy to show that the matrix H formed as shown is positive-definite.

There are two difficulties with this procedure. The first is that, for general matrices, computing $\mathbf{H}$ is prohibitively expensive, requiring order N^3 operations; $\mathbf{LU}$ decomposition will require only a third of this for a full general matrix and produce an "exact" solution. For sparse systems, it is also undesirable to compute $\mathbf{H}$, as this $\mathbf{H}$ may be less sparse than the original matrix $\mathbf{A}$. The solution is not to compute $\mathbf{H}$ at all. In the conjugate gradient algorithm, whenever a vector v is multipled by $\mathbf{H}$, we simply multiply by $\mathbf{A}$ and then by $\mathbf{A^\wedge}$. Each of these matrix times vector operations requires order N^2 operations for a full matrix, which is quite affordable.

The second problem is that the condition number of the matrix $\mathbf{H}$ (see Chapter 3 of *C Tools*) is the square of the condition number of the matrix

A. Thus, if the matrix **A** is ill-conditioned, then the matrix **H** is extremely ill-conditioned. The rejoiner to this valid complaint is that the conjugate gradient method generally does very well on ill-conditioned problems. If the problem is badly conditioned, then you may expect trouble however you propose to solve it and should look carefully at the results whatever method is used.

How well does the conjugate gradient method perform and how many iterations are needed? This of course depends on the initial guess in general as well as the nature of the **H** matrix. If the spectral condition number of the matrix is K, then the number of iterations required for the conjugate gradient method to achieve a specified accuracy is of the order of the square root of K (for large K). This compares very favorably to that of the steepest desent method, which has a requirement for order of K iterations. This is obviously much more costly for large K. The steepest descent method dates from about 1847 and is attributed to Cauchy in the book by Dahlquist, Bjork and Anderson. Cauchy should not feel badly about his method being superceded over a century later!

We present two versions of the conjugate gradient method in the attached codes. One treats the symmetric positive-definite matrix case, and the other the general matrix case. You will see that the latter is quite similar to the former, except for some multiplications by the transpose of the matrix. We have not explicitly included provisions for sparse matrices, as these vary widely depending upon the nature of the sparsity. Is it random, banded, block, or some special pattern?

Preconditioning, Splitting, Accelerating

Suppose we are solving the problem **Ax** = **b**. If we multiply by another matrix **B**, we have **BAx** = **Bb** or **Cx** = **c** where **C** = **BA** and **c** = **Bb**. If there is nothing pathalogical about **B** (if it does not have a zero determinant), then the system **Cx** = **c** will have the same solutions as the original system. However, the eigenvalues of **C** will not be the same as those of **A**. Consider one choice we already know about. If **B** = **A^**, then each eigenvalue will be squared, and the spectral condition number will obviously also be squared. This of course is quite undesirable. It is clear we want the opposite effect. If **B** were the inverse of **A**, then **C** would be the identity matrix **I**, all the eigenvalues would be the same, namely one, the spectral condition number would also be one, and we would have instant convergence. Of course, if we knew the inverse of **A** exactly, we wouldn't need to solve the problem with the conjugate gradient (or any other) method. However, it is often possible to get an approximation to the inverse of **A**, which might be insufficiently good to give us the answer by itself but would be appropriate for a preconditioning matrix.

One of the most popular methods employing this device, which is known as "preconditioning," is called the ICCG, for Incomplete Cholesky Conjugate Gradient Method. The basic idea is to develop the Cholesky or LL^ factorization of the symmetric sparse matrix **A** (recall for symmetric matrices the **U** of the **LU** decomposition is the transpose of **L**, namely L^), however neglecting any "fill" elements in **L** or the inverse of **L** – we only compute those elements for which the **A** matrix elements are nonzero. This gives rise to the word "incomplete" in the IC of ICCG. Clearly, such an incomplete determination of **L** would not give us an accurate inverse of **A**. It would give a good basis for preconditioning, however. The ICCG is applicable to symmetric matrices whose properties (eigenvalue distributions) are not known a priori.

For many **A** matricies which arise from the application of finite-difference schemes to problems, **B** matrices may be found that reduce the range of eigenvalues and hence the spectral condition number, giving much improved convergence. Such schemes usually produce symmetric positive-definite matrices **A**. Once **B** is determined, the cost of preconditioning is an additional matrix times vector multiplication each iteration. This is generally preferable to forming the product **BA**, which may be less sparse and which requires order n^3 operations for full matrices, more than solving the system by **LU** decomposition. Preconditioning may be vital to make the computational workload managable. This preconditioning is related to the so-called acceleration procedures that have been developed for many iterative schemes for solving the linear systems that arise from finite-difference approximations to elliptic partial differential equations.

Assume we have an approximate, incomplete factorization of the matrix **A** as **LU**. We can define the residual matrix **R** = **A** − **LU**. If the matrix **A** is "well behaved," **R** will in some sense be small and **LU** will be a good approximation to **A**. For example, if **A** is "diagonally dominant" (meaning roughly that the diagnonal elements are large compared to the off-diagonal elements), this will be the case. Letting **M** = **LU**, the equation **Ax** = **b** which we wish to solve becomes, since **A** = **M** + **R**, **Mx** = **b** — **Rx**. We have a number of options at this point. We can now regard this equation as an iterative method. If the k th iterate of the solution vector **x** is denoted x_k as above, we can solve $Mx_{k+1} = Rx_k + b$ for x_{k+1}, since **M** is factored into **LU** and the solution for x_{k+1} is relatively inexpensive. Alternatively, we could use a conjugate gradient iteration with **C** = **M** as the preconditioning matrix. Again, it is easy to invert **C** as it is already factored. (see Chapter 3 of *C Tools*, specifically subroutine invm().)

Other acceleration methods rely on the "splitting" of the A matrix, as it is called, into M and R matrices as shown, where M is easily invertible (e.g., M is tridiagonal) or gives rise to a system as above which is easily solved, and iteration is used as mentioned in the previous paragraph. Refer to Axelsson and Barker, Hageman and Young, or Birkhoff and Lynch. Table 1.1 lists some of the common or "classical" operator splittings used.

TABLE 1.1

Typical Splittings of A= M+ R

$A = L + D + U$ by definition. D is diagonal, L and U are the upper and lower triangular. If A is symmetric, as required by the SSOR method, U is the transpose of L.

METHOD	M	R
Jacobi	D	$L + U$
Gauss-Seidel	$D + L$	U
SOR	$(1/w)D + L$	$U + (1 - 1/w)D$
SSOR	$M = 1/(2-w)(D/w+L)(D/w)^{-1}(D/w+U)$	

$$R = 1/(2 - w)(D/w + L)(D/w)^{-1}[(1/w - 1)D - L](D/w + L)^{-1}$$
$$[(1 - 1/w)D - U]$$

In the Succesive Over-Relaxation (SOR) and Symmetric SOR (SSOR), w is the "acceleration" parameter, and should be between 0 and 1 for SOR and between 0 and 2 for SSOR.

Sparse Matrix Storage

There are many ways to store and manipulate sparse matrices. The tradeoffs involve overhead vs. efficiency. Dahlquist, Bjorck, and Anderson discuss possible methods as do Pissanetsky and Wait in their books. Linked lists can be constructed for rows, or columns, or both (see Horowitz and Sani).

"Skyline" storage is perhaps more efficient in storage usage. The diagonal elements are stored, the upper triangle is stored by column starting with the highest nonzero element in any column, and the lower triangle is stored by row in a similar fashion (starting with the leftmost element). The books by Dhatt and Touzot and Pissanetsky discuss skyline storage. The former book has FORTRAN routines which use the method.

Bandwidth Reduction

By rearranging the rows and columns one may achieve a more compact sparse matrix. This is called bandwidth reduction. If the equations come from a set of finite-difference equations on some mesh, this amounts to re-sequencing the mesh points. Various heuristic methods which produce improvements but do not guarantee to be optimal exist. The "reverese Cuthill-McKee" method is the most popular. This method is discussed in Dahlquist et al. and the other books cited above.

C Program Tools: The Conjugate Gradient Method

Two sample programs are given. Program cgs() performs the CG iteration for positive-definite matrices (which must be symmetric). A rank two test problem is employed, so it should take two iterations to achieve an exact solution (neglecting roundoff effects). The "exact" result, determined by Cramer's rule, is printed first. Intermediate result vectors are illustrated and then the final answer is given.

The subroutine cg() is for general matrices, and has calls to subroutine mvt() to multiply vectors by the transpose of the **A** matrix. It is tested on two problems—the symmetric problem, which was used to test subroutine cgs(), and an asymmetric matrix.

A library of programs to manipulate vectors, VECTOR.C, is used by the routines cg() and cgs(). The routines in this library have application to a variety of problems involving vectors and matrices, as will be seen in the following chapters. One routine, pv(), is the analog for vectors of printm() in Chapter 2, and is designed to print a vector in a convenient, readable form. Other routines perform basic vector operations. They are contained in *C Tools*.

For use on actual (e.g., sparse) problems, the routines cg() and cgs() and those in the vector package would have to be modified somewhat. First, the diagnostic calls to the print routine pv() would have to be removed to prevent a flood of output. The vector and matrix processing routines would have to be modified from the "full" storage model to an appropriate sparse model.

TABLE 1.2

Programs Of Chapter 1

Name	*Purpose*
cg	performs conjugate gradient iteration on general matrix problem **Ax=b**
cgs	performs conjugate gradient iteration for **Ax=b** where A is a symmetric, positive-definite matrix

---

References

The Conjugate Gradient method should be viewed as a family of methods, that has branched off in many directions beside solving linear systems. The original paper by M. R. Hestenes and E. Stiefel (*J. Res. Nat. Bur. Stand.* **49**,409,1952) was actually a development of earlier work on conjugate direction methods by L. Fox, H. D. Huskey, and J. H. Wilkinson (*Quart. J. Mech. Applied Math.***1**, 149, 1948). It is related to work by C. Lanczos on iterative solutions of equations and eigenvalue determination(*J. Res. Nat. Bur. Stand.* **49**,33 (1952). As mentioned above, it was in disfavor due to roundoff destroying the conjugacy property, until J. K. Reid ("On the method of conjugate gradients for the solution of large sparse systems of linear equations," in *Proceedings of the Conference on Large Sparse Systems of Linear Equations*, New York: Academic Press, 1971) pointed out that such problems merely delay convergence, and that viewed as an iterative method, it had attractive features for sparse systems.

D. S. Kershaw (*J. Comp. Phys.* **26**,43,1978) popularized the ICCG method. Preconditioning is important in producing a method which converges rapidly enough to be competative with other schemes for the common equations of mathematical physics. The use of the conjugate gradient method in electromagnetic problems has a strong advocate in T. Sarkar- see *IEEE Trans. Antennas and Propagation,* **AP**- **23**,398 (1984) and an earlier review and comparison with other methods in the same journal, **AP**-**29**,847,1981. There is much discussion of preconditioning methods in the literature, in the references cited below and in C. P. Jackson and P. C. Robinson, *International J. Numerical Methods Engineering*, **21**,1315 (1985). These methods are suited to parallel processing; see, e.g., L. M. Adams and E. G. Ong, in *Parallel Computations and Their Impact on Mechanics*, (ed: A. K. Noor) (New York: Am. Soc. Mechanical Engineers, 1988), p. 171.

References Cited in Text:

O. Axelsson and V. A. Barker, *Finite Element Solution of Boundary Value Problems* (New York: Academic Press, 1984).

G. Birkhoff and R. Lynch, *Numerical Solution of Elliptic Problems* (Philadelphia, PA: SIAM, 1984).

G. Dahlquist, A. Bjorck, N. Anderson, *Numerical Methods* (Englewood Cliffs, New Jersey: Prentice Hall, 1974).

G. Dhatt and G. Touzot, *The Finite Element Method Displayed* (New York: Wiley Interscience, 1984).

L. A. Hageman and D. M. Young, *Applied Iterative Methods* (New York: Academic Press, 1981).

E. Horowitz and S. Sahni, *Fundamentals of Data Structures* (Rockville, MD: Computer Science Press, 1983).

S. Pissanetsky, *Sparse Matrix Technology* (New York: Academic Press, 1984).

L. E. Scales, *Introduction to Non-Linear Optimization* (New York: Springer-Verlag, 1985).

R. Wait, *Numerical Solution of Algebraic Equations* (New York: J. Wiley, 1979).

Program Listing And Test Problem Output

(Listing begins next page.)

```
/* conjugate gradient solver for symmetric positive definite
systems

from Handbook of C tools for Scientists and Engineers by L. Baker


int cgs() returns integer count of iterations used.

main() is test driver for spd system.  As system is of second order,
    two iterations should produce "exact" answer (neglecting
    roundoff).

DEPENDENCIES:
   requires routines in vector.c
*/

#include <ftoc.h>

int cgs(a,x,y,r,p,ar,ap,n,m,xold)
int n,m;
float a[],x[],y[],r[],p[],ar[],ap[],xold[];
{
    float gamma,rnew,alpha,beta,rlen;
    float resid;
    double dot();
    int i,k; int j;
    vset(x,0.,n);
    vcopy(y,r,n);
    vcopy (x,xold,n);
    beta=0.;
    vcopy(r,p,n);
    pv(x,n);
    pv(r,n);
    pv(p,n);
    k=n<<1;
    DOFOR(i,k)
    {
        /* ith iteration*/
```

```
      mv(a,p,ap,n,n);
/*   pv(ap,n);*/
      alpha=dot(p,ap,n);
      rlen=dot(r,r,n);
      if(alpha==0. || rlen==0.) return(i);
      alpha=rlen/alpha;

      /*update*/
      vv(x,x,p,alpha,n);
      gamma=-alpha;
      vv(r,r,ap,gamma,n);
      rnew=dot(r,r,n);
      beta=rnew/rlen;
      if(beta==0.)return(-i);
      vv(p,r,p,beta,n);
/*   pv(p,n);  */

   for(j=0,resid=0.;j<n;j++)
      {resid+=(x[j]-xold[j])*(x[j]-xold[j]);}
printf(" at %d iteration x=%e\n",i,resid);
   if( resid<1.e-5)break;
   vcopy(x,xold,n);
/*   pv(x,n);*/
   }
   return(n);
}

main(argc,argv)
int argc; char **argv;
{
   float a[20],p[20],x[20],r[20],y[20],ar[20],ap[20],work[800];
   int n,m,cgs(),iter,isym,k;
   float d,x1,x2;
   isym=0;
   /* try bigger system to see if still works? */

   n=m=2;
   y[0]=0.;y[1]=1.;
```

```
    a[0]=1.;a[3]=4.;a[2]=.5-isym;a[1]=.5;
    x[0]=1.;x[1]=1.;
    d=1./(a[0]*a[3]-a[1]*a[2]);
    k=n;
    x1= d*(y[0]*a[3]-y[1]*a[1]);
    x2= d*(y[1]*a[0]-y[0]*a[2]);
    printf(" x1= %f x2=%f\n",x1,x2);
/*  n=m=20;
    for(iter=0;iter<n;iter++)
    {y[iter]=1.;
    for (isym=0;isym<iter;isym++)
      a[iter+n*isym]=a[isym+n*iter]=.2;
    a[iter+n*iter]=2.;
    }      */
    iter=cgs(a,x,y,r,p,ar,ap,n,m,work);
    printf(" iterations=%d\n",iter);
    pv(x,n);
    exit(0);
}
```

```
x1= -0.133333 x2=0.266667
printing vector from 0 to 1
0.00000e+00 0.00000e+00
printing vector from 0 to 1
0.00000e+00 1.00000e+00
printing vector from 0 to 1
0.00000e+00 1.00000e+00
at 0 iteration x=6.25000e-02
at 1 iteration x=1.80556e-02
at 2 iteration x=0.00000e+00
iterations=2
printing vector from 0 to 1
-1.33333e-01 2.66667e-01
```

```
/* conjugate gradient solver for general matrices

from More C tools for Scientists and Engineers by L. Baker


cg() returns integer count of iterations used. see text for details

main() test driver. tests solver on both symmetric positive definite
    and asymmetric system. As system is or rank 2, exact answer
    should be obtained after two iterations, neglecting roundoff.

DEPENDENCIES:
    requires programs in vector.c

*/


#include <ftoc.h>
#define tol 1.e-10

int cg(a,x,y,r,p,ar,ap,n,m,xold)
int n,m;
float a[],x[],y[],r[],p[],ar[],ap[],xold[];
{
float gamma,rnew,alpha,beta,rlen,change;
double dot();
int i,j,k;
vset(x,0.,n);
vcopy(x,xold,n);
/*vcopy(y,r,n);*/
mvt(a,y,r,n,n);/* set r to a[t]*y, not y*/
beta=0.;
vcopy(r,p,n);
pv(x,n);
pv(r,n);
pv(p,n);
k=n<<1;printf(" max iterations allowed %d\n",k);
DOFOR(i,k)
```

```
{
/* ith iteration*/
/* for symm case, was mv(a,p,ap,n,n) only*/
   mv(a,p,ar,n,n);
   pv(ar,n);
   mvt(a,ar,ap,n,n);/*new*/
alpha=dot(p,ap,n);
rlen=dot(r,r,n);
if(alpha==0. || rlen==0.) return(i);
alpha=rlen/alpha;

/*update*/
vv(x,x,p,alpha,n);
gamma=-alpha;
vv(r,r,ap,gamma,n);
rnew=dot(r,r,n);
beta=rnew/rlen;
if(beta==0.)return(-i);
vv(p,r,p,beta,n);
change=0.;
for(j=0;j<n;j++)change+=(x[j]-xold[j])*(x[j]-xold[j]);
printf(" change in x %e\n",change);
if(change<tol)return i;
vcopy(x,xold,n);
pv(p,n);
pv(x,n);
}
return(n);
}

main(argc,argv) int argc; char **argv;
{
float a[4],p[2],x[2],r[2],y[2],ar[2],ap[2],work[4];
int n,m,cg(),iter,isym,k;
float d,x1,x2;
DOFOR(isym,2)
{/* isym=0 symmetric case =1 asymmetric*/
n=m=2;
```

```
y[0]=0.;y[1]=1.;
a[0]=1.;a[3]=4.;a[2]=.5-isym;a[1]=.5;
/*guess*/
x[0]=1.;x[1]=1.;
d=1./(a[0]*a[3]-a[1]*a[2]);
k=n;
x1= d*(y[0]*a[3]-y[1]*a[1]);
x2= d*(y[1]*a[0]-y[0]*a[2]);
printf(" x1= %f x2=%f\n",x1,x2);
iter=cg(a,x,y,r,p,ar,ap,n,m,work);
printf(" iterations=%d\n",iter);
pv(x,n);
}
exit(0);
}
```

x1= -0.133333 x2=0.266667
printing vector from 0 to 1
0.00000e+00 0.00000e+00
printing vector from 0 to 1
5.00000e-01 4.00000e+00
printing vector from 0 to 1
5.00000e-01 4.00000e+00
max iterations allowed 4
printing vector from 0 to 1
2.50000e+00 1.62500e+01
change in x 5.87256e-02
printing vector from 0 to 1
-1.38127e-01 2.21525e-02
printing vector from 0 to 1
3.00578e-02 2.40462e-01
printing vector from 0 to 1
-1.27051e-01 1.95466e-02
change in x 2.73833e-02
printing vector from 0 to 1
-2.69178e-07 -1.69283e-06
printing vector from 0 to 1
-1.33333e-01 2.66667e-01
printing vector from 0 to 1
-1.11559e-06 -6.90592e-06
change in x 8.21565e-15
iterations=2
printing vector from 0 to 1
-1.33333e-01 2.66667e-01
x1= -0.117647 x2=0.235294
printing vector from 0 to 1
0.00000e+00 0.00000e+00
printing vector from 0 to 1
-5.00000e-01 4.00000e+00
printing vector from 0 to 1
-5.00000e-01 4.00000e+00
max iterations allowed 4
printing vector from 0 to 1
1.50000e+00 1.62500e+01

change in x 6.05030e-02
printing vector from 0 to 1
-9.60387e-02 -9.67698e-03
printing vector from 0 to 1
-3.05093e-02 2.44074e-01
printing vector from 0 to 1
-1.00877e-01 9.31142e-03
change in x 7.67008e-03
printing vector from 0 to 1
-1.04179e-07 1.09834e-06
printing vector from 0 to 1
-1.17647e-01 2.35294e-01
printing vector from 0 to 1
4.44994e-07 4.44547e-06
change in x 3.60822e-15
iterations=2
printing vector from 0 to 1
-1.17647e-01 2.35294e-01

CHAPTER 2

Block Matrix Methods

Chapter Objectives

In this chapter we present tools to:

– solve sparse matrix problems when the matrix is in "block" form

– apply those tools to solve two-point boundary value problems.

Introduction

As noted in Chapter 3 of *C Tools*, finite-difference and finite-element approximations to continuous systems (systems of differential, integral, or integro-differential equations) generally produce linear systems of equations to be solved which are sparse. If one equation, such as Poisson's equation for electrostatics, is to be solved, then often a simple band system is the result, and this may be solved by a special solver for such systems, as in the LINPACK package.

In this chapter, we consider the case where the sparse system results in a matrix with a "block" structure, that is, where the matrix $\mathbf{A}$ of the resulting linear system to be solved, $\mathbf{A}\mathbf{x} = \mathbf{b}$, can be viewed as composed of submatrices or blocks. These submatrices may be treated as elements of the matrix in a manner completely analogous to the numbers comprising a matrix. The result is a family of very efficient methods for solving such systems.

For concreteness, we will consider the solution of a two point boundary value problem consisting of a set of N differential equations to be solved and a total of N boundary conditions, which are imposed at either a "top" or a "bottom" boundary. We shall further assume that the equations are all linear and that they are discretized by means of a specific second order finite-difference method which we will present.

We will discuss extensions to time-dependent and multi-dimensional problems, boundary layers and stretched grids, and eigenvalue and nonlinear problems briefly at the end of this chapter, and in more detail in the next chapter.

The Two-Point Boundary Value Problem

In this class of problems we have an independent variable which ranges between fixed limits, say x_{top} to x_{btm}, and a system of ordinary differential equations in a set of dependent variables y[i]. A system of ordinary differential equations of arbitrary order may be reduced to a system of first-order equations. For example, the harmonic oscillator equation $y'' + Ky = 0$ can be replaced by the system: y[0]' = y[1], y[1]' = − y[0]. We assume in what follows that the system to be solved has been put into this form.

Next, the problem must be discretized. Let y[j][i] denote the value of the ith variable at the jth gridpoint. We show the finite-difference "mesh" of gridpoints in the accompanying figure. We will assume that the intervals

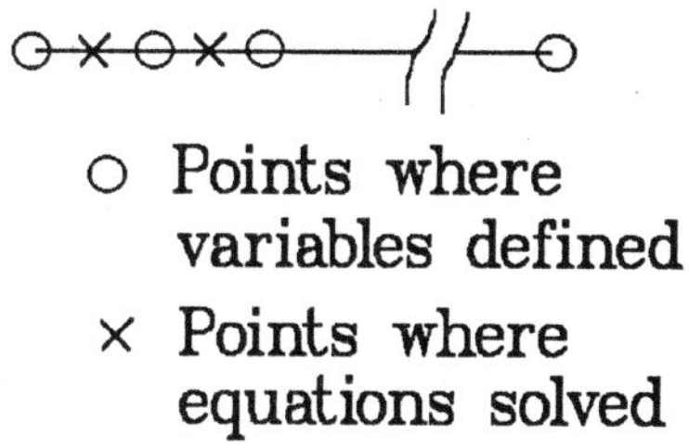

○ Points where
   variables defined
× Points where
   equations solved

Fig. 2.1. Arrangement of Gridpoints for Bidiagonal Solution

dx between the successive gridpoints at which the variables are defined, and which are also the intervals between the collocation points at which the equations are solved, are all equal in what follows, discussing generalizations later. A simple scheme which is of second order accuracy in dx can be developed by imposing the differential equations (the collocation method discussed in Chapter 3 of *C Tools*) midway between the points at which the dependent variables are defined. Then the value of the ith variable at the point between gridpoints j and j+1 is given by

{ y[j][i] + y[j + 1][i] }/2

while the derivative of the same variable at that point is

{ y[j + 1][i] − y[j][i] }/dx .

The boundary conditions are another matter. If the boundary conditions are, e.g., Dirichlet boundary conditions, i.e., a constraint on the value of the dependent variable at the boundary, this may be simply imposed at the boundary itself. If the boundary condition is of Neumann form, i.e., involves the first derivative of the dependent variable, then we would use a representation of the form {y[top] − y[top − 1]}/dx = value. This boundary condition is not second-order, as it is centered on the first cell instead of the boundary itself. There are a number of possible improvements. One is to use "guard" cells outside of the actual boundaries of the problem. Another is to use various symmetry properties. These improvements are all problem specific. In general, for an nth order system, i.e., one with n dependent variables, n first order ordinary differential equations and a total of n boundary conditions are required for a unique solution.

The boundary conditions mentioned above are fairly typical. For example, consider the steady state heat diffusion equation in one dimension, $T'' = 0$, for the temperature T. We may write y[j][0] = T, y[j][1] = T' = dT/dx. Dirichlet boundary conditions on T correspond to an imposed boundary temperature. An imposed value for the heat flux can in this case be written as a Dirichlet boundary condition on the variable T', i.e., T' = (heat flux)/diffusion constant. Neumann conditions would have to be used in this formulation to impose a symmetry condition such as $T'' = 0$. In addition, periodic boundary conditions, where the variable is required to have the same value at the top and bottom of the region, often arise in problems in which part of a large system is being modeled.

The vector of dependent variable values is arranged in the normal C ordering, with the last index varying most rapidly. Thus, all of the dependent variables at the first gridpoint, j = 0, a boundary, are stored adjacent to one another at the head of the y "matrix", next the dependent variables at the next gridpoint, etc. It will be convenient to think of y as a vector array rather than a matrix in what follows, so that the notation an ideas of Chapter 3 can be applied.

The equations to be solved at the first collocation point, halfway between the boundary and the first point are the first elements of the matrix **M** of the system to be solved, **My = b**. Here we can, following Carl Baum, call **M** a "supermatrix" whose elements are ordinary matrices called "submatrices." The **y** and **b** are profitably viewed a vectors of vectors, either "supervectors" or "composite vectors" in the terminology of Issacson and Keller. The general structure of the M matrix for the finite-difference discretization discussed above will be:

$$M = \begin{pmatrix} D[0]\,A[0]\ 0 & 0 & 0 \\ 0 & D[1]\,A[1]\ 0 & 0 \\ . & . & . & . & . \\ Bc1\ Bc2\ 0 & Bc3\ Bc4 \end{pmatrix}$$

where the sub-matrices that form the diagonal of **M** are stored as an array of matrices (just as **y** is stored as an array of arrays). The above-diagonal sub-matrices are stored as a similar array. The boundary conditions are grouped in four matrices as shown. If it were not for them, the matrix would be in upper triangular form, and no "forward" solution would be necessary. Because they exist, however, it is necessary to use Gaussian elimination to zero them out. This results in no net "fill-in" if the matrices are expendable, as they may be re-used to store the matrix along the bottom row in the column currently being processed. We use Gaussian elimination to cancel **Bc1**, modifying **Bc2** in the process. Then the modified **Bc2** is zeroed, with the third "column" of the last "row" of **M** now no longer a zero matrix. This is then eliminated, etc., until we have an upper triangular matrix equation. That is then solved exactly as it was in Chapter 3 of *C Tools*, except that in there the **R** matrix was full whereas here only the diagonal directly above the main diagonal contains nonzero element matrices.

Let us consider a concrete example to see how the sub-matrices D, A, and the boundary condition matrices are constructed. Consider our old friend the "harmonic oscilator" equation, $Y'' + KY = 0$, so-called because, when the independent variable is time, this describes the motion of an harmonic oscillator, such as a weight suspended by a spring. If the independent variable x is considered as a spatial variable, then this equation may be viewed as the one-dimensional form of the wave equation (Helmholtz's equation in which K may be viewed as $K = \omega^2/c^2$ where c is the wave speed and ω the angular frequency). Then the sub-matrices A,D and the B matrices are all second order, i. e., 2 x 2. Each row represents an equation (or boundary conditions). Let the variables be $Y' = Z$, $Z' = -KY$, with the discretized variables assigned as y...[0] = Y and y...[1] = Z. The first equation, Y'=Z, is then expressed at the collocation point midway between the j and j+1 st points, as:

$$\{\ y[j + 1][0] - y[j][0]\}/dx\ -\ \{y[j + 1][1] + y[j][1]\}/2 = 0$$

Let dxi = 1/dx. Then, in the first row of matrix **D**, which will include contributions from y[j][...] we have a — dxi in the position corresponding to the Y variable, and a —1/2 corresponding to the Z variable. Completing the process for the second equation, the matrices will look like:

$$D = \begin{pmatrix} -dxi & -.5 \\ .5K & -dxi \end{pmatrix}$$

for the sub-matrices on the diagonal, and

$$A = \begin{pmatrix} dxi & -.5 \\ .5K & dxi \end{pmatrix}$$

for the above diagonal sub-matrices. The formation of the four boundary condition matrices is similar. Note that the row corresponds to the equation or boundary condition, the column to the variable.

Block Matrix Solver

The block solver we present is specifically designed to treat the block bi-diagonal system discussed above. A wide variety of boundary conditions may be specified, including the Dirichlet and Neumann boundary conditions discussed above. In addition to such boundary conditions which are local to each boundary, periodic boundary conditions, e.g., y[0][top]=y[0][btm] may be imposed.

One uses Gaussian elimination just as in Chapter 3 of *C Tools*, except now the elements of the matrix are matrices themselves, not numbers. Instead of dividing by a number, one multiplies by the inverse of the matrix. Because matrix multiplication is not commutative, care needs to be taken to perform the multiplications in the correct order. Because the band structure of the matrix is preserved (if no pivoting is used), the process can be performed with only the "fill-in" produced by the occurance of periodic boundary conditions. This can be accomodated within one of the two workspace matrices supplied to the working subroutine (see below), which are used in the inversion of the element sub-matrices.

Time-Dependent Problems

The methods discussed above can easily be generalized to handle the problem of, say, the time evolution of the temperature in a one-dimensional body. One merely discretizes the time variable as well as the spatial, and solves the resulting equation at a given time based upon the values of the variables at previous times. The partial differential equation:

$$\frac{d^2 T}{dt^2} = \frac{d^2 T}{dx^2}$$

would be discretized the with the time derivative term represented as $\{T[t + dt] - T[t]\}/dt$. The spatial derivative could be discretized in a variety of ways. We could write the system in the form $Z = dT/dx$, $dT/dt = dZ/dx$. This leaves us with many options as to how to discretize dT/dx and dZ/dx in time. If we use only values at time t, we have a simple "explicit" scheme. In that case, we wouldn't have to solve any equations, just evaluate the terms. The matrix M would be purely diagonal. The initial conditions would have to satisfy the boundary conditions, however, and the finite-difference equations could not destroy this. Alternatively, we can write a "fully implicit" scheme by writing the spatial derivatives in terms of the unknown values at $t + dt$. This would give a system very similar to the steady state systems or time-independent systems we have treated. In fact, they are the limit of the time-dependent system for infinite timestep. Such implicit schemes are typically safer than other schemes. If the timestep is too large for other schemes, the results can be grossly wrong, as the schemes become unstable, and the finite-difference solutions no longer even approximate the solution to the differential equations as intended. See Chapter 12 of *C Tools* for a discussion of implicit vs. explicit schemes in solving ODE's, and see Lapidus and Pinder or Richtmyer and Morton, for examples of discretizing PDE's and for stability limits on timesteps.

The "Crank-Nicholson" scheme would be half-way between implicit and explicit, i.e., dT/dx would be written:

$$\{T[t + dt,x + dx] + T[t,x + dx] - T[t + dt,x] - T[t,x]\}/2dx$$

Indeed, the interpolation between explicit and implicit could be done by an adjustable parameter. The virtue of the Crank-Nicholson version is that, being time centered, it is second order accurate in time. The danger is instability (see the above references) .

Nonlinear Problems And Eigenvalue Problems

The methods used above need no generalization to parameters, e.g., diffusion coefficients, in space or in time. If the equations are nonlinear, however, then some iterative method is required. Such a nonlinear problem will arise if the diffusion coefficient is a function of temperature, for example. To solve such problems, the Newton-Raphson iteration of Chapter 6 of *C Tools* may be combined with the methods of this chapter. Briefly, we start off with an initial guess as to the solution "vector" **y**. Using the Newton-Raphson method, the nonlinear equations are linearized about this guess, and those linear equations are solved precisely as the the linear equations here are solved. The block structure of the **M** matrix will be as for the linear problem, if the same types of discretization is used for the derivatives. See Chapter 12 of *C Tools* for more discussion.

I have solved eigenvalue problems by a similar method. In such problems, a solution satisfying the boundary conditions and the ODE's is possible only if a parameter (the eigenvalue) takes on a certain set, usually discrete, of values. For example, our "harmonic oscillator" or wave equation has the parameter k. If we were interested in the normal vibrational modes of a string, "clamped" at both ends to have zero vibrational amplitude, we would see that the equation could only be satified if the value of k allowed a half-integral (1/2,1,3/2,...) number of wavelengths between x[top] and x[btm]. Eigenvalue problems can be treated in this formalism by treating the term kx as a nonlinear term in the two variables k and x, augmenting the system by the equation $k' = 0$ and the boundary condition $k' = 0$. Which eigenmode you will find will depend critically upon your initial guess. With the boundary conditions discussed, some effort must be devoted to avoiding the trivial solution $x = 0$. One expedient would be to divide the equations by, say, x^2, to try to prevent the trivial solution from being found. In the case mentioned, one could use symmetry and find the even modes by solving the problem over the half-interval with the boundary condition x=1 at the middle. This could not find all modes, of course. For the linear system described, one would generally have to find some way to fix the amplitude of the solution, as with homogeneous boundary conditions the solution of the linear equation can have any amplitude. Thus, even if it were not an eigenvalue problem, the vibrating string problem would need some attention to be suitable for numerical treatment.

My Ph. D. thesis involved, in part, solving such eigenvalue problems ("Modal Analysis of Convection in a Rotating Fluid," L. Baker and E. A. Spiegel, *J. Atmospheric Sciences*, **32**,1909,1975). The block bi-diagonal equations were set up and solved by a neat program developed by Dr. Eric Graham called BODEL. One could write statments such as:

D(X) – Y = 0

D(Y) – KX = 0

and the BODEL interpreter would turn this in the proper code to solve the problem. No, don't write me for BODEL—I don't have it. Now, programs like SMP or MACSYMA can generate FORTRAN code to solve such equations.

"Stretched" Grids

It is often undesirable to use a uniform grid. Some regions of the problem require more resolution than others, and to use a uniform grid to resolve the variation in these regions would place many points in regions of little variation or interest. An example would be "boundary layers" in viscous fluid flow, in which the area near the wall requires much better resolution than the bulk of the flow, as tangential fluid velocities can fall to zero at the wall in a layer of very small thickness if the Reynolds number is high. Similarly, "skin depth" problems in electromagnetics, "critial layers" in fluid shear flows, and the region near the "critical surface" in laser absorbsion, all tend to require better resolution than the remainder of the problem being solved.

Care must be used in stretching grids. One approach, to vary the interval dx, can easily give bad results if the intervals do not change smoothly (see de Rivas for a good discussion of the problem). A more reliable approach is to use a stretched coordinate, say z(x), rewriting dy/dx as z' dy/dz, etc. The intervals dz are uniform, but by proper choice of z(x), the effect can be to place more points where desired. One good choice for such a function is given in G. Roberts, *Proceedings 2nd International Conference on Numerical Methods*, Berlin: Springer, 1971, p.171. For a problem defined in the region $-a < x < a$, to be transformed to the domain 0z , with similar boundary layers at both boundaries, Roberts recommends the function:

$$z = (n + 1)/2 + (n - 1)/2 \ \{\log\{(b + x)/(b - x)\}$$
$$/\log\{(b + a)/(b - a) \} \ \}$$

where $b^2 = a^2 /(1- d/a)$ and d is a scale length for the boundary layer to be resolved.

We will return to grid selection in Chapter 3, where we will discuss ratio zoning and adaptive grids.

Test Problem

The test problem is the Helmhlotz or harmonic oscillator equation as discussed above, with x[top] $-$ x[btm] $= 2\pi$. The boundary condition is adjustable by the user, with Y = 1 imposed at the bottom and Z{top} + coefficient Z{btm} = 0. If the coefficient = 0, then we have the usual trigonometic solution, with y = cos (x) and z = $-$ sin (x). If the coefficient is $-$ 1, then we have a simple periodic boundary condition on the Z variable. There is no unique solution for this latter problem, the result depending upon the vagaries of roundoff! For y = A cos (x + q), we merely need the condition A cos(q) = 1 to satisfy the boundary conditions.

The user can, however, verify that (within computational accuracy), the boundary conditions and equations are satisfied.

The program includes a few general purpose linear algebra routines not used previously. Subroutine invert() uses the programs of Chapter 3 of *C Tools*, lufact() and invm(), to invert a matrix in place, mmult() multiplies two matrices, mmultg() does the same but without the assumption of mmult that the three matrices all have the same number of columns, vdif() occurs in Chapter 4's programs, mset() sets a matrix to a value (typically, zero), mm() copies a matrix, as in Chapter 4.

References

de Rivas, E. K., *J. Computational Phys.*, **10**,202-210,1972.

G. H. Golub and C. F. van Loan, *Matrix Computations* (Baltimore: Johns Hopkins, 1983).

E. Issacson and H. B. Keller, *Analysis of Numerical Methods* (New York: John Wiley, 1966).

L. Lapidus and G. F. Pinder, *Numerical Methods for Partial Differential Equations in Science and Engineering* (New York: Wiley Interscience, 1982).

R. D. Richtmyer and K.W. Morton, *Difference Methods for Initial-Value Problems* (New York: Wiley Interscience, 1967).

In the Collected Algorithms from CACM, algorithm 546, called BLOCK-SOLV, provides a block matrix solver, as does algorithm 603.

Program Listing And Test Problem Output

(Listing begins next page.)

```
/* routines to solve block matrix problems

from More C tools for scientists and engineers by L. Baker

CONTENTS:

bs()    solves a block-bidiagonal matrix
msub()    subtracts two matrices to yeid a third
invert() uses the lufact() and invm() routines to invert a matrix.
    the original matrix is left unaltered.
mm()   move a matrix
mmult()   multiply two matrice to form a third.
mmultg   generalized version of mmult. dimensioning of
    matrix storage can differ from actual number of columns
mset   set a matrix to a value (usually used to zero a matrix)
vdif   difference two vectors (also in VECTOR.C)

test problem: a simple two-point boundary value problem with
second-order differencing.  The harmonic oscillator equation is
solved.


DEPENDENCIES:

invert() uses lufact() and invm() from Chapter 2,
    files LUF.C and LUINV.C to invert a matrix (block)

*/


/*#include "libc.h"
#include "math.h"
*/
#define DOFOR(i,to) for(i=0;i<to;i++)
#define INDEX(i,j) [j+(i)*coln]
#define IND(i,j,k) [j+(i)*k]
/* next is for element matrices such as q,r,bt,bt2,bb2,bb*/
#define IE(i,j)    [j+(i)*n]
```

```
/* next is for the main matrices a and b note that
"natural" C ordering is NOT used
   it would have been:  [k+(j)*n+n*n*i]
this would have spread the blocks all over the place unless
the first subscript were the block index, with j and k the within block
indices.
*/
#define IM(i,j,k)  [ j+(i)*n+(k)*nsq]
/* to locate submatrix, IM(0,0,k) reduces to: */
#define IN(k) [(k)*nsq]


int bs(b,a,bt,bt2,bb2,bb,c,q,r,pivot,n,np)
int n,np,pivot[];
float a[],b[],c[],bt[],bt2[],bb2[],bb[],q[],r[];
/* assumed matrix problem in form:
   b1 a1 0  ...               c1
   0  b2 a2 0


   ............       =


   .....         bnp anp
   bt bt2 ...    bb2 bb       cb

*****************************CAVEAT:*******************
backsweep is simplified by the assumption that cb is c(np+1)
q,r must have dimensions of at least nsq=n*n
*/
{
float *cb,*cp;
float *work;
int nsq,coln,i,index,j,k,info,np1,invert();
np1=np-1;
nsq=n*n;
work=q;
cb=&(c[(np)*n]);
coln=n;
```

```
DOFOR(i,np)
   {
   info=invert(&(b IN(i)),pivot,work,n);
if(info!=0)printf(" bomb i=%d\n",i);
   if(info!=0)return(1);
   mmult(bt,&(b IN(i)),r,n,n,n,n);
   mmult(r,&(a IN(i)),q,n,n,n,n);
   msub(bt2,q,bt,n,n,coln);
   mv(r,&(c[i*n]),q,n,n);
   vdif(cb,q,cb,n);
   if(i<(np-3))
      {
      mset(bt2,0.,n,n,coln);
      }
   else
   if(i==(np-3))
      {
      mm(bb2,bt2,n,n,coln);
      }
   else
   if(i==(np-2))
      {
      mm(bb,bt2,n,n,coln);
      }
   }
info=invert(bt,pivot,work,n);
if(info!=0)return(2);
mv(bt,cb,r,n,n);
vcopy(r,cb,n);
/* if cb were not c[np*n] then here would include:
   mv(&(a IN(np1)),cb,r,n,n);
   msub(r,&(c IN(np1),r,n,n,coln);
   mv(&(b IN(np1),r,&(c IM(0,0,np-1),n,n);
AND
   next loop ranges from j=np-2 not np-1
*/
for(j=np-1;j>=0;j--)
   {
```

```
   k=j+1;
   cp=&(c[j*n]) ;
   mv(&(a IN(j)),&(c[k*n]),r,n,n);
   vdif(cp,r,q,n);
   mv(&(b IN(j)) ,q,cp,n,n);
   }
return(0);
}

msub(a,b,c,m,n,coln)
int coln;
float a[],b[],c[];
{
int i,j;
DOFOR(i,n)
   {
   DOFOR(j,n)c INDEX(i,j) = a INDEX(i,j) - b INDEX(i,j);
   }
return;
}
```

/*------------------ invert matrix m----------------*/

```
int invert(m,pivot,work,n)
float m[],work[];
int pivot[],n;
{int info;
lufact(m,n,n,pivot,&info);
if(info!=0)return(info);
invm(m,n,n,pivot,work);
return(0);
}
```

/*----------- multiply two matrices---------------------*/

```
mmult(a,b,c,m,n,o,coln) int n,m,o,coln;
float a[],b[],c[];
/* c=a*b matrices actually a(m,n) b(n,o) c(m,o) with coln columns*/
```

```
{
int i,j,k;
double sum;
DOFOR(i,m)
  {
  DOFOR(j,o)
    {
    sum=0.;
    DOFOR(k,n)sum+= a INDEX(i,k)* b INDEX(k,j);
    c INDEX(i,j)=sum;
    }
  }
return;
}
```

```
/*---------------multiply two matrices-generalized
   the dimensions of the actual matrices do not have to
   be the same as the storage limits, i.e. the actual number
   of columns could be less than the array dimension-----------*/
```

```
mmultg(a,b,c,m,n,o,cola,colb,colc) int o,n,m,cola,colb,colc;
float a[],b[],c[];
/* c=a*b matrices actually a(m,n) b(n,o) c(m,o) */
{
int i,j,k;
double sum;
DOFOR(i,m)
  {
  DOFOR(j,o)
    {
    sum=0.;
    DOFOR(k,n)sum+= a IND(i,k,colc)* b IND(k,j,colb);
    c IND(i,j,colc)=sum;
    }
  }
return;
}
```

```
/*-------- difference of two vectors-------------------------------*/

vdif(a,b,c,n) int n;
float a[],b[],c[];
{
int i;
DOFOR(i,n)c[i]=a[i]-b[i];
return;
}


/* ----------- set a matrix to value s ----------------------*/

mset(f,s,n,m,coln) int n,m,coln;
float f[],s;
{
int i,j;
DOFOR(i,n)
   {
   DOFOR(j,m) f INDEX(i,j)=s;
   }
return;
}


/* ------------- copy a matrix --------------------*/

mm(from,to,n,m,coln) int n,m,coln;
float to[],from[];
/* matrix move*/
{
int i,j;
DOFOR(i,n)
   {
   DOFOR(j,m) to INDEX(i,j)= from INDEX(i,j);
   }
return;
}
```

```
/* test driver for routines to solve block matrix problems

test problem: a simple two-point boundary value problem with
second-order differencing.  The harmonic oscillator equation is
solved.

from More C tools for scientists and engineers by L. Baker

CONTENTS:
   main()

DEPENDENCIES:
   none
*/


/*#include "libc.h"
#include "math.h"
*/
#define DOFOR(i,to) for(i=0;i<to;i++)
#define INDEX(i,j) [j+(i)*coln]
#define IND(i,j,k) [j+(i)*k]
/* next is for element matrices such as q,r,bt,bt2,bb2,bb*/
#define IE(i,j)    [j+(i)*n]
/* next is for the main matrices a and b note that
"natural" C ordering is NOT used
   it would have been:  [k+(j)*n+n*n*i]
this would have spread the blocks all over the place unless
the first subscript were the block index, with j and k the within block
indices.
*/
#define IM(i,j,k)  [ j+(i)*n+(k)*nsq]
/* to locate submatrix, IM(0,0,k) reduces to: */
#define IN(k) [(k)*nsq]

/*---------------- test driver--------------------*/

main(argc,argv) int argc;char **argv;
```

```
{
int pivot[4],info,i,j,k,np,n,nsq,bs();
double x,dx,dxi,v;
double sin(),cos();
float bc;
float bb[4],bb2[4],bt[4],bt2[4],c[24],a[44],b[44],*cb,q[4],r[4];
x=2.*3.1415926535;
np=10;
dx=x/np;
dxi=1./dx;

n=2;
nsq=n*n;
cb=&(c[np*n]);
/*setup problem*/
DOFOR(i,np)
   {
   mset(&(a IN(i)),0.,n,n);
   mset(&(b IN(i)),0.,n,n);
   /* equation 0: y'=z */
   a IM(0,0,i)=dxi;
   b IM(0,0,i)=-dxi;
   a IM(0,1,i)=-.5;
   b IM(0,1,i)=-.5;
   c [ i*n ]=0.;
   /*equation 1: z'=-y*/
   a IM(1,1,i)=dxi;
   b IM(1,1,i)=-dxi;
   a IM(1,0,i)=.5;
   b IM(1,0,i)=.5;
   c [ i*n +1 ]=0.;
   }
/* boundary conditions*/
mset(bb,0.,n,n,n);
mset(bt,0.,n,n,n);
mset(bb2,0.,n,n,n);
mset(bt2,0.,n,n,n);
/* y=1 at bottom*/
```

```
bb[0]=1.;
cb[0]=1.;
/*periodic b.c. z(top)=z(btm) if bb[3]=-1. */
/* z=0. at top if bb[3]=0.*/
bt[3]=1.;
/*printf(" enter coef in coef*z(top)+z(btm)=0. 0,-1 probably\n");
scanf("%f", &bc);*/
bc=0.;
printf(" echoing coef=%f\n",bc);
bb[3]=bc;
cb[1]=0.;
info=bs(b,a,bt,bt2,bb2,bb,c,q,r,pivot,n,np);
/*answer*/
if(info!=0)
   {printf(" info=%d,trouble\n",info);
   exit(0);
   }
printf(" z   z'  \n");
DOFOR(i,np+1)
   {
   j=i*n;
   v= i*dx;
   printf(" %f %f %f %f\n",c[j],cos(v),c[j+1], -sin(v));
   }
exit(0);
}
```

echoing coef=0.000000
z z'
1.019373 1.000000 -0.000000 -0.000000
0.836232 0.809017 -0.582955 -0.587785
0.352616 0.309017 -0.956443 -0.951057
-0.257703 -0.309017 -0.986261 -0.951057
-0.775423 -0.809017 -0.661695 -0.587785
-1.014518 -1.000000 -0.099368 -0.000000
-0.889076 -0.809017 0.498664 0.587785
-0.444170 -0.309017 0.917515 0.951057
0.160335 0.309017 1.006684 0.951057
0.707229 0.809017 0.734131 0.587785
1.000000 1.000000 0.197789 0.000000

CHAPTER 3

Partial Differential Equations: Multigrid Methods

Chapter Objectives

In this chaper we will:

– explain the multigrid method

– present C programs which solve a two-point boundary value problem and a two-dimensional boundary value problem using the multigrid method

Introduction

In this chapter, we discuss the solution of partial differential equations. These equations differ radically in the methods required as well as necessary boundary conditions depending upon whether they are elliptic, parabolic, or hyperbolic in character. In transonic flows, the equations can even change character within the problem. We discuss here a standard elliptic problem, involving the solution of Poisson's equation, solved here in one spatial dimension. Parabolic and hyperbolic problems, typified by the heat (diffusion) equation and the wave equation, can be solved by methods combining the initial value methods discussed in previous chapters for treating the time-like independent variable(s) and methods similar to those in this chapter for the space-like variables if there are more than one. We shall use a method suitable for multi-dimensional problems called the multigrid method.

PDE's and Poisson's Equation

The partial differential equations (PDE's) of interest in mathematical physics are generally of second order. If the problem has two independent variables that are x and y, we can write the general linear equation in dependent variable u as:

$$A\frac{d^2u}{dx^2} + B\frac{d^2u}{dy^2} + 2C\frac{d^2u}{dx\,dy} + D\frac{d\,u}{d\,x} + E\frac{d\,u}{d\,y} + F\,u = 0$$

where the coefficients A-G are independent of u and its derivatives, but may depend upon x and y. The "discriminant" is $AB - C^2$ (note the factor of 2 in front of C in the equation above). If $A - G$ were constants, we could view the left-hand side operator as a quadratic form and diagonalize it, rotating to a coordinate system x', y', which the cross product term (proportional to C) would be nulled out to zero. Then the transformed A', B' would correspond to an elliptic quadratic form if both were positive, and hyperbolae if A' and B' were of different signs. In the orignial independent variables, if the discriminant is positive, we have an elliptic system, if it is negative, a hyperbolic system, if zero, a parabolic system. These concepts generalize to problems with more than two independent variables, to nonlinear problems, and to higher order problems. See, e.g., P. R. Garabedian's *Partial Differential Equations* (NY: John Wiley, 1964), or A. G. Webster's *Partial Differential Equations of Mathematical Physics,* (NY: Dover Publ., 1966).

What is of importance in numerical analysis is that these different classes of partial differential equations (PDE's) have solutions of very different character. In elliptic problems, boundary conditions must be specified for all of the boundary surface. Every point in the x,y plane within the solution domain is affected by every other point. An example of an elliptic problem is the one we will consider in this chapter, Poisson's equation, which is of the form:

$$\frac{d^2u}{dx^2} + \frac{d^2u}{dy^2} + Gu = 0$$

for rectangular coordinate systems.

In contrast, a hyperbolic system has directions in the x-y plane, called characteristics, along which information propagates from point to point at a finite speed. Generally, one of the variables, say y, is time (lets call it t in this context), and such a problem represents the flow of some quantity in time. The canonical example of such a hyperbolic system is the wave equation:

$$\frac{d^2u}{dx^2} - \frac{d^2u}{dt^2} + Gu = 0$$

In such problems, the boundary conditions should not be specified for all bounding x and t but only for, say, all x and t = 0 (an initial value problem or IVP). It would overspecify the problem to constrain the values of u at the final time, t = t[end], as well.

Finally, we come to parabolic problems. These are in some sense intermediate between the other two, and most typically correspond to a time-dependent diffusion problem:

$$K\frac{d^2u}{dx^2} - \frac{du}{dt} = 0$$

As in elliptic problems, there is no finite limit to the speed at which a change at one point of the x-t plane can affect another. As in hyperbolic problems, the boundary conditions appropriate to the equation are those of an IVP.

Poisson's equation describes the electric field in a region produced by electrical charges within and/or by assigning certain electrical potentials to conductors on the boundary of the region (which, by causing surface charge distributions to form on these surfaces, produces the same effect). As the electric force has an infinite range, we have an elliptic problem, since a charge anywhere can affect the electric potential anywhere through its field. The plan is to discretize the partial derivatives into finite-differences, and to then solve the resulting linear system.

We first need to select a grid of x and y values on which to solve the system. Electric field problems often require the kind of "stretched" grids discussed in Chapter 2 to put resolution in regions where it is needed. This is because the electric fields can "concentrate" at edges and points, resulting in regions which require much more resolution than others. Such a system of stretching should be easy to implement and to specify if the general user isn't to feel burdened excessively in setting up the problem. Often, a simple "ratio" zoning method is used in which each zone is a fixed multiple of the adjacent zone size, for user convenience. More general schemes are easily implemented. As in Chapter 2, we formulate finite-difference expressions for the necessary derivatives as functions of the values the independent variables take at the gridpoints. We then have to solve a system of equations of the typical form (for a two dimensional problem):

A u[l + 1][m] + B u[l][m] + C u[l − 1][m] + D u[l][m + 1]

+ E u[l][m −1] = F

where the coefficients A–F depend only upon the two coordinates and their differences, and not on u. If they depend upon u, the problem will be nonlinear and methods similar to Chapter 6 of *C Tools* must be used.

We could view u[l][m] as a composite vector as in Chapter 2 and directly solve the system. The matrix of the system would be initally very sparse, as each point is linked by the finite-difference equations directly to its nearest neighbors only. The matrix **A** for **Au** = **b** would be of the general form of a "striped" matrix, with nonzero diagonal lines of nonzero elements, similar to tridiagonal or bidiagonal matrices (see Chapter 2) but with additional diagonal stripes of nonzero elements at a distance from the main diagonal corresponding to the maximum index in one dimension.

If we arranged u in the composite vector so that the neighboring points in the z direction for the same r are adjacent withing the vector (i.e., the normal ordering for u[l][m] for C row–major storage), then the a–e correspond to the A–E of the finite difference form of the equation. The separation between the main diagonal and the two distant diagonals with the a and c coefficients is the number of gridpoints in the z direction. A band solver could be used to directly solve this system with Gaussian elimination. However, there would be tremendous fill-in of the diagonals between the main diagonal and those with the a and c coefficients. This suggests that an iterative solver should be used (see Chapter 1). There are many options, and we discuss here one method specifically developed for PDE's as the one presented here, the Multigrid method.

Multigrid Methods

One recent development in iterative methods for elliptic PDE's is the idea of "multigrid" methods. The idea is to solve the problem crudely, on a coarse grid, then use the approximate solution found to interpolate onto a finer grid, solving the problem (iteratively), then propagating the refinements onto the coarse grid again (the so-called "smoothing" step), etc. See W. Hackbusch, *Multigrid Method and Applications*, Berlin: Springer, 1985.

To explain the concept of multigrid methods, consider a concrete example. Suppose we want to solve the Poisson equation $\nabla^2 u = \rho$ on a simple rectangular mesh. If i is the index in the x direction and j the index in the y direction, with the solution represented as u[i][j], then a simple discretization of the finite-difference equations for dx = dy would be:

$$(u[i + 1][j] + u[i - 1][j] + u[i][j + 1] + u[i][j - 1]$$
$$- 4u[i][j]) = \rho \, dy \, dx$$

One simple iterative scheme, the Gauss-Seidel method, to solve this system of equations would look something like this:

```
for (i=1;i<x;i++)
    for (j=1;j<x;j++)
        u[i][j]=
        ( ρ dx dy-u[i+1][j]-u[i-1][j]-u[i][j+1]-u[i][j-1])/4
```

where we have solved the first equation for u[i][j] and repeatedly applied this. We assume that boundary conditions at i = 0,jmax and j = 0,jmax are applied as appropriate. The two nested for loops are repeated until the maximum change in any u value is below a specified threshold. The problem with this approach is that it often takes many iterations to achieve reasonable accuracy. This is because of the local nature of the iteration: u[i][j] knows directly only its immediate neighbors. It takes an iteration for information to move one gridpoint.

Multigrid methods attempt to overcome this problem by defining a sequence of coarser grids. Not only is less work done on each grid, as they have fewer points, but as the points are further apart, information travels greater distances per iteration. Therefore, the global onvergence is faster. Given the partial differential equation to be solved, we assume the problem is discretized using a specified mesh of grid points to give a system of equations for the independent variables at those gridpoints. Let the system to be solved be $\mathbf{Au} = \mathbf{f}$ for the unknown u. Here we assume that the boundary conditions have been incorporated into the system. Let v be an approximation to the u which exactly solves the finite-difference system, and let $\mathbf{e} = \mathbf{u} - \mathbf{v}$ represent the error vector. Then $\mathbf{Av} - \mathbf{f} = \mathbf{r}$ will define the residual error vector r, which will not be a vector of zeroes unless $\mathbf{v} = \mathbf{u}$. Then, if A is a linear operator, i. e., satisfies the condition $\mathbf{A}(\mathbf{x} + \mathbf{y}) = \mathbf{Ax} + \mathbf{Ay}$ for all x and y, we have $\mathbf{Ae} = \mathbf{Au} - \mathbf{Av}$
$= \mathbf{f} - (\mathbf{f} - \mathbf{r}) = \mathbf{r}$. Thus, instead of solving $\mathbf{Au} = \mathbf{f}$ for u, it is equivalent to solve $\mathbf{Ae} = \mathbf{r}$ and then correct v via $\mathbf{u} = \mathbf{v} + \mathbf{e}$. The "trick" is that in order to solve the fundamental problem $\mathbf{Au} = \mathbf{f}$ on our mesh, we accelerate convergence by solving problems of the form $\mathbf{Ae} = \mathbf{r}$ on coarser meshes. The residual r is "restricted" from the finer mesh, while the solution e is interpolated as a correction to the v on the finer mesh. To apply a multigrid method, we need to specify four things:

the geometry of the meshes
the method(s) of solving $\mathbf{Ae} = \mathbf{r}$
the methods for interpolating and restricting between grids
the method of sequencing between meshes

Note that multigrid methods require more storage, as we must save values on each mesh. As the meshes get progressively smaller, the result is a geometric series of points. Thus, in one dimension, if the meshes have half the number of points of the next finer mesh, we use about twice as much storage, while in two dimensions about 4/3 as much storage. Note also that while on the finest mesh we are solving the system $\mathbf{Au} = \mathbf{f}$, on all coarser meshes we are solving a different problem, $\mathbf{Ae} = \mathbf{r}$, where r is defined by the error residual of the problem on the next finer mesh.

Mesh Geometry

The simplest and most popular choice is to let the number of mesh points in any direction be a power of two. Then, each coarse mesh uses half the resolution of the next finer mesh in any direction. Thus, a one-dimensional mesh cuts the number of points in half between two adjacent meshes, while a two-dimensional grid would cut the number of points by 4 (two in each direction). Two possible choices in a two-dimensional mesh are illustrated:

```
x   o   x           o   x   o
o   o   o           x   o   x
x   o   x           o   x   o
```

where x (or o) indicates a point in both the coarse and fine mesh while the other symbol indicates a point that is only in the finer mesh. The arrangement on the right is often called a red-black ordering after the coloring of a checkerboard.

Solution Method

We will use the Gauss-Seidel method discussed above. It can be proved to converge if the A matrix is diagonally dominant, i. e., if the $A[i][i]$ term exceeds in magnitude the sum of the $A[i][j]$ terms for $j \neq i$. Other choices, such as a conjugate gradient iteration, are possible. Because we expect the multigrid approach to couple distant points efficiently and cheaply, it is not cost-effective to use a complicated iteration method.

Interpolating And Restricting

For restriction, i. e., going from the fine to the coarse mesh, the obvious choice is to use the values at the coarse meshpoints of the corresponding points in the fine mesh. This is called "injection." Another possibility is called "full weighting," in which neighboring points on the fine mesh are used. In one dimension, then, at a point with index 2j in the fine mesh and j in the coarse mesh,

$$v[coarse][j]=(v[2j-1]+2v[2j]+v[2j+1])/4$$

For interpolation, (called "prolongation" by some, such as Wesseling) the obvious method is: for points in the fine mesh corresponding to those in the coarse, take the value of the coarse mesh. For other points, interpolate between the nearest points of the coarse mesh.

With appropriate interpolation and restriction methods, and an approximate solution method for $\mathbf{Ae} = \mathbf{r}$ on each mesh, it is possible to apply these methods to nonlinear problems (see Brandt). He suggests restricting ("escalating" in his terminology) from fine to coarse by solving on the coarser grid   Ae[coarse] = **r** + A{Rv[fine]}   where R{ } is the restriction operator and v[fine] are the values on the next finer mesh. For interpolation, the corrections to the finer mesh values due to the coarser mesh corections are taken to be of the form I{ e[coarse] − R{e[fine]} } where I is the interpolation operator. (See Peyret and Taylor.)

Mesh Sequence

How should we progress through the meshes? The most obvious method is the so-called V-cycle, after its appearance on a diagram in which the meshes are shown from top (fine) to bottom (coarse) and progress is from left-to-right. In the V-cycle method, we first solve on the finest grid, then the next coarser, then the next, etc., until we reach the coarsest mesh. We then go back up through the sequence, correcting each solution with the next coarser mesh's solution and relaxing. This fundamental V-cycle is repeated until the desired accuracy is achieved. In the W-cycle, we do not proceed directly back to the the finest mesh. We proceed from the coarsest mesh to the next coarsest mesh, then back to the coarsest, then back up two levels, back to coarsest, etc. This is done symmetrically in time, stopping before we have gone all the way to the finest mesh. The result looks something like the letter W if there are only a few levels. The Full Multigrid (FMV) scheme differs in a number of ways from the V and W cycles. We start with the coarsest mesh, assuming that the initial guess for solution u and errors e on all finer meshes are zero. We proceed up one level, back to the coarsest, then two, then back down to coarsest, then three, etc., until we reach the finest mesh. See Briggs for a complete discussion of the virtues of the FMV scheme, and McCormick for a number of articles on various aspects of the method as well as a sample FORTRAN code.

There is much active research going on as to optimal grid sequencing, multigrid methods for irregular regions, nonlinear problems, etc.

The Program

To illustrate the mutigrid method, we have set up a program which solves a one-dimensional Poisson problem. The reader can choose the form: W,V, or full multigrid method. The simple Gauss-Seidel iteration is used. The two-dimensional version of the same problem is solved on a red-black grid in which the updates are only done to the "red" gridpoints. Output to PLOT.DAT is plotted in Chapter 11 and below.

Mesh Generation

As remarked above and discussed in Chapter 2, a uniform grid is often not the best choice. But one must be careful to make the grid vary smoothly so as not to introduce large errors in the finite difference scheme. One can use ratio zoning, it which the successive d and D values are the previous values multiplied by factors of the form $(1 + e)$ and $(1 + f)$ respectively, where |e| and |f| are < 1 (no larger than .2 at the very most, and .1 if you wish some safety margin).

There is considerable interest in sophisticated grid generators which "fit" the grid to the boundary surfaces. Usually, an elliptic solver is employed to place the grid points. Generally, and orthogonal grid is desirable for simplicity in the finite-difference expressions. An even greater level of sophistication is the so-called "adaptive grid" in which the grid points are moved during computation based upon the solution, to resolve regions of large gradients. The general idea is to place the grid points according to a variational formulation, which is solved by an elliptic solver. The variational integral to be minimized contains a number of "penalty' terms to enforce desirable properties on the grid, including orthogonality, and to put increased resolution (minimizing the grid spacing for fixed number of points) where, say, the magnitude of the derivative of some variable is large. A good overall reference is J. F. Thompson, et al.

What Method To Use

There are a wide variety of methods available for solving PDE's. For one dimensional problems, use direct (non-iterative solvers similar to that discussed in Chapter 2. For problems with three spatial dimensions, direct solvers are too expensive in general and an interative method should be used. For problems with two spatial dimensions, direct and iterative solvers are roughly competitive. As to iterative methods, the basic point interative methods (Gauss-Seidel, Jacobi, successive overrelaxation or SOR, etc.), often have convergence problems and should probably be avoided. Conjugate gradient family methods should only be used if a good preconditioning can be achieved. The ADI method is useful in the general case in which the boundaries are irregular, regions are held at fixed potential, etc. Conversely, if the boundaries of the region are regular (e.g., a rectangle), and if the differential operator is fairly simple, the direct methods, such as those using cyclic reduction, hold the upper hand. For a review and critical comparison of the various methods for solving elliptic potential problems, such as the one treated in this chapter, see Hickney and Eastwood. For a more general comparison of methods, see Axelsson and Barker.

References

W. F. Ames, *Numerical Methods for Partial Differential Equations*, 2nd ed. (New York: Academic Press, 1977).

O. Axelsson and V. A. Barker, *Finite Element Solution of Bounary Value Problems* (New York: Academic Press, 1984).

G. Birkhoff and R. E. Lynch, *Numerical Solution of Elliptic Problems* (Philadelphia: Society of Industrial and Applied Mathematics (SIAM), 1984).

A. Brandt, *Mathematics of Computation*, **31**,333,1977.

W. L. Briggs, *A Multigrid Tutorial* (Philadelphia: SIAM, 1987).

R. W. Hockney and J. W. Eastwood, *Computer Simulation Using Particles* (New York: McGraw-Hill International, 1981).

E. Isaacson and H. B. Keller, *Analysis of Numerical Methods* (New York: J. Wiley, 1966).

S. F. McCormick (ed.), *Multigrid Methods* (Philadelphia: SIAM, 1987).

R. Peyret and T. D. Taylor, *Computational Methods for Fluid Flow*

(Berlin & New York: Springer, 1983).

D. Potter, *Computational Physics* (New York: J. Wiley Interscience, 1973).

J. F. Thompson, Z. U. A. Warsi, C. W. Mastin, *Numerical Grid Generation* (New York & Amsterdam: North Holland, 1985).

E. L. Wachspress, *J. SIAM* **8**,403,1960 and **10**,339,1962.

P. Wesseling, *J. Computational Physics,* **79**,85, 1988.

Program Listing And Test Problem Output

(Listing begins next page.)

```
/* 1d multigrid simple test
from More C Tools for Scientists and Engineers by L. Baker*/
/* dimension to two times n */
float x[100],v[100],u[100],f[100];
/* x=grid v=answer f=drive  A for Laplacian, i.e Poisson Ay=f */

/*problem size, coarsest grid allowed*/
#define n 32
#define ncoarsest 4

/*relaxtion parameters*/
#define n0 1
#define n1 2
#define n2 2
#define dx .1
float bc0=1.,bc1=2.;/*boundary conditions*/

float av(i,m,y)
int i,m;  float *y;
{/* evaluate Av. use Av-f for residual*/
if(!i) return y[0];
if(i==(m-1))return y[m-1];
return (y[i+1]+y[i-1]-2.*y[i])/(dx*dx);
}

float residual(i,m,f,v)
int i,m;float *f,*v;
{
float av();
return f[i]-av(i,m,v);
}

correct(m,v,v2h)
int m; float *v,*v2h;
{/*coarse to fine*/
int i,mfine;
mfine=m<<1;
for(i=0;i<m;i++)/*don't touch boundary points*/
```

```
   {/* i=0 set v 0,1 from v2h 0,1. i=m-1, set 2m-1*/
   if(i!=(m-1))
      {
      v[2*i]+=v2h[i];/*add correction term*/
      v[2*i+1]+=.5*(v2h[i]+v2h[i+1]);
      }
   else
      {
      v[2*i]+=.5*(v2h[i]+v2h[i-1]);
      v[2*i+1]+=v2h[i];
      }
   }
}

restrict(m,coarsef,finef,v)
int m; float *finef,*coarsef,*v;
{/*fine to coarse f*/
int i,mfine,j,finetop;
float coef,residp,residm,residc;
float residual();
mfine=m<<1;
finetop=mfine-1;
coef=dx*dx;
for(i=1;i<m;i++)
   {
   /* restrict  f2h = (fh-Av)*/
   j=i<<1;
   residc= residual(j  ,mfine,finef,v);
   residm= residual(j-1,mfine,finef,v);
   residp= residual(j+1,mfine,finef,v);
   coarsef[i]=.25*(residp+residm+2.*residc);/*full weighting*/
   /*coarsef[i]=residc*/;/*injection*/
   }
   /* error residual  Ae=r;*/
   coarsef[0]= finef[0]-v[0];
   coarsef[m-1]=finef[finetop]-v[finetop];

}
```

```
relax(m,u,f)
int m;
float *u,*f;
{
int i,k;
float fip,fim,coef;
coef=dx*dx;
/* solve approx. by sor iteration Au=f for u*/
u[0]=f[0];u[m-1]=f[m-1];/*boundary conditions Av=f a=1*/
for(i=1;i<m-1;i++)
    {/* laplacian  u"= (u+ + u-  -2*u)/dx^2=f */
    u[i]= ( u[i+1]+u[i-1] -f[i]*coef )*.5;
    }
}


mvcycle(nn,hin,v,f)
int hin,nn; float *v,*f;
{
/* perform MV scheme cycle  v initial guess returns v*/
int h,i,m,mu=1;/* mu=1 for V scheme =2 for W scheme*/
float *nextgridf,*nextgridv;
h=hin;
m=nn;
/*printf(" enter mvcycle with h=%d n=%d\n",h,nn);*/
for(i=0;i<n1;i++)relax(nn,v,f);
if(ncoarsest!=nn)
    {
    nextgridf= &(f[m]);
    nextgridv= &(v[m]);
    m>>=1;
    h<<=1;
    restrict(m,nextgridf,f,v);
    for(i=0;i<m;i++) *nextgridv++=0.;
    for(i=0;i<mu;i++)mvcycle(m,h,nextgridv ,nextgridf);
    correct(m,v,nextgridv);
    }
for(i=0;i<n2;i++)relax(nn,v,f);
```

```
}



fullmgv(nn,hin,v,f)
int nn,hin;float *v,*f;
{
int i,j,m,h;
float *nextgridf,*nextgridv;
h=hin;
/*printf(" enter full with h=%d n=%d\n",h,nn);*/
if(nn!=ncoarsest)
   {
   m=nn>>1;
   h<<=1;
   nextgridf= &(f[nn]);
   nextgridv= &(v[nn]);
   restrict(m,nextgridf,f,v);
   for(i=0;i<m;i++) *nextgridv++=0.;
   fullmgv(m,h,nextgridv ,nextgridf);
   correct(m,v,nextgridv);
   }
for(i=0;i<n0;i++)mvcycle(nn,hin,v,f);
}


main()
{
int i,j,k,l,m,twon;
float resid,error;
float residual();
/*init*/
twon=2*n;
for(i=0;i<n;i++)
   {x[i]= i*dx;
   v[i]=0.;/*initial guess*/
   f[i]=0.;
   }
/*boundary conditions */
```

```
/*iterate*/
  /*initialize f,v all grids*/
  for(i=0;i<twon;i++)
    {v[i]=0;f[i]=0.;}
  /* b.c. for Av=f*/
  k=n;j=0;
  f[j]=bc0;f[k+j-1]=bc1;
/* special test- v already ok*/
/*   for (i=0;i<n;i++)
     v[i]=bc0+(bc1-bc0)*i/((float)(n-1));
*/
while(1)
  {
/*   for (i=0;i<n;i++)
     printf(" resid %e for v %e\n",residual(i,n,f,v),v[i]);
*/
  fullmgv(n,1,v,f);
  /*calc. resid.*/
  resid=0.;
  for (i=0;i<n;i++)
    {
    error = residual(i,n,f,v);
    printf(" error[%d]=%f v=%f\n",i,error,v[i]);
    resid+=error*error;
    }
  if(resid < .01) break;
  else printf("RESIDUAL = %f IN MAIN\n",resid);
  }
printf(" fini\n");
}
```

```
error[0]=0.000000 v=1.000000
error[1]=0.973558 v=1.358533
error[2]=1.799345 v=1.707331
error[3]=1.658440 v=2.038135
error[4]=2.314544 v=2.352355
error[5]=2.080679 v=2.643429
error[6]=2.666879 v=2.913696
error[7]=2.349997 v=3.157295
error[8]=2.784371 v=3.377394
error[9]=2.433777 v=3.569649
error[10]=2.767563 v=3.737566
error[11]=2.382207 v=3.877808
error[12]=2.549171 v=3.994227
error[13]=2.159905 v=4.085155
error[14]=2.231359 v=4.154484
error[15]=1.873875 v=4.201499
error[16]=1.852560 v=4.229775
error[17]=1.526737 v=4.239526
error[18]=2.442884 v=4.234010
error[19]=2.055550 v=4.204064
error[20]=3.834629 v=4.153563
error[21]=3.333879 v=4.064716
error[22]=4.100943 v=3.942530
error[23]=3.286910 v=3.779335
error[24]=3.142810 v=3.583271
error[25]=2.185965 v=3.355778
error[26]=1.420951 v=3.106426
error[27]=-5.806494 v=2.842864
error[28]=0.521922 v=2.637367
error[29]=0.260973 v=2.426651
error[30]=-0.000024 v=2.213326
error[31]=0.000000 v=2.000000
RESIDUAL = 196.048248 IN MAIN
error[0]=0.000000 v=1.000000
error[1]=1.123893 v=1.450703
error[2]=1.564550 v=1.890167
error[3]=1.938426 v=2.313985
error[4]=2.294207 v=2.718420
```

error[7]=-0.023389 v=1.202111
error[8]=-0.021863 v=1.231621
error[9]=-0.029504 v=1.261349
error[10]=-0.027871 v=1.291373
error[11]=-0.036037 v=1.321675
error[12]=-0.034261 v=1.352337
error[13]=-0.042367 v=1.383343
error[14]=-0.040412 v=1.414771
error[15]=-0.047374 v=1.446604
error[16]=-0.044787 v=1.478911
error[17]=-0.048542 v=1.511665
error[18]=-0.044227 v=1.544905
error[19]=-0.042534 v=1.578588
error[20]=-0.035584 v=1.612695
error[21]=-0.028348 v=1.647159
error[22]=-0.020099 v=1.681906
error[23]=-0.012374 v=1.716853
error[24]=-0.005794 v=1.751925
error[25]=-0.008118 v=1.787055
error[26]=-0.004911 v=1.822265
error[27]=-0.035024 v=1.857525
error[28]=-0.000858 v=1.893135
error[29]=-0.000441 v=1.928754
error[30]=0.000000 v=1.964377
error[31]=0.000000 v=2.000000
RESIDUAL = 0.023821 IN MAIN
error[0]=0.000000 v=1.000000
error[1]=-0.000989 v=1.031071
error[2]=-0.000143 v=1.062152
error[3]=-0.002301 v=1.093235
error[4]=-0.001073 v=1.124340
error[5]=-0.003886 v=1.155457
error[6]=-0.002730 v=1.186612
error[7]=-0.006199 v=1.217794
error[8]=-0.004733 v=1.249038
error[9]=-0.008821 v=1.280330
error[10]=-0.007534 v=1.311710
error[11]=-0.012136 v=1.343165

error[12]=-0.010622 v=1.374742
error[13]=-0.015306 v=1.406425
error[14]=-0.013781 v=1.438261
error[15]=-0.017786 v=1.470235
error[16]=-0.015724 v=1.502386
error[17]=-0.018036 v=1.534695
error[18]=-0.015211 v=1.567184
error[19]=-0.015080 v=1.599825
error[20]=-0.010824 v=1.632617
error[21]=-0.009549 v=1.665518
error[22]=-0.006604 v=1.698514
error[23]=-0.007379 v=1.731575
error[24]=-0.005698 v=1.764711
error[25]=-0.012994 v=1.797904
error[26]=-0.011194 v=1.831226
error[27]=-0.034308 v=1.864661
error[28]=-0.005722 v=1.898438
error[29]=-0.002861 v=1.932273
error[30]=0.000012 v=1.966137
error[31]=0.000000 v=2.000000
fini

```
/* 2d multigrid simple test
From More C Tools for Scientists and Engineers by L. Baker*/
/* dimension to 2(n+1)**2 where n is a power of 2 */
float x[2000],v[2000],u[2000],f[2000];
/* x=grid v=answer f=drive  A for Laplacian, i.e Poisson Ay=f */
#include <stdio.h>
/*problem size, coarsest grid allowed*/
#define n 16
#define ncoarsest 2

#define INDEX(I,J) [J+(I)*maxj]
#define INDX(I,J,k) [J+(I)*((k)+1)]
/*relaxtion parameters*/
#define n0 1
#define n1 2
#define n2 2
#define dx .1
float bc0=1.,bc1=2.,mult;/*boundary conditions*/

float av(i,j,m,y)
int i,j,m;  float *y;
{/* evaluate Av. use Av-f for residual*/
int maxj;
maxj=m+1;
/* boundary conditions residuals*/
if(!i||!j||i==(m)||j==(m))return y INDEX(i,j);
return (y INDEX(i,j+1)+y INDEX(i,j-1)+
   y INDEX(i+1,j)+y INDEX(i-1,j)-4.*y INDEX(i,j) )/dx*dx;
}

float residual(i,j,m,f,v)
int i,j,m;float *f,*v;
{
int maxj;
float av();
maxj=m+1;
return f INDEX(i,j)-av(i,j,m,v);
}
```

```
correct(m,v,v2h)
int m; float *v,*v2h;
{/*coarse to fine red points only */
int i,j,mfine,maxj;float save;
mfine=m<<1;
maxj=m+1;/*coarse*/
/*printf(" correcting coarse=%d\n",m);*/
for(j=0;j<=m;j++)
for(i=0;i<=m;i++)/*don't touch boundary points*/
   {/* i=0 set v 0,1 from v2h 0,1. i=m-1, set 2m-1*/
   if(i!=(m) && i && j && j!=(m) )
      {
      /* prevent correction of i==0 boundary here*/
      if(i)  /* agrees with comment, but not actual usage in MULTIG*/
         {
      save= v INDEX(2*i,2*j+1);
      /* multiply correction by 2 to account for no corr. of black*/
      v INDX(2*i,2*j+1,mfine)+=.5*mult*(v2h INDEX(i,j)+v2h INDEX(i,j-1));
/*printf("v %d %d was %f now %f\n",2*i,2*j+1,save,v INDX(2*i,2*j+1,mfine));*/
         }
/*add correction term*/
      save= v INDEX(2*i+1,2*j);
      v INDX(2*i+1,2*j,mfine)+=.5*mult*(v2h INDEX(i,j)+v2h INDEX(i-1,j));
/*printf("v %d %d was %f now %f\n",2*i+1,2*j,save,v INDX(2*i+1,2*j,mfine));*/
         }
/* if i==m but 2*i+1 would not be boundary- don't correct!
/*   else
      {;
      if(!i)
         {
         v INDX(0,2*j+1,k)+=.5*(v2h INDEX(i,j)+v2h INDEX(i,j-1));
         }
      else if(!j)
         {
         v INDX(2*i+1,j,k)+=.5*(v2h INDEX(i,j)+v2h INDEX(i-1,j));
         }
      else if (i==(m))
```

```
          {
          v INDX(2*i+1,2*j,k)+=.5*(v2h INDEX(i,j)+v2h INDEX(i,j-1));
          }
       else
          {
          v INDX(2*i,2*j+1,k)+=.5*(v2h INDEX(i,j)+v2h INDEX(i-1,j));
          }
       }
    */
}
}


restrict(m,coarsef,finef,v)
int m; float *finef,*coarsef,*v;
{/*fine to coarse f*/
int i,mfine,j,k,l,finetop,maxj;
float coef,residp,residm,residc,residq,residr;
float residual();
maxj=m+1;/*coarse*/
mfine=m<<1;
finetop=mfine;
coef=dx*dx;
for(j=1;j<m;j++)
for(i=1;i<m;i++)
   {
   /* restrict  f2h = (fh-Av)*/
   k=i<<1;l=j<<1;
   residc= residual(k ,l  ,mfine,finef,v);
   residm= residual(k-1,l  ,mfine,finef,v);
   residp= residual(k+1,l  ,mfine,finef,v);
   residq= residual(k ,l+1,mfine,finef,v);
   residr= residual(k ,l+1,mfine,finef,v);/*full weighting*/
   coarsef INDEX(i,j)=.125*(residp+residm+residq+residr+4.*residc);
   /*coarsef INDEX(i,j)=residc*/;/*injection*/
   }
   /* error residual  Ae=r;*/
for(j=0;j<m;j++)
   {
```

```
      coarsef INDEX(0,j)= finef INDX(0,j,mfine)-v INDX(0,j,mfine);
      coarsef INDEX(m,j)=finef INDX(finetop,j,mfine)-v INDX(finetop,j,mfine) ;
      }
for(i=0;i<m;i++)
   {
   coarsef INDEX(i,0)= finef INDX(i,0,mfine)-v INDX(i,0,mfine);
   coarsef INDEX(i,m)=finef INDX(i,finetop,mfine)-v INDX(i,finetop,mfine) ;
   }
}

relax(m,u,f)
int m;
float *u,*f;
{
int i,j,k,maxj;
float fip,fim,coef;
coef=dx*dx;
maxj=m+1;
/* solve approx. by sor iteration Au=f for u*/
/*boundary conditions Av=f a=1*/
for(i=0;i<=m;i++)
   {
   u INDEX(i,0)=f INDEX(i,0);
   u INDEX(i,m)=f INDEX(i,m);
   u INDEX(0,i)=f INDEX(0,i);
   u INDEX(m,i)=f INDEX(m,i);
   }
/*brute force*/
for(j=0;j<=m;j++)
for(i=0;i<=m;i++)
   {
/*   u INDEX(i,j)= ( u INDEX(i,j-1)+u INDEX(i,j+1)+u INDEX(i+1,j)
      +u INDEX(i-1,j)-f INDEX(i,j)*coef )*.25;
      */
/*printf(" before: u %f f %f i,j %d %d\n",u INDEX(i,j), f INDEX(i,j) ,i,j);*/
   }

/* red-black*/
```

```
for(k=0;k<2;k++)
for(j=1+k;j<m;j+=2)
for(i=1;i<m;i++)
  {/* laplacian  u"= (u+ + u  -4*u)/dx^2=f */
  u INDEX(i,j)= ( u INDEX(i,j-1)+u INDEX(i,j+1)+u INDEX(i+1,j)
    +u INDEX(i-1,j)-f INDEX(i,j)*coef )*.25;
  }
for(j=0;j<=m;j++)
for(i=0;i<=m;i++)
  {
/*   u INDEX(i,j)= ( u INDEX(i,j-1)+u INDEX(i,j+1)+u INDEX(i+1,j)
    +u INDEX(i-1,j)-f INDEX(i,j)*coef )*.25;
    */
/*printf(" after: u %f f %f i,j %d %d\n",u INDEX(i,j), f INDEX(i,j) ,i,j);*/
  }
}


mvcycle(nn,hin,v,f)
int hin,nn; float *v,*f;
{
/* perform MV scheme cycle  v initial guess returns v*/
int h,i,m,mu=1,msq;/* mu=1 for V scheme =2 for W scheme*/
float *nextgridf,*nextgridv;
h=hin;
m=nn;

/*printf(" enter mvcycle with h=%d n=%d\n",h,nn); */
for(i=0;i<n1;i++)relax(nn,v,f);
if(ncoarsest!=nn)
  {
  msq=(m+1)*(m+1);
  nextgridf= &(f[msq]);
  nextgridv= &(v[msq]);
  m>>=1;
  msq=(m+1)*(m+1);
  h<<=1;
  restrict(m,nextgridf,f,v);
```

```
  for(i=0;i<msq;i++) *nextgridv++=0.;
  for(i=0;i<mu;i++)mvcycle(m,h,nextgridv ,nextgridf);
  correct(m,v,nextgridv);
  }
for(i=0;i<n2;i++)relax(nn,v,f);
}


fullmgv(nn,hin,v,f)
int nn,hin;float *v,*f;
{
int i,j,m,msq,h;
float *nextgridf,*nextgridv;
h=hin;

/*printf(" enter full with h=%d n=%d\n",h,nn);*/
if(nn!=ncoarsest)
  {
  m=nn>>1;
  h<<=1;
  msq=(nn+1)*(nn+1);
  nextgridf= &(f[msq]);
  nextgridv= &(v[msq]);
  restrict(m,nextgridf,f,v);
  msq=(m+1)*(m+1);
  for(i=0;i<msq;i++) *nextgridv++=0.;
  fullmgv(m,h,nextgridv ,nextgridf);
  correct(m,v,nextgridv);
  }
for(i=0;i<n0;i++)mvcycle(nn,hin,v,f);
}


FILE *plot;

main()
{
int i,j,k,l,m,twon,np,maxj,kount=0;
float resid,error,stopr;
float residual();
```

```
/*init*/
/* n, m, etc powers of two np 2**n+1. index runs 0-n, b.c. at 0,n */
np= n +1;maxj=np;
twon=2*np;
printf(" enter 1<=mult<=2,stop resid.");
scanf("%f %f",&mult,&stopr);
printf(" mult=%f stopping resid=%f\n",mult,stopr);
  /*initialize f,v all grids*/
  for(i=0;i< twon;i++)
  for(j=0;j<= n ;j++)
    {
    v INDEX(i,j)=0.;f INDEX(i,j)=0.;}
  /* b.c. for Av=f*/
l=n;
for(i=0;i<= n ;i++)
  {
  f INDEX(i,0)=bc0;
  f INDEX( n , i)=bc1;
  f INDEX( 0 ,i) =bc0;
  f INDEX(i, l ) =bc1;
  }
/* special test- v already ok*/
/*   for (i=0;i<n;i++)
    v[i]=bc0+(bc1-bc0)*i/((float)(n-1));
*/
while(1)
  {
/*   for (i=0;i<=n;i++)
  for (j=0;j<=n;j++)
    printf(" resid %e for v %e %d %d\n",
      residual(i,j,n,f,v),v INDEX(i,j),i,j);
*/
  fullmgv(n,1,v,f);
  /*calc. resid.*/
  resid=0.;
  for (j=0;j<=n;j++)
  for (i=0;i<=n;i++)
    {
```

```
      error = residual(i,j,n,f,v);
/*      printf(" error[%d][%d]=%f v=%f f=%f\n",
        i,j,error,v INDEX(i,j),f INDEX(i,j));
*/
      resid+=error*error;
      }
   kount++;
   if(resid < stopr ) break;
   else printf("RESIDUAL = %f IN MAIN at %d iteration\n",resid,kount);
         }
printf(" fini\n");
plot=fopen("plot.dat","w");
resid=1./((double)np);
fprintf(plot," %d %d\n",np,np);
for(i=0;i<2;i++){for(j=0;j<=n;j++)fprintf(plot,"%le ", j*resid);}
for(i=0;i<=n;i++){for(j=0;j<=n;j++)fprintf(plot,"%le ",v INDEX(i,j) );fprintf(plot,
}
```

enter 1<=mult<=2,stop resid. mult=1.000000 stopping resid=0.00001
RESIDUAL = 3.584443 IN MAIN at 1 iteration
RESIDUAL = 0.542412 IN MAIN at 2 iteration
RESIDUAL = 0.147893 IN MAIN at 3 iteration
RESIDUAL = 0.066587 IN MAIN at 4 iteration
RESIDUAL = 0.040397 IN MAIN at 5 iteration
RESIDUAL = 0.027727 IN MAIN at 6 iteration
RESIDUAL = 0.019843 IN MAIN at 7 iteration
RESIDUAL = 0.014390 IN MAIN at 8 iteration
RESIDUAL = 0.010480 IN MAIN at 9 iteration
RESIDUAL = 0.007643 IN MAIN at 10 iteration
RESIDUAL = 0.005576 IN MAIN at 11 iteration
RESIDUAL = 0.004069 IN MAIN at 12 iteration
RESIDUAL = 0.002969 IN MAIN at 13 iteration
RESIDUAL = 0.002167 IN MAIN at 14 iteration
RESIDUAL = 0.001581 IN MAIN at 15 iteration
RESIDUAL = 0.001154 IN MAIN at 16 iteration
RESIDUAL = 0.000842 IN MAIN at 17 iteration
RESIDUAL = 0.000614 IN MAIN at 18 iteration
RESIDUAL = 0.000448 IN MAIN at 19 iteration
RESIDUAL = 0.000327 IN MAIN at 20 iteration
RESIDUAL = 0.000239 IN MAIN at 21 iteration
RESIDUAL = 0.000174 IN MAIN at 22 iteration
RESIDUAL = 0.000127 IN MAIN at 23 iteration
RESIDUAL = 0.000093 IN MAIN at 24 iteration
RESIDUAL = 0.000068 IN MAIN at 25 iteration
RESIDUAL = 0.000049 IN MAIN at 26 iteration
RESIDUAL = 0.000036 IN MAIN at 27 iteration
RESIDUAL = 0.000026 IN MAIN at 28 iteration
RESIDUAL = 0.000019 IN MAIN at 29 iteration
RESIDUAL = 0.000014 IN MAIN at 30 iteration
RESIDUAL = 0.000010 IN MAIN at 31 iteration
fini

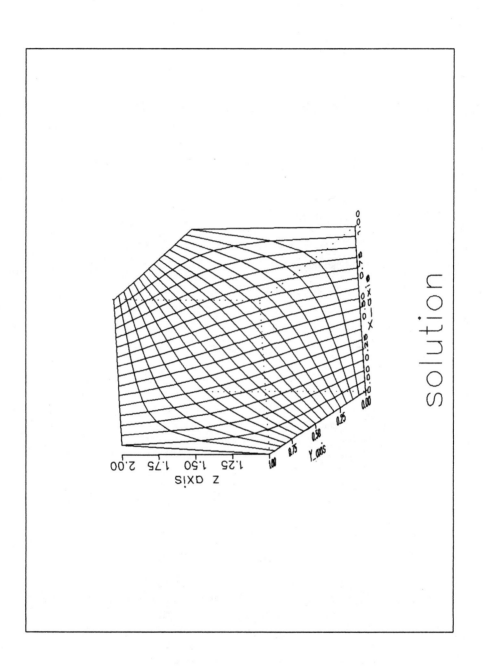

Chapter 4

Gaussian Quadrature and Related Methods

Chapter Objectives

In this chapter you will find C tools to:

– perform Gaussian quadrature

– efficiently evaluate integral powers of a variable

In addition, we will discuss the many varieties of integration methods related to Gaussian quadrature and their applications.

What Is Gaussian Quadrature?

In the previous chapter, we have discussed general methods of integration and a particular technique for obtaining integrals of prescribed accuracy. One pays a price for adaptive quadrature, however, in the cost of function evaluations. We describe in this chapter methods that are much more economical and provide accurate answers if the integrand is not pathological (i.e., contains singularities or other "tricky" features). We will also discuss the application of related methods to a variety of problems which implicitly contain integration, such as transport problems, and as a sidelight discuss an economical, recursive method for computing the integral powers of a number. We will continue to use the notation of the previous chapter, so please review it briefly if you have not already read it.

Orthogonal Polynomials, Gaussian Quadrature

In the preceding chapter, we stated that an integration method was obtained by fitting a prescribed function, which we can easily integrate, to a portion of the function to be integrated. In Gaussian quadrature, the function used for the fit is a sum of polynomials which are orthogonal over the interval of integration (orthogonal means that any pairwise product of the polynomials over that interval integrates to zero. For a full discussion of orthogonal polynomials see, for example, Wilf. This fitting can be done very economically if we properly choose the points at which we do the fitting. Unlike the Newton-Cotes family of methods in which those points were equally spaced, the points in Gaussian quadrature have to be chosen, it turns out, as the zeros of a polynomial.

Another way of looking at the problem is the following. We want to obtain a formula for the integral of a function f(x) between the x[min] and x[max] of any panel which is of the form:

$$\sum_{i=1}^{N} c_i \, f(x_i)$$

If we use a Newton-Cotes formula, the x[i] are constrained to be x[min],x[min + dx],...x[max] (where dx= (x[max] − x[min])/(N − 1)). We therefore have N free parameters, c[i], i = 1...,N. We can therefore expect to obtain a formula which will be exact for functions f which are polynomials up to degree N − 1. Gauss suggested that if we view the x[i] as free parameters, we now have 2N parameters, and can hope to obtain formulae which exactly integrate functions f which are polynomials up to degree 2N − 1. He then showed how to do this. Briefly, one uses Lagrange interpolation with orthogonal polynomials. To construct a polynomial which goes through the points (x[1],y[1]),(x[2],y[2]),..., Lagrange interpolation constructs a sum of terms each of which evaluates to y[i] at the corresponding x[i] and vanishes at the other values of x[i]:

$$y[1]\frac{(x-x[2])(x-x[3])...}{(x[1]-x[2])(x[1]-x[3])...} + y[2]\frac{(x-x[1])(x-x[3])...}{(x[2]-x[1])(x[2]-x[3])...} + ...$$

and similarly for the terms proportional to y[3], etc. Gauss constructed an interpolating polynomial for f (where f is assumed to be a polynomial of degree 2N −1 or less, whose integral we attempted to determine exactly), from the Nth polynomial of an orthogonal sequence of polynomials, P(N,x) (which will in general be an Nth degree polynomial—see Wilf, op. cit.) in exactly the same fashion, as the sum of terms of the form:

$$L(i) = P(N,x) / \{(x - x[i]) \, P'(N,x[i])\}$$

Note that the derivative of P(N,x) with respect to x, P′(N,x), is used as a shorthand way of writing the other factors of the denominator in Lagrange interpolation. Then

$$S = \sum_{i=1}^{N} L[i]f(x[i])$$

is a polynomial of degree N-1, which, by construction, is the Lagrange interpolating polynomial through the f(x[i]). But P(N,x) must have zeros at the values x[i] if the L(i) are to remain finite. We have thus determined the abscissa values x[i], and need only determine the c[i]. We leave the details to Wilf or a similar text. For "standard", Nth order Gaussian quadrature, which will be exact for integrating polynomials of degree 2N-1 or less, over the range -1 < x < 1 :

$$c[i]= 2 /\{(1-x[i]^2)P'\,(N,x[i])^2\}$$

where the P are Legendre polynomials and x[i] are their zeros. (Again, we refer you to Wilf or similar works for details about the Legendre and similar orthogonal polynomials, to the general expression for c[i], and for recurrence relations that make the evaluation of the polynomials and their derivatives simple). The roots of the polynomials can be determined with a root finder such as discussed in Chapter 5 of *C Tools*, assuming you wish to construct your own analogues of Gaussian quadrature formulae for some special purpose.

Pitfalls

Gaussian quadrature does very well if the function is a polynomial, or well approximated by a polynomial. It will obviously do less-well on a function which is not well fitted by polynomials. Rational functions, that is the ratio of polynomials, can obviously give problems, especially near zeros of the denominator. It is well known that interpolating a function with a polynomial can be dangerous. Polynomial fits tend to oscillate wildly if the polynomial is of large degree. For this reason, it is dangerous, in general, to use a high order Gaussian quadrature unless you check cases with an adaptive quadrature method, or perhaps by subdividing the interval and doing separate Gaussian quadratures over each interval, summing the results and comparing with the result for the single interval.

The Gaussian quadrature method uses Legendre polynomials, which are orthogonal over the interval [− 1,1]. Any integral between finite limits can be transformed to this interval by simply transforming the variable x to the variable z defined by:

$$z= 2 (x - \{x[max] + x[min]\}/2)/(x[max] - x[min]).$$

Of course, the integral evaluated in this "stretched" coordinate system must be scaled back to that in the original range by a factor of (x[max]-x[min])/2.

Related Methods: Other Orthogonal Polynomials

The results above can be generalized in a number of ways. First, assume we are integrating the function f multiplied by some weighting function w(x). We can carry over all of the above results by using polynomials orthogonal over the interval when multiplied by w. We can also extend the results to infinite intervals by using appropriate w and the corresponding orthogonal polynomials.

For just about any choice of interval and suitable weight function for that interval, orthogonal polynomials may be found, and consequently formulas analogous to Gaussian quadrature. For Gaussian quadrature, the weight function is w(x)=1. Over the same interval, $-1 < x < 1$, if we use the weight function w(x)= $1/\sqrt{(1 - x^2)}$, we find that the appropriate orthogonal polynomials are Tchebycheff (also spelled Chebyshev or many other ways) polynomials, for example. We may then find the integral of w(x)f(x) over the specified interval in a manner entirely similar to Gaussian quadrature.

Of more interest are formulae for the intervals $0 < x < \infty$ and $- \infty < x < \infty$. For the former case, with a weight function w(x) = exp($- x$), we may use Laguerre polynomials and for the latter, Hermite polynomials, with w(x) = exp($-x^2$). The coefficients (and requisite zeros of these polynomials) are tabulated in M. Abramowitz and I. Stegun, *Handbook of Mathematical Functions*, Dept. of Commerce, National Bureau of Standards, 1964—also reprinted by Dover Publ., NY.

Related Methods: Lobatto Quadrature

Between having the integration points prescribed as in Newton—Coates and freely chosen to be optimal, there are intermediate possibilities. Lobatto quadrature is an example in which the endpoints of the interval, i.e., x[max] = 1 and x[min] = −1 are to be used as quadrature points, with the remaining points to be chosen "optimally" (where optimal usually is taken to mean in the same sense as for Gaussian quadrature, namely to integrate exactly the highest order polynomial possible). There are at least two possible reasons for adopting such a method of integration. The prescribed points might be known as boundary conditions or function values that can easily be evaluated. Alternatively, they may be values of x of special interest; here we are thinking of transport problems, which we will discuss below. Table 4.1 summarizes some of the variants on Gaussian quadrature.

TABLE 4.1

Gaussian Quadrature And Its Relatives

METHOD	POLYNOMIAL	INTERVAL	WEIGHT	ERROR	NOTES
Gauss	Legendre	$-1 < x <$	1	2n	
Radau	"	"	1	2n–1	f(-1) used
Lobatto	"	"	1	2n–2	f(-1),f(1)used
Jacobi	Jacobi	$0 < x < 1$	x^k	2n	
Legendre	Legendre	"	$\sqrt{(1-x)}$		
Legendre	"	"	$1/\sqrt{(1-x)}$	2n	
Chebyshev	Chebyshev	$-1 < x < 1$	$1/\sqrt{(1-x^2)}$	2n	
"	"(2nd kind)	"	$\sqrt{(1-x^2)}$	2n	
Laguerre	Laguerre	$0 < x < \infty$	$\exp(-x)$	2n	
Hermite	Hermite	$-\infty < x < \infty$	$\exp(-x^2)$	2n	
Filon	–	finite	sin/cos tx	—	

POLYNOMIAL is the name of the family of orthogonal polynomials used in obtaining the formulae.

"ERROR " is the order of the derivative in the error term of the formula with N function evaluations. For an error deriv. of m, the formula will be exact for polynomials of degree m-1 or less.

Application To Transport Problems

A standard numerical method for solving the equations for the transport of, e.g., neutrons, is the spherical harmonics method, sometimes called the P—N method. This involves (in problems involving one-spatial dimension, as transport through "slabs" or a sphere) expansion of the intensity I in Legendre polynomials. The application of Gaussian Quadrature, the significance of particular "ray" directions at the zeros of the Legendre polynomial, etc., should suggest themselves, and indeed they are related. See Richtmyer and Morton, *Difference Methods in Initial-Value Problems* (NY: J. Wiley (Interscience),1967 second edition) for a discussion of the relationships in their Chapter 9. The topic doesn't deserve much coverage in a chapter on numerical integration in a book such as this. However, let us note the value of Lobatto quadrature in such methods, as demonstrated by J. Morel of Los Alamos National Laboratories, and others.

Application To Spectral Line Transport

We present one final application of Gaussian-Hermite quadrature for your amusement. In a problem involving the transport of an approximately Gaussian (in this case, I mean a function of the form $\exp(-x^2)$; Carl Friedrich Gauss has his name attached to many things) spectral line, I found it desirable to discretize the spectral line by representing its values at the points used for Gaussian-Hermite quadrature. But the tabulated values in Abramowitz and Stegun only went up to twenty points, and I needed more resolution. Since evaluating Hermite polynomials is a fairly simple exercise, you only need a root solver to complete the task. For example, for 28 points, the abscissas (x[i] at which f is evaluated) and the corresponding weights by which f should be multiplied (the weights presented here include the factor of $\exp(x[i]^2)$ and are required to cancel the similar factor implicitly contained in the integral are as follows:

abscissa	wt
.208067	.4162404
.624837	.4175135
1.043535	.4201116
1.465537	.4241439
1.892326	.4298914
2.324749	.4373327
2.767765	.4471895
3.221112	.4600081
3.689134	.4768166
4.176637	.4993444
4.690756	.5307748
5.243285	.5777941
5.857015	.6579890
6.591605	.8447289

(There are only 14 tabulated abscissas, since the other 14 have equal weights and abscissa values which are the negatives of these. In the case of odd-order schemes, the abscissa x=0. occurs in the formulae as well.) You might find it amusing to duplicate or extend these results, particularly if you can use them.

Algorithm 331 of the Collected Algorithms of the CACM presents a program in ALGOL which obtains the abscissas and weights for Gaussian quadrature formulae for arbitrary weight functions.

Test Problem: Integral Powers

For our test problem, we use a Gaussian quadrature formula for N=3, which should be exact for polynomials up to the fifth degree. Indeed it is, and for the sixth degree problem, whose exact answer is 1/7, it still does very well.

The programs of the Chapter are listed in Table 4.2. In addition to a third order Gaussian quadrature routine (exact up to 5th degree polynomials), routines for calculating the type double value of x^n for integral (positive, zero, or negative) n is included. An efficient recursion scheme is used, with an auxiliary routine powr() and a global variable used to reduce the overhead due to argument passing. Evaluation of the nth power of x requires of the order of the logarithm to the base two of n multiplications with this method. This is not optimal (for n = 9 will require 4 multiplications, whereas an optimal scheme will form x^3 and square the result, using a total of three multiplications), but is quite a bit simpler than an optimal scheme (see Knuth for a detailed discussion of the problem).

Table 4.2 lists the subroutines and functions presented in this chapter.

TABLE 4.2

Programs Of Chapter 4

gq3	3rd order Gaussian Quadrature
power	calculate x^n for type double x, type int n
powr	auxiliary routine used by power

References

D. E. Knuth, *The Art of Computer Programming, Vol. 2: Seminumerical Algorithms*, 2nd edition (Reading, Mass: Addison Wesley, 1981).

H. S. Wilf, *Mathematics for the Physical Sciences* (New York: Dover, 1962).

Program Listing And Test Problem Output

(Listing begins next page.)

```
/* Gaussian Quadrature routine

from More C tools for Scientists and Engineers by L. Baker

includes function power() for computing arbitrary integral power of
a floating point variable x

*/



/*#include "libc.h"*/
#define DOFOR(i,to) for(i=0;i<to;i++)

int expn;

main(argc,argv) int argc;char **argv;
{
double gq3(),power();
int n;

DOFOR(n,7)
   {
   expn=n;
   printf(" integral 0-1 x to %d = %f \n",n, gq3(0.,1.,power) );
   }
exit(0);
}


double gq3(left,right,f)
double left,right,(*f)();
{
double a,b,y;

a=.5*(left+right);
b=right-left;
y=.3872983*b;
y=.2777777777*( (*f)(a+y) +(*f)(a-y) );
```

```
y=b*(y+ .4444444444*(*f)(a));
return(y);
}

double zprwr;/* making it global reduces the recursive call overhead*/

double power(x)
double x;
{double powr();
/* returns x**expn */
zprwr=x;
if (expn<0)
  {expn=-expn;
   return(1./powr(expn));
   }
return (powr(expn));
}

double powr(n)
int n;
{
double y;
if (n==0) return(1.);
if(n==1)return(zprwr);
  y=powr(n>>1);
  y=y*y;
if( n&1 )
  /* n is odd*/
  return( zprwr*y);
else
  return(y);
return(0.);/* keep DeSmet happy*/
}
```

integral 0-1 x to 0 = 1.00000
integral 0-1 x to 1 = 0.500000
integral 0-1 x to 2 = 0.333333
integral 0-1 x to 3 = 0.250000
integral 0-1 x to 4 = 0.200000
integral 0-1 x to 5 = 0.166667
integral 0-1 x to 6 = 0.142500

CHAPTER 5

The Complex Error Function and Relatives

Chapter Objectives

In this chapter we will:

– develop the use of continued fractions for function approximation

– apply this technique to the approximation of a number of functions of interest

These are the complex error function and some of its relatives: the plasma dispersion function, the Fresnel integrals, and Dawson's integral.

Introduction

In this chapter we employ a powerful method for functional approximation, based on the use of continued fractions. This has been used in conjunction with our complex arithmetic package to produce a program for evaluating the plasma dispersion function and its derivative, based upon a FORTRAN program by Dr. B. S. Newberger. While this function may not be of interest to most readers, we have used it as the kernel of a set of programs to evaluate more popular functions, the error function and the Fresnel sine and cosine integrals, and Dawson's integral.

The Plasma Dispersion Function

This function may be looked upon as the Hilbert transform of the Gaussian function $\exp(-x^2)$. That is, it is

$$Z(z) = \frac{-1}{\sqrt{\pi}} P \int_{-\infty}^{\infty} \frac{e^{-x^2}}{z - x} dx$$

where the P indicates that the Cauchy principal value of the integral is to be taken, and the variable z is complex. It is $Z(z) = \frac{w(z)}{\sqrt{\pi} \, i}$ where w(z) is the complex error function. Thus computing this function easily gives us the complex error function.

As its name implies, the Plasma Dispersion function appears in dispersion relations in warm plasmas. The exponential or Gaussian factor arises from the Maxwellian distribution of particle velocities. The denominator is a difference between the particle velocity and a wave (phase)velocity, there being a resonant coupling between waves and particles with the same velocity.

The Voigt function is essentially the real part of the plasma dispersion function, and may be viewed as the convolution of the Gaussian and Lorentz functions. This function gives the shape of a spectral line which is broadened by quantum mechanical effects (the "natural" line shape is a Lorentzian profile of the form $1/(f^2 + a^2)$ where f is the frequency), and the thermal motion of the emitting atoms or molecules, which by the Doppler effect produces a Gaussian distribution of the emitted spectral lines.

Allied Functions

Error Function

We will use simpler rational approximations to the error function in Chapter 8, where we will discuss the Gaussian probability integral. We will also present an inverse error function based upon such rational approximations. Here, we merely need the fact that

$$Z(z) = i \sqrt{\pi} e^{-z^2} [1 + erf(iz)]$$

where erf() is the error function. Note that it is of an imaginary argument.

Fresnel Functions

The Fresnel functions are to the error function what the sine and cosine integrals are to the exponential integral, as discussed in the previous chapter. These functions arise in optics problems as well as antenna theory, generally in the context of the diffraction of electromagnetic (or acoustic) waves at an edge or wedge. See, for example, Balanis' Antenna Theory for both a discussion of diffraction theory which employs the Fresnel integrals as well as an appendix tabulating the functions. Relton's Applied Bessel Functions gives an example of a problem concerning the proper curvature for the bend of rails for a railway (the solution of which involves the Fresnel functions). The Fresnel integrals are given by

$$C(z) = \int_0^z \cos(\pi t^2/2) \, dt$$

and

$$S(z) = \int_0^z \sin(\pi t^2 / 2) \, dt$$

These may be found "simultaneously" as the real and imaginary parts of the plasma dispersion function of appropriate argument, appropriately scaled (see the program code).

Dawson's Integral

The function $D(x) = e^{-x^2} \int_0^x e^{t^2} \, dt$ may be expressed in terms of the plasma dispersion function (see, e.g., Abramowitz and Stegun where it is related to the error function of an imaginary argument).

Numerical Method

The computation of the plasma dispersion function follows the general pattern of the functional approximations encountered previously. First, symmetry relations are used to transform a problem in which the complex variable z is not in the first quadrant, i.e., does not have both real and imaginary parts positive, into a problem in which this is the case. Here, if the transformed variable z has real part less than 10 and imaginary part less than 1, a rational approximation is employed, based upon expressing the PDF in terms of Kummer's Confluent Hypergeometric Function. This is evaluated by a recurrence relation. The rational approximation to Kummer's function is of the form A[n](z)/B[n](z), where A[n] and B[n] are polynomials of the same degree n (that is, we are using a diagonal Pade approximant as discussed above in Chapter 14), and the polynomials are evaluated by means of recurrences of the form A[n](z) = (1 + zF[n]) A[n − 1](z) + G[n]A[n − 2](z).

For larger arguments, a continued fraction approximation is employed. A continued fraction is a fraction whose denominator is a (continued) fraction, whose denominator is a (continued) fraction, etc., infinitely if desired. That is, they are expressions of the form:

$$\cfrac{p[1]}{q[1] + \cfrac{p[2]}{q[2] + \cfrac{p[3]}{q[3] + \ldots}}}$$

These are often written, for compactness, as

$$[\frac{p[1]}{q[1] +}, \frac{p[2]}{q[2] +}, \ldots]$$

Most of the continued fractions used are infinitely continued expressions for functions of interest. If we truncate the expansion at some point, i.e. we set p[k] = 0, the resulting fraction is called the kth convergent to the infinite continued fraction.

There are many books on continued fractions (see the references below). The best book describing the numerical applications of continued fractions I've found is Nonweiler's.

For a functional approximation we know the forms of the p[i] and the q[i]. If we know a priori how many terms to retain to get the desired accuracy, we may evaluate that convergent by so-called "backward" evaluation, evaluating r[k] = p[k]/q[k], r[j] = p[j]/(q[j] + r[j + 1]) for j = k − 1,k − 2,...1 with r[1] being the values of the kth convergent.

Generally, however, we wish to use forward evaluation, evaluating the first, second, etc., convergents until the nth and n + 1st converents are the same, to the required accuracy. There are a variety of methods for doing so. The simplest method, which we shall use here, is to use the recurrence relation where the nth converent to the continued fraction is written as A[n]/B[n], and

$$A[n] = A[n − 1]q[n − 1] + A[n − 2]p[n]$$

$$B[n] = B[n − 1]q[n − 1] + B[n − 2]p[n]$$

with A[− 1] = B[0] = 1,A[0] = B[− 1] = 0. While this simple method is easy to program and adequate for our needs, more sophisticated methods are available when these recurrences run into problems; we shall present one such method, due to Lentz and modified by Barnett and Thompson, in a later chapter. The A[n] and B[n] tend to grow exponentially and generally need to be rescaled to avoid overflows, even though their ratio is well behaved.

Such continued fraction representation are found, for example, in Luke, Slater, and Higher Transcendental Functions.

Thus, functions that can be represented as some form of such a function can be approximated with a continued fraction representation. Algorithms 191 and 192 of the *Collected algorithms from the CACM* given ALGOL procedures for computer hypergeometric and confluent hypergeometric functions, while Luke's book gives a number of FORTRAN programs for the confluent hypergeometric functions.

Continued fraction and rational (Pade) approximations are intimately related. See, for example, Sullivan's article. A good reference with many examples is Khovanskii.

The classic paper on the convergence of continued fractions is that of Scott and Wall. Briefly, it is necessary that odd terms form a divergent series. Consequently, continued fractions may perform poorly for small x, or when the a and b coefficients are all near one. The continued fraction for the "golden ratio" has all the a's and b's equal to one, and is therefore one of the slowest converging fractions.

The Program And Test Results

The program presented here uses the complex arithmetic package discussed in *C Tools*. Each line of output contains the (real) value of the argument, and x (which ranges from .4 to 2.), the error function, the complementary error function (1 − the error function), and the cosine and sine Fresnel integrals, and Dawson's integral. Note that the test programs do not exercise the value calculated for the derivative of the plasma dispersion function. The iterated complementary error function is also provided. It is defined by: i^0 erfc(z) = erfc(z) and $i^n erfc(t) = \int_z^\infty i^{n-1} erfc(t)\, dt.$

One sometimes sees the following method for performing complex multiplications advocated. To calculate (a+bi)(c+di), form A = (a+b)(c+d), B = ac, C = bd. Then the real part of the product is B − C, and the imaginary part is A − B − C. This method uses three multiplications and five additions/subtractions, compared to four and two, respectively, for the simple method used in Complex.h. While this may result in a savings when software emulation or very old machine architectures are used, for typical floating point processors such as the 80387 family, a multiplication generally costs only slighly more than an addition. Thus the subtle method will be slower than the obvious one.

TABLE 5.1

Programs of Chapter 5

printc	print complex number
dawson	Dawson's integral
fresnel	Fresnel integrals
pdisp	plasma dispersion function
cfbig,cfsmall	aux. routines uded by pdisp
cexp	complex exponential
ierfc	iterated complementary error function
cerf	complex error function

References

M. Abramowitz & I. Stegun, *Handbook of Mathematical Functions* (New York: Dover, 1965).

A. R. Barnett, D. H. Feng, J. W. Steed, and L. J. B. Goldfarb, *Comput. Phys. Commun.* **8**,377,1974.

Bateman Manuscript Project, *Higher Transcendental Functions* (A. Erdelyi, ed., NY: Krieger Publ. Co., 1981).

Collected Algorithms from (C)ACM (CALGO), (New York: Association for Computing Machinery, Vol. 1 1980; continuing).

H. S. Hall and S. R. Knight, *Higher Algebra* (London: MacMillan and Co.,1936).

A. Ya Khinchin, *Continued Fractions* (Chicago: University of Chicago Press, 1961 3rd (Russian) edition).

A. N. Khovanskii, *The Applications of Continued Fractions and Their Generalizations to Problems in Approximation Theory* (Groningen, The Netherlands: P. Noordhoff N. V., 1963).

W. J. Lentz, *Applied Optics*, **15**,668,1976.

Y. Luke, *Algorithms for the Computation of Mathematical Functions* (New York: Academic Press, 1977).

B. S. Newberger, *Computer Physics Communications*, **42**,305 1986.

T. R. F. Nonweiler, *Computational Mathematics: An Introduction to Numerical Approximation* (New York: Ellis Horwood/Halsted Press, a division of J. Wiley, 1984).

L. J. Slater, *Confluent Hypergeometric Funtions* (Cambridge: University Press, 1960).

W.T. Scott and H. S. Wall, *Am . J. Math*, **69**, 551, 1947.

Sullivan, J., "Pade approximants via the continued fraction approach," *Am. J. Physics*, **46**, May 1978, p.489.

I. J. Thomspon and A. R. Barnett, *J. Comp. Physics*, **64**,490,1986.

Program Listing And Test Problem Output

(Listing begins next page.)

```
/*
package of routines that compute the plasma dispersion
function for complex arguments, returning a complex value

allied functions computed are the error function and the Fresnel integrals

routines for handling complex arithmetic in C are included

from More C tools for scientists and engineers by L. Baker

*/

int iterp;/* global to return count used*/

/* for below, x,y are complex structures, and one is returned*/
#include "complex.h"
struct complex    ci,c1,c0,o,o2,ir;

#define min(a,b) (((a)<(b))? (a): (b))
#define abs(x) ((x)?  (x):-(x))

main (argc,argv) int argc; char **argv;
{
/*FILE*/int *fopen(),*fileid;
int i;double erf(),erfc,a,z,x,y,si,ci,q,dawson(),ierfc();
fileid=fopen("PLOT.DAT","w");
fprintf(fileid," 4 \n");
q=1/.56418958;
printf(" ierfc %e %e\n",ierfc(.1,2),ierfc(.5,2));
printf(" ierfc %e %e\n",ierfc(.1,4),ierfc(.5,4));
printf(" ierfc %e %e\n",ierfc(.1,6),ierfc(.5,6));
printf(" scaled ierfc %e %e\n",q*ierfc(.1,1),q*ierfc(.5,1));
printf(" scaled ierfc %e %e\n",4.*ierfc(.1,2),4.*ierfc(.5,2));
printf(" scaled ierfc %e %e\n",32.*ierfc(.1,4),32.*ierfc(.5,4));
printf(" scaled ierfc %e %e\n",384.*ierfc(.1,6),384.*ierfc(.5,6));
printf(" scaled ierfc %e %e\n",122880.*ierfc(.1,10),122880.*ierfc(.5,10));
for (i=0;i<50;i++)
{
```

```
   x=(i+1)*.1;
   y=erf(x,&erfc);
   fresnel(x,&ci,&si);
   z=dawson(x);
printf(" x=%f %f %f %f %f %e %d\n",x,y,erfc,ci,si,z,iterp);
fprintf(fileid,"%f %e %e %e %e\n",x,y,erfc,ci,si);
};


exit(0);
}

printc(z) struct complex *z;
{
printf("%f %f",z->x,z->y);
}


double erf(z,erfc)
double *erfc,z;
{
struct complex cz1,cz,c4,czeta,czsp;
int iter;
double erff,exp();
c4.y=.5641895835;
c4.x=0.;
CMPLX(cz,0.,z);
iter=40;
pdisp(&cz,1.e-5,&czeta,&czsp,iter);
/*printf(" erf "); printc(&czeta);printc(&czsp);printf("\n");*/
CMULT(cz1,c4,czeta);
erff=1.+cz1.x*exp(-z*z);
*erfc=1.-erff;
return (erff);
}


double dawson(x) double x;
{
double eps=1.e-5;
```

```
int iter=30;
struct complex z,ans,derans;
z.x=x;z.y=0;
pdisp(&z,eps,&ans,&derans,iter);
return (-.5*ans.x);
}


/* compute the Fresnel integrals */

fresnel (z,fci,fsi) double z,*fci,*fsi;
{
int iter;
double rtip,aa;
struct complex ci,c1,c2,c3,cz,cc,czeta,czp,cdum,cdu1;
aa=.8862269255;
c1.x=aa;
c1.y=aa;
ci.x=0.;ci.y=1.;
c2.x=0.;
c2.y=1.570796327;
c3.x=-.5641895835;
c3.y=c3.x;
CTREAL(cz,c1,z);
iter=20;
pdisp(&cz,1.e-5,&czeta,&czp,iter);
/*printf(" fresnel "); printc(&czeta);printc(&czp);printf("\n");*/
CTREAL(cdum,c2, (z*z) );
cexp(&cdum,&cdu1);
CMULT(cdum,cdu1,czeta);
CMULT(cdu1,cdum,ci);
CTREAL(cdu1,cdu1,-.5);
cdu1.x=cdu1.x-aa;
CMULT(cdum,cdu1,c3);
*fci=cdum.x;
*fsi=cdum.y;
return;
}
```

```
/* compute the plasma dispersion function and its derivatives
iter is maximum iteration count allowed, eps desired error
zetai is the input argument, zeeo the value of the function
and zeeprimo the first derivative (both output)

*/
int itmax=20,lhpsw;
struct complex zeta,zee,zeeprim;
struct complex w,ww,g1,g2,ofo,z,zetasq,zp,bp,bpp1,bs,rz,iz;
struct complex crtpi,a1,a2,a3,b1,b2,b3,t1,t2,u1,u2,v1,v2,cdum,cdu2,cdu3,cdu1;
double pi=3.141592653589,sqrt(),rtpi,flhp,csw,xi1,ct1,ct2,cp1,app1,dreal;


pdisp(zetai,eps,zeeo,zeeprimo,iter) int iter;double eps;
struct complex *zetai,*zeeprimo,*zeeo;
{ci.x=0.;
ci.y=1.;
c1.x=1.;
c1.y=0.;
crtpi.x=0.;
crtpi.y=1.772453851;
c0.x=0.;c0.y=0.;
CASSN(zeta,zetai);
if(iter>0) itmax=iter;
if( zeta.x< 0.){lhpsw=-1;CONJG(cdum,zeta);CSUB(zeta,c0,cdum);}
   else {lhpsw=1;}
flhp=lhpsw;
if( zeta.y<0.) csw=-1.;
   else csw=1.;

CMULT(zetasq,zeta,zeta);
CMPLX(w, zeta.x, (csw*zeta.y));
CMULT(ww,w,w);
/*printf(" pdf w,ww ");printc(&w);printc(&ww);printf("\n");*/
if ( abs(zeta.y)>=1. || cabs(zeta)>10.)
```

```
{
/* continued fraction approx for  abs( Im(zeta) ) >1 */
cfbig(eps);
}
else
{/* abs(zeta)<1*/
cfsmall(eps);
}
if(lhpsw==-1){
    CONJG(cdum,z);
    CSUB(z,c0,cdum);
      };
CLET(zee,z);
/*printf(" zee=");printc(&zee);printf("\n");*/
if(lhpsw==-1) {
    CONJG(cdum,zeta);
    CSUB(zeta,c0,cdum);
        };
CMULT(zetasq,zeta,zeta);
if(cabs(zeta)>10.)
  {
  CLET(cdum,c1);cdum.x=cdum.x-csw;
  CMULT(cdu2,cdum,zetasq);
  CTREAL(cdu2,cdu2,-.5);
  cexp(&cdu2,&cdu3);
  CMULT(cdu1,cdum,cdu3);
  CMULT(zp,cdu1,crtpi);
  CLET(u1,c1);
  CLET(u2,c0);
  cdum.x=3.5;cdum.y=0.;
  CSUB(cdum,cdum,ww);
  cdu2.x=-1.5;cdu2.y=0.;
  CDIV(v1,cdu2,cdum);
  CLET(v2,c0);
  CLET(t1,v1);
  CLET(t2,c0);
  iterp=1;
  while(1==1)
```

```
    {
    app1= -(iterp+1)*(iterp+2.5);
    cdum.y=0;
    cdum.x=1.5+2*iterp;
    CSUB(bp,cdum,ww);
    CLET(bpp1,bp);bpp1.x=bpp1.x+2.;
    CMULT(bs,bpp1,bp);
    CTREAL(cdum,u1,app1);
    CADD(cdu2,cdum,bs);
    CDIV(u2,bs,cdu2);
    CSUB(cdum,u2,c1);
    CMULT(v2,v1,cdum);
    CADD(t2,v2,t1);
    CSUB(cdum,t2,t1);
    if(cabs(cdum)<eps || iterp>itmax) break;
    iterp++;
    CLET(u1,u2);
    CLET(t1,t2);
    CLET(v1,v2);
    }
    CMULT(cdum,zp,zeta);
    CTREAL(cdum,cdum,-2.);
    CSUB(cdu1,t2,ww);
    cdu2.x=cdu1.x+1.5;
    cdu2.y=cdu1.y *csw;
    CDIV(zeeprim,c1,cdu2);
    CTREAL(zeeprim,zeeprim,-1.);
    CADD(zeeprim,zeeprim,cdum);
if(lhpsw==-1)
    {
    CONJG(cdum,zeeprim);
    CLET(zeeprim,cdum);
    }
/*printf(" zeeprim=");printc(&zeeprim);printf("\n");*/
}
else
  {
  CMULT(cdum,zeta,z);
```

```
   CADD(cdum,c1,cdum);
   CTREAL(zeeprim,cdum,-2.);
   };
CSET(zeeprimo,zeeprim);
CSET(zeeo,zee);
return;
}
cfbig(eps)double eps;
{
iterp=1;
CLET(a1,c1);
CLET(a2,c0);
cdum.x=2.5;cdum.y=0.;
CSUB(cdum,cdum,ww);
cdu2.x=-.5;cdu2.y=0.;
CDIV(b1,cdu2,cdum);
CLET(b2,c0);
CLET(t1,b1);
CLET(t2,c0);/*printf(" big\n");
printc(&a1);printc(&a2);printc(&b1);printc(&b2);printc(&t1);printc(&t2);*/
while(1)
   {
   app1=-(iterp+1)*(iterp+.5);
   dreal=.5+2*iterp;
   CLET(bp,c0); CSUB(bp,bp,ww);
   bp.x=bp.x+dreal;
   CLET(bpp1,bp);bpp1.x=bpp1.x+2.;
   CMULT(bs,bp,bpp1);
   CTREAL(cdum,a1,app1);
   CADD(cdum,cdum,bs);
   CDIV(a2,bs,cdum);
   CSUB(cdum,a2,c1);
   CMULT(b2,b1,cdum);
   CADD(t2,t1,b2);
   CSUB(cdum,t2,t1);
/*printc(&a1);printc(&a2);printc(&b1);printc(&b2);printc(&t1);printc(&t2);
printc(&bp);printc(&bpp1);printc(&bs);printf(" %d\n",iterp);
*/
```

```
    if( cabs(cdum) < eps || iterp>itmax) break;
    iterp++;
    CLET(a1,a2);
    CLET(b1,b2);
    CLET(t1,t2);
    }
CLET(cdum,c1);cdum.x=cdum.x-csw;
CTREAL(cdum,cdum,-.5);
CMULT(cdu2,cdum,zetasq);
cexp(&cdu2,&cdu3);
CLET(cdum,c1);cdum.x=cdum.x-csw;
CMULT(cdu2,cdum,cdu3);
CMULT(cdum,cdu2,crtpi);
CSUB(cdu3,t2,ww);
CLET(cdu2,cdu3);
cdu3.x=cdu3.x+.5;
cdu1.x=cdu3.x;
cdu1.y= csw*cdu2.y;
CDIV(cdu3,zeta,cdu1);
CADD(z,cdum, cdu3);
}

cfsmall(eps)double eps;
{
xi1=1.;
CLET(b1,c1);
CLET(a1,c1);
ct1=2.5;
cp1=.5;
cdum.x=ww.x/ct1;cdum.y=ww.y/ct1;
CADD(b2,cdum,c1);
CTREAL(cdum,ww,.6666666666);
CSUB(a2,b2,cdum);
iterp=1;
/*printf(" small");*/
/* recursive calculation of kummer function*/
while(1==1){
    ct2=ct1*ct1;
```

```
        CTREAL(cdum,ww,(cp1/(ct2+ct1+ct1)));
        CADD(g1,c1,cdum);
        CTREAL(cdum,ww,(xi1*(xi1+cp1)/(ct2*(ct2-1.))));
            CMULT(g2,cdum,ww);
        CMULT(cdum,g2,a1);
        CMULT(cdu2,g1,a2);
        CADD(a3,cdum,cdu2);
        CMULT(cdum,g2,b1);
        CMULT(cdu2,g1,b2);
        CADD(b3,cdum,cdu2);
        CDIV(cdu2,a2,b2);
        CDIV(cdu3,a3,b3);
        CSUB(cdum,cdu3,cdu2);
/*printc(&a1);printc(&a2);printc(&a3);printc(&b1);printc(&b2);printc(&b3);
printc(&g1);
printc(&g2);printf("%f %f %f %d\n",ct1,ct2,xi1,iterp);
*/
      if( cabs(cdum) <eps || iterp>itmax)break;
      CLET(a1,a2);
      CLET(b1,b2);
      CLET(a2,a3);
      CLET(b2,b3);
      ct1=ct1+2.;
      xi1=xi1+1.;
      iterp++;
        }
CMPLX(ofo,cdu3.x,(csw*cdu3.y));
CSUB(cdum,c0,zetasq);
cexp(&cdum,&cdu2);
CMULT(cdum,cdu2,crtpi);
CMULT(cdu2,zeta,ofo);
CTREAL(cdu2,cdu2,2.);
CSUB(z,cdum,cdu2);
/*printf(" ofo,z,iter"); printc(&ofo);printc(&z);printf(" %d\n",iterp);
*/
}


/* complex exponential function */
```

```
cexp( x,ans) struct complex *x,*ans;
{
double y,exp(),sin(),cos();
y = exp ( x->x);
ans->x= y*cos (x->y);
ans->y= y*sin (x->y);
return;
}

double ierfc(x,n) double x;int n;
{
double erf(),y,z,sqrt(),exp(),exch;
int k;
y=erf(x,&z);
if(!n)return z;
y=2./sqrt(pi)*exp(-x*x);
/* y=i^-1,z=i^0*/
for(k=1;1;k++)
   {
   y=(.5*y-x*z)/k;
   if(k==n)break;
   exch=z;
   z=y;
   y=exch;
   }
return y;
}


cerror(a,b,eps)double eps; struct complex *a,*b;
{
struct complex dummy;
pdisp(a,eps,b,&dummy,20);
dummy.x=b->y;/* dummy=-i * b */
dummy.y=-b->x;
CTREAL((*b),dummy,.564189583);
}
```

```
ierfc 1.98393e-01 6.99647e-02
ierfc 2.30069e-02 6.04400e-03
ierfc 1.80542e-03 3.73927e-04
scaled ierfc 8.32738e-01 3.53855e-01
scaled ierfc 7.93573e-01 2.79859e-01
scaled ierfc 7.36220e-01 1.93408e-01
scaled ierfc 6.93283e-01 1.43588e-01
scaled ierfc 6.28971e-01 8.84744e-02
x=0.100000 0.112463 0.887537 0.099998 0.000524 9.93360e-02 1
x=0.200000 0.222703 0.777297 0.199921 0.004188 1.94751e-01 1
x=0.300000 0.328627 0.671373 0.299401 0.014117 2.82632e-01 2
x=0.400000 0.428392 0.571608 0.397481 0.033359 3.59943e-01 2
x=0.500000 0.520500 0.479500 0.492344 0.064732 4.24436e-01 2
x=0.600000 0.603856 0.396144 0.581095 0.110540 4.74763e-01 2
x=0.700000 0.677801 0.322199 0.659652 0.172136 5.10504e-01 2
x=0.800000 0.742101 0.257899 0.722844 0.249341 5.32102e-01 3
x=0.900000 0.796908 0.203092 0.764823 0.339776 5.40724e-01 3
x=1.000000 0.842702 0.157298 0.779893 0.438259 5.38080e-01 3
x=1.100000 0.880206 0.119794 0.763807 0.536498 5.26207e-01 3
x=1.200000 0.910314 0.089686 0.715437 0.623401 5.07274e-01 3
x=1.300000 0.934008 0.065992 0.638550 0.686333 4.83398e-01 4
x=1.400000 0.952285 0.047715 0.543096 0.713525 4.56507e-01 4
x=1.500000 0.966105 0.033895 0.445261 0.697505 4.28249e-01 4
x=1.600000 0.976348 0.023652 0.365462 0.638888 3.99940e-01 4
x=1.700000 0.983790 0.016210 0.323827 0.549196 3.72559e-01 4
x=1.800000 0.989091 0.010909 0.333633 0.450939 3.46773e-01 5
x=1.900000 0.992790 0.007210 0.394471 0.373347 3.22974e-01 5
x=2.000000 0.995322 0.004678 0.488253 0.343416 3.01341e-01 5
x=2.100000 0.997021 0.002979 0.581564 0.374273 2.81885e-01 5
x=2.200000 0.998137 0.001863 0.636286 0.455705 2.64511e-01 6
x=2.300000 0.998857 0.001143 0.626562 0.553152 2.49053e-01 6
x=2.400000 0.999311 0.000689 0.554961 0.619690 2.35313e-01 6
x=2.500000 0.999593 0.000407 0.457413 0.619182 2.23083e-01 6
x=2.600000 0.999764 0.000236 0.388937 0.549989 2.12164e-01 6
x=2.700000 0.999866 0.000134 0.392494 0.452917 2.02375e-01 7
x=2.800000 0.999925 0.000075 0.467492 0.391528 1.93551e-01 7
x=2.900000 0.999959 0.000041 0.562376 0.410141 1.85556e-01 7
x=3.000000 0.999978 0.000022 0.605721 0.496313 1.78272e-01 7
```

```
x=3.100000 0.999988 0.000012 0.561594 0.581816 1.71602e-01 7
x=3.200000 0.999994 0.000006 0.466320 0.593349 1.65462e-01 8
x=3.300000 0.999997 0.000003 0.405694 0.519286 1.59788e-01 8
x=3.400000 0.999998 0.000002 0.438492 0.429649 1.54523e-01 8
x=3.500000 0.999999 0.000001 0.532572 0.415248 1.49620e-01 8
x=3.600000 1.00000 0.000000 0.587953 0.492309 1.45039e-01 8
x=3.700000 1.00000 0.000000 0.541946 0.574980 1.40752e-01 9
x=3.800000 1.00000 0.000000 0.448095 0.565619 1.36722e-01 9
x=3.900000 1.00000 0.000000 0.422333 0.475202 1.32929e-01 9
x=4.000000 1.00000 0.000000 0.498426 0.420516 1.29351e-01 9
x=4.100000 1.00000 0.000000 0.573696 0.475798 1.25964e-01 10
x=4.200000 1.00000 0.000000 0.541719 0.563199 1.22760e-01 10
x=4.300000 1.00000 0.000000 0.449441 0.553996 1.19720e-01 10
x=4.400000 1.00000 0.000000 0.438333 0.462268 1.16832e-01 10
x=4.500000 1.00000 0.000000 0.526026 0.434273 1.14084e-01 10
x=4.600000 1.00000 0.000000 0.567237 0.516192 1.11473e-01 11
x=4.700000 1.00000 0.000000 0.491426 0.567145 1.08978e-01 11
x=4.800000 1.00000 0.000000 0.433797 0.496750 1.06596e-01 11
x=4.900000 1.00000 0.000000 0.500161 0.435067 1.04320e-01 11
x=5.000000 1.00000 0.000000 0.563631 0.499191 1.02133e-01 12
```

CHAPTER 6

Statistical Functions

"If your experiment needs statistics, you should have done a better experiment." —Ernest Rutherford

Chapter Objectives

In this chapter we will develop tools to:

– calculate a wide variety of functions of use in statistics,including the most popular distributions (normal, Student's t, chi-quare, and F) and their inverses

– simulate a handy "desk calculator" main program to drive these routines

The applications of these functions are discussed. It is especially rare to find programs to determine these inverses. Generally, a Newton- Raphson iteration (see Chapter 6 of *C Tools*) is used to find the inverse in the programs below.

Applications Of Statistics—Why Rutherford Was Wrong

Many of us are not blessed with the good fortune of being able to abide by Lord Rutherford's dictum. Observational sciences, for example, cannot rely upon precisely controlled laboratory conditions. An astronomer can neither build a star in his lab nor request a supernova at some appointed time. Statistics has played a role in many of the more interesting questions of recent astronomy. Are the galaxies uniformly distributed, or in clusters? Are these clusters uniformly distributed or in superclusters? Are quasars associated with galaxies of very different redshifts, or are these just coincidental situations in which a nearby galaxy is along the line-of-sight to a distant quasar? If Lord Rutherford were alive today and still working at the forefront of particle physics, he'd probably have to eat his words.

It has been my hope to make this book more balanced than others in its presentation of statistical methods as well as the more "conventional" numerical analysis methods. Part of this effort is to present the functions which are of most use in statistics.

In this chapter, we continue to apply the continued fraction approximation method discussed in the previous chapter. These methods are used to evaluate the incomplete gamma and beta functions, which in turn supply us with the chi-square, F and student's-t, and generalized t (Hotelling T) distribution functions.

In addition we include a more compact version of the error function, which will supply us with the Gaussian probability integral, and we develop from this the inverse of the error function. Thus, the four basic functions of statistics, chi-square, F, t, and probability integral are calculable from functions presented in the code of this chapter. We will use the programs developed here in interpreting the results of the analysis of variance problems of Chapter 8, for example. For that purpose, we have included a small "calculator" version of the test program along with the test driver that produces tables of these statistics. Our programs produce the confidence level given the statistic, rather than the other way around, as most tables do. It is generally more useful, especially in significance testing, to do things this way. Sometimes, however, as in determining confidence intervals via the t statistic, this is not the case. We discuss this difficulty.

I have encountered disagreements between tables as to the values of student's-t for a given confidence and number of degrees of freedom. This is due to the existence of "one-sided" and "two-sided" tests. This will be discussed in detail below, but be forewarned of the possible confusion.

First, we will briefly discuss the functional approximations used, and then describe the statistical applications for the functions.

Error Function, Z Scores, Probability Integral

The error function, erf(x), is defined as:

$$erf(x) = \frac{2}{\sqrt{\pi}} \int_0^x e^{-t^2} dt$$

is also useful to define the complementary function, erfc(x) = 1 − erf(x). This will not be the last complementary function defined in this chapter. We present a simpler approximation which is more compact and faster, based upon Hasting's approximations and contained, for example, in Abramowitz and Stegun. The erf() is plotted in Fig. 6.1.

If y = erf(x), we need a function giving x = ierf(y) for determining z scores, for example. As I was unable to find one ready-made, I made one by applying the Newton–Raphson iteration (Chapter 6 of *C Tools*) to

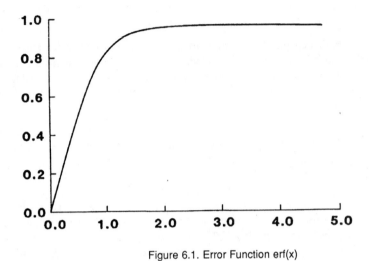

Figure 6.1. Error Function erf(x)

another of Hasting's approximations. The approximation selected for this purpose was different from that used in erf(x), in order that each iteration would require only algebraic operations and no log() or sqrt() operations. The iteration converges extremely rapidly, with three or four iterations quite sufficient for excellent accuracy. The program is written for clarity. Those of you who wish to optimize it somewhat can determine 6. *.0000430638, etc., and replace the calculation in the code (most C compilers will not optimize the program by performing this calculation at source time). Figure 6.2 displays this function (the horizontal scale is expanded by plotting against the variable x/5 instead of x).

The probability integral as generally defined (Dwight) such that $P(x)=$ erf($x/\sqrt{2}$). This is defined as the integral from $-x$ to x of exp($-x^2/2$). Of more value is the cumulative normal distribution, which is the integral from $-\infty$ to x. These functions, and the inverse of the cumulative normal distribution, are contained in the subroutine package of this chapter.

One standard use of these functions is the conversion between "p-scores" and "z-scores". The former is merely the percentile of the individual score, i.e., a p-score of .9 means the individual's score exceeds 90% of the individuals tested. Thus, its abscissa on the normal distribution z must be such that 90% of the area under the curve lies to the left, if we assume the population is normally distributed. This condition is satisfied for z = 1.82. Note that for p = .5, z = 0. The functions cump() and icump() perform the transformations between p and z. In general, if the sample size is large enough (typically N>30), the z distribution may be used. For smaller samples, Student's t plays the same role and should be used. We illustrate in our examples below the relationship of z and t for large N.

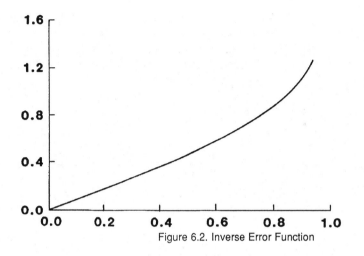

Figure 6.2. Inverse Error Function

Gamma And Incomplete Gamma Functions

The gamma function is defined as

$$\Gamma(x) = \int_0^\infty t^z e^{-t} dt$$

while the incomplete gamma functions are defined as

$$P(a,x) = \frac{\int_0^x t^{a-1} e^{-t} dt}{\Gamma(a)}$$

and $\gamma(a,x) = P(a,x)\Gamma(a)$. The function $\Gamma(a,x) = \Gamma(a)(1-P(a,x))$ is also called an incomplete gamma function.

We use a function loggam(x) which returns $\log(|\Gamma(x)|)$. It uses a rational approximation due to Hastings for $1 < x < 2$, Stirling's formula for large x, and various transformations for all other values The function returns $\Gamma(x)$ for all valid arguments x.

If you need the actual gamma function, use the function gamma(x) provided (Fig. 6.3). First, the logarithm of the gamma function is evaluated using either Stirling's approximation for $|x| > 2$ or an approximation due to Hastings. If $x > 0$, no further work need be done. If x, the result is multiplied by

$$((double)(2*((int) (- x))\%2) -1))$$

What this does is the following. Suppose $x = -2.5$. Then $-$ x is 2.5. The typecast to integer turns this into 2. The modulus operator %2 returns the remainder of this upon division by 2, which is zero. Finally, $2*0 -1 = -1$, which is typecast back to a floating point number, -1. This final typecast is done automatically by C when an assignment to a floating point number is

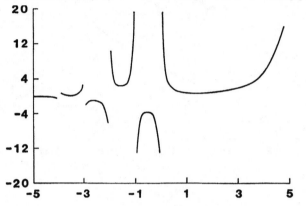

Figure 6.3. The Gamma function

made, and is therefore omitted from the program code below. Exactly the same result would follow from $x = -.5$, or $x = -4.5$, etc. If x were -1.5, say, then 1%2 would be 1, and $2*1 -1= +1$, so the resultant gamma function would be positive, as it would be for $x = -3.5$, etc.

The incomplete gamma function may be found by means of a continued fraction representation,

$$\gamma(a,x) = \cfrac{\exp(- x)\, x^a}{x + \cfrac{(1 - a)}{1 + \cfrac{1}{x + \cfrac{(2 - a)}{1 + \cfrac{2}{x + (3 - a)}}}}}$$

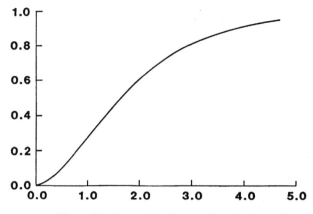

Figure 6.4. Incomplete Gamma Function for a=.2

due to Legendre and can be found on page 136 of Volume II of Erdelyi, and Abramowitz and Stegun as 6.5.31, which is useful for large x (x > 1 + a). It is evaluated using the methods of Chapter 5. For small x, Abramowitz and Stegun give an expansion suitable for small x for γ(a,x). Together, these are used to calculate P(a,x). The incomplete gamma function is plotted versus x for a typical a = .2 in Fig. 6.4. It will be needed to calculate Chi-Square.

Beta And Incomplete Beta Functions

The beta function B(a,b) is defined as Γ(a)Γ(b)/Γ(a+b). The incomplete beta function I_x(a,b)=B_x(a,b)/B(a,b) is given by

$$\frac{\int_0^x t^{a-1}(1-t)^{b-1}dt}{B(a,b)}$$

The arguments should satisfy 0<x<1, and a>0, b>0. This function may be found by evaluation of the continued fraction approximation 26.5.8 on p. 944 of Abramowitz and Stegun; they note that it gives best results for $x < \dfrac{a-1}{a+b-2}$. For larger x , the variables may be transformed by z = 1 − x, which merely exchanges the role of a and b in the integral but improves convergence. This expansion derives from Gauss' continued fraction expansion for the ratio of two hypergeometric functions, F(a,b,c+1;z)/F(a,b,c;z), found in Vol. I of Erdelyi, p.88. As Bx(p,q) =$p^{-1}x^p$ F(p,1 − q;p + 1;x), let a = c = p and b = $-$ q. Using F(a,b;c;z) = F(b,a;c;z) and F(p,$-$q;p;z) = $(1 - z)^q$ (see Abramowitz and Stegun), $B_x(p,q) = p^{-1}x^p(1 -z)^q$ C where C is Gauss's continued fraction. The other continued fraction, 26.5.9, is less well-behaved. We use Lentz's method, which is mentioned in the previous chapter. Instead of evaluating A_n and B_n and forming the nth convergent $h_n = A_n/B_n$, we form the ratios $D_n = b_{n-1}/B_n$ and $C_n = A_n/A_{n-1}$ and the ratio $D_n = h_n/h_{n-1}$. This avoids the problem of A_n and B_n growing large and having to be renormalized with loss of accuracy. On the other hand, it costs us a division instead of a multiplication for each step. Thompson and Barnett added a check to prevent division by zero. They advocate this method strongly, so we have adopted it. (We did not change Newberger's code in the previous chapter because of the maxim: "If it ain't broke, don't fix it.") The F distribution and student's t may be expressed in terms of the incomplete beta distribution.

Chi-Square

If a number of variables are selected from a normal distribution, and they are squared and added, the resultant sum is distributed according to the chi-square distribution. It is thus a function of two variables, the sum and the number of degrees of freedom (or variables summed over). Notice that while it is possible to apply the chi-square distribution for one degree of freedom, special care must be taken (see below). Note also that the distribution is skewed, as a sum of squares cannot be negative.

By its definition, it should be clear that the chi-square distribution should be useful for tests concerning the variance (square of the standard deviation), as it is a positive definite sum of squares. The variance of a set of N observations x[i] is the sum of

$$(x[i] - \bar{x})/(N -1)^2 = \{\Sigma\ x[i]^2 -\ (\Sigma\ x[i])^2/N\}/(N -1)$$

The principal use for chi-square is with contingency tables. Suppose we have an expected distribution of observations. The classic example is Mendel's experiments on inheritance. By the Hardy-Weinberg law, if fraction s of the gene pool is for the dominant trait and t = 1 $-$ s is for the recessive trait, then the fraction t^2 should be homozygous for the recessive trait (and display it), the fraction 2ts will be heterozygous (have both genes) and appear to exhibit the dominant trait while being carriers of the recessive gene, while the remainder will be homozygous for the dominant trait (and exhibit it). There is, by the way, some suspicion that Mendel fudged his results as they are "too good." (The classic discussion of this is R. A. Fisher's paper in Ann. Sci, 1, 115, 1936.) The observed distribution may be compared with the theoretical distribution by calculating for each expected characteristic the sum

$$\sum \frac{(observed\ frequency - expected\ frequency)^2}{expected\ frequency}$$

which has a chi-square distribution. Once this number is calculated, we can use the program of this chapter to calculate the associated cumulative chi-square value. This will give us the confidence level associated with this figure, i.e., the likelihood that the deviations of the observed from the expected distribution are caused by chance. If there is one degree of freedom, as in our example, the skewness of the chi-square distribution results in a bias which must be corrected by rewriting the sum tested as

$$\sum \frac{(observed\ frequency - expected\ frequency - .5)^2}{expected\ frequency}$$

The chi-square distribution may also be used to compare the variances of samples to see if they are significantly different (indicating that the sample populations are distinct). This is called Bartlett's test. Suppose the ith group consists of k observations, called k[i]. We compute

$$\{2 \log(\bar{s})\sum (k[i]-1)\ -\ \sum 2 \log s[i])(k[i]-1)\}/c$$

where s[i] are the variances of each sample, $\bar{s}$ is the mean of the variances, and c is a correction factor (similar to the .5 required above for 1 degree of freedom), and is

$$c = 1 + \{\sum 1/(k[i] -1)\ \ -1/\sum(k[i] -1)\}/3(n -1)$$

The test then proceeds as for the goodness of fit case (contingency table problem).

For more details as to the correction factors for chi-square and for examples, see Mann. Figure 6.5 plots the chi-square distribution for 10 degrees of freedom. (Plots in books often show the probability density function; the chi-square distribution is then the integral, i.e., the area under this distribution.) This plot may be interpreted to show, for example, that for a $\chi^2 = 4$ with ten degrees of freedom there is roughly a 5% chance that our expected law does not explain the data, i.e., a 96% confidence our postulated law is good.

The Chi-square probability function $P(\chi^2|v) = \gamma(a,x)/\Gamma(a)$.

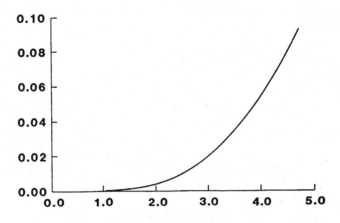

Figure 6.5. Chi-Square for 10 Degrees of Freedom

Student's t

One definition of the t (or student's t) distribution is that if z is a standard normal random variable (i.e., a normally distributed random variable with zero mean and unit variance), and X is a chi-square distribution with N degrees of freedom, then t = z/√(X/N) possesses a t distribution. The significance of this is that the means of a set of observations drawn from a normal distribution are distributed according to the t distribution. For large N, t approaches equality with z.   Figure 6.6 plots t for ten degrees of freedom.

The t distribution may be written in terms of the incomplete beta distribution as $1 - I_x(N/2,1/2)$ where x = $n/(n + t^2)$.

Every table of student's-t values I encounter is slightly different. Some present one-sided values and others two-sided values without a word of warning, which can easily cause confusion and error. Two-sided tests are appropriate when the test is intended to distinguish only if the observation is within or out of bounds, without noting whether it is too high or too low compared to those bounds. The confidence factors for two-sided tests are twice those for one-sided tests, i.e. if a t variable is significant at the 5% level in a 1-sided test, the same t value corresponds to a 10% confidence level in a 2-sided test (alternatively, 95% and 90% levels in some books). Often one sees a confidence level of C/2 specified for a t variable. This means that if one wants a 90% confidence that the true mean, say, is within the bounds specified, which is a two-sided test, one should look up in the appropriate one-sided table the value for a 95%. There is then a 5% pos-

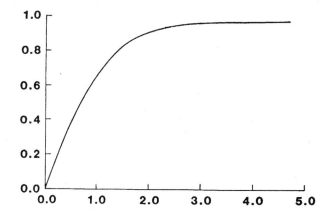

Figure 6.6. Student's t for 10 Degrees of Freedom

sibility that the value is too low and another 5% that it is too high, resulting in a 10% overall probability that the true mean is out of bounds.

Our definition of t is in accord with that of Abramowitz and Stegun (section 26.7.1), and the values tabulated by the programs are in accord with table 26.10 of their book for the same confidence levels. However, the confidence levels in other books are often expressed as one minus the confidence levels here, and are often half or one minus half the confidence levels listed here. This is due to the fact that some books use confidence levels appropriate to one-sided tests, while the others use values for two-sided tests. For example, the original tables of Fisher and Yates gave two-sided values. The book by Mann reproduces these two-sided values, and, for example, Merritt presents two-sided confidence limits. On the other hand, when Crow, Davis, and Maxfield adapted the same table, they altered the confidence levels to one-sided tests (the confidence levels given as table headings are halved from the corresponding numbers in the original). They warn the reader. S. A. Lippman also adapts and abridges the same table due to Fisher and Yates, and changes to one-sided tests, but he does not state clearly that this has been done. We have chosen to print confidence factors and complementary confidence factors for both one-sided and two-sided tests with explicit identification of each.

It should be clear from the distribution that the t distribution is useful for testing hypotheses about means. For example, if two sample means are different, what is the likelihood that they are actually from the same population, and that the differences are merely due to chance? Similarly, if a mean is computed based upon a sample, what is the likelihood that the actual population mean is within a certain interval of the computed mean? There are numerous special versions of these tests, depending upon whether the sample variance is known or unknown, etc. See the texts by Mendenhall and Sincich, and by Harnett (references below) for a complete discussion. A typical test might be to determine if a population of unknown variance, with measured mean m, has true mean M. Form $t = (m - M)/(s/\sqrt{n})$, where s is the variance of the observed measurements and n is their number. Then using the t distribution with $n - 1$ degrees of freedom, find the appropriate confidence level. Note that one degree of freedom is lost because we have used the measured variance instead of the true population variance.

One problem of great interest: having found a regression or correlation coefficient b (see Chapter 5), what is the likelihood that the actual value is B? An important special case is $B = 0$. In that case we are testing whether the apparent correlation is due to chance, and the actual correlation is zero. For a single variable linear regression line, $y = a + bx$, which may be found by a simple version of the methods of Chapter 5, the test statistic

is
$$t = \frac{b}{\sqrt{\frac{(n-2)\,SD}{n\,SE}}} \qquad \text{where}\quad SD = \sum (x[i] - \bar{x})^2 \qquad \text{and}$$

$$SE = \frac{1}{n} \sum (y[i] - a - bx[i])^2 \quad \text{the sums over the observation points. Note}$$

that these expressions for SD and SE may not be the most computationally convenient (see the expression for the variance calculation given above). A similar relation holds for a if b is replaced by a. These results generalize to multiple regression. The simple model may be viewed as regression on two variables, a and b, the former always having a coefficient of unity in the regression equations. The least squares solution of $y = Ax$ may be written as

$$x = A^+ \; y \; = \; (A^\wedge A)^{-1} \; A^\wedge \; y$$

where A^+ is the pseudoinverse (see Chapter 5 of *C Tools*), and $(A^\wedge A)$ is the unnormalized covariance matrix. Call the elements of its inverse c[i][j]. (Note that the SVD may be used instead of forming the matrix $A^\wedge A$ and inverting. It is preferable to use the SVD for this problem.) A one-tailed test of the null hypothesis x[i] = 0, i.e., a test that the alternative to the null hypothesis is that, say, x[i]>0 (or x[i]<0), can be performed using student's-t. Then t = x[i]/(s $\sqrt{}$ (c[i][i])), with s = (y^y-xA^y)/(m −n) where m is, as in Chapter 5 of *C Tools*, the number of observations (the number of components of the y vector) and n the number of parameters in the fit (the number of components of the x vector). The one-tailed or one-sided test is then t > t(C) or t < − t(C) where C is the confidence level and the latter test is used if x[i] is negative. A two-sided test would have the same test statistic, but we would be testing the null hypothesis x[i] = 0, and we would reject the null hypothesis if |t| < t(C/2) when using a table of one-sided values. If using our calculator program, merely enter the calculated t value, and the appropriate confidence levels for one-sided or two-sided tests will be printed and identified. All the t tests are based upon m − n −1 degrees of freedom.

Similarly, if we want the range about x[i] in which the true regression parameter lies with some confidence level C, we can use x[i] ± t(C/2) s √(c[i][i]) where again t() is the one-sided value, or use the two-sided value for t(C).

In the case where a confidence interval is desired, one has to find the value of t for a given confidence interval and degrees of freedom, rather than having t as a given. Simply use the inverse-student's-t function provided.

F Distribution

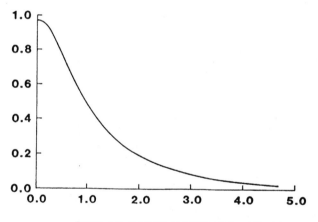

Figure 6.7. F for 10 and 5 Degrees of Freedom

The F distribution is that of (U[1]/n[1])/(U[2]/n[2]), where U[i] is a chi-square distributed random variable of n[i] degrees of freedom. The cumulative F distribution is given by the expression $I_x(n[2]/2, n[1]/2)$ with x = n[2]/(n[2] + n[1]F). Note that the t distribution is a special case of the complementary F distribution (i.e., 1 − F), in which F = t and v_2 = 1. The principal use of the F statistic is in analysis of variance. Figure 6.7 shows the F distribution for 10 and 5 degrees of freedom.

Generalized Student's t: Hotelling and Mahalanobis

Wilks discusses in Section 18.4 the problem of comparing a vector of means (i.e., testing the hypothesis that two vectors of mean values are equal). This is the multidimensional generalization of the t test above. The problem is of interest in discriminant analysis (see Chapter 5) and analysis of covariance. Using the inverse of the covariance matrix C^{-1} (see Chapter 5) we form the statistic

$$T^2 = nD^2 = \sum (x[i] - \bar{x}) \, C^{-1} \, (x[j] - \bar{x})$$

which is Hotelling's generalized student ratio T. The quantity D is Mahalanobis' distance between the sample and population. Either statistic is likely to be encountered in discussions of discriminant analysis or multivariate analysis It can be shown that $H(T,k,n) = 1 - I_x ((n - 1)/2, k/2)$ where $x = (n-1)/(n -1 + T^2)$. Here k is the dimension of the vector of means. Note that for $k = 1$, the Hotelling distribution is the student t distribution for $T = t$ and $n -1$ degrees of freedom. You may encounter in books other similar tests that employ the F distribution. It will be seen that Hot(T,k,n) is the complementary F distribution for $F = T^2 (n -k)/\{k(n -1)\}$, $n[2] = n -1$, $n[1] = k$. For example, in the problem cited, form $J = (n -1 -k) \, T^2 /(n -2)k$ and use an F test with k and $n -1 -k$ degrees of freedom. This test is given by Hand.

Another application of interest in multivariate analysis of variance (MANOVA) as well as discriminant analysis (Chapters 7, 4 and 5 of *C Tools*) is testing for the significance of the difference between the means of two samples. The Mahalanobis distance D may be formed similarly as

$$D^2 = (m - m') \, C^{-1} \, (m - m') \, \{n[1] + n[2] -2\}$$

where m and m' are k-dimensional vectors of the group means (centroids in the terminology of some authors), with n[i] members in the ith group. Then Hotelling's T is given by

$$T^2 = n[1]n[2]/(n[1]) + n[2]) \, D^2$$

An F test may alternatively be used with k and $n[1] + n[2] -k -1$ degrees of freedom, with $F = T^2 \{n[1]+n[2] - k -1\} k/\{n[1] + n[2] -2\}$ (see Maindonald). Hand gives an equivalent test in slightly different form.

See the books by Hand and by Wilks for more applications and examples.

Noncentral Distributions

The F, t, and chi-square distributions all have noncentral versions with a positve non-centrality parameter, λ. This parameter is zero for the usual or central distribution. See Abramowitz and Stegun for the definitions as infinite sums (26.4.25,26.6.18,26.7.9). We use these sums (it typically requires only a few terms for convergence for reasonable parameters). We also provide inverse functions.

Inverse Distributions

As discussed above, one sometimes needs the critical value of t, F or chi-square for a given confidence instead of determining at what confidence level a given value is significant. This is available from our subroutine package. A function, invnr(), uses a Newton-Raphson iteration (see Chapter 6 of *C Tools*) to determine the inverse of our the desired function. This routine could be of fairly general use for determining the inverse of functions.

Wilcoxon And Mann-Whitney Tests

Following Owen, we present recursive routines for the Wilcoxon Matched Pair Signed Rank test and the Mann-Whitney two-sample statistic.

It is non-parametric, i. e., does not assume that the sample is drawn from a population of a specific, known distribution (usually normal).

Test Program

The test program has two drivers. One produces the table of chi-square, t and F statistics which may be compared with values tabulated in Abramowitz and Stegun and which produced the numbers plotted in the figures of this chapter. The other is a "calculator" version intended for use by obtaining values from the keyboard. Note that a return carriage will recover the previous value for that parameter, easing the burden on the user if many examples of the same statistic with the same number of degrees of freedom are to be evaluated. Comments are added to the listing to explain the purpose of each calculation.

TABLE 6.1

Functions of Chapter 6

gamma(x)	gamma function
loggam(x)	logarithm of gamma function of x
incgam(a,x)	incomplete gamma function
chisq(x,nu)	chi-square for n degrees of freedom (all arguments are type double)
incbeta(a,b,x)	incomplete beta function
studt(t,nu)	student's-t distribution for nu degrees of freedom
fdist(x,n1,n2)	F distribution
tinv(a,nu)	inverse of the student's-t distribution for nu degrees of freedom
chiinv(a,nu)	inverse of chi-square distribution
cump(x)	cumulative (normal) probability
wilcoxs(n)	Wilcoxon matched-pair signed rank test
mannw(n,m,u)	Mann-Whitney two-sample statistic
wilcoxon(n,m,u)	Wilcoxon cummulative. Called by mannw
ks(d,n)	Kolmogorov-Smironov one-sample statistic
invnr(narg,x,nu1,nu2,value,iguess)	
	Used for determining the inverse function value z such that value(z,nu1,nu2)=x. A Newton-Raphson iteration is used. The initial guess iguess is used for z. The actual number of degree-of-freedom arguments to be used is narg.
erf(x)	error function
ierf(x)	inverse of error function
icump(x)	inverse of cumulative probability function
finv(x,n1,n2)	inverse of F distribution

References

M. Abramowitz and I. A. Stegun, *Handbook of Mathematical Functions* (Wash. DC: Superintendent of Documents, 1964 also New York: Dover,1965).

E. L. Crow, F. A. Davis, M. W. Maxfield, *Statistics Manual* (New York: Dover, 1960).

E. B. Dwight, *Table of Integrals and Other Mathematical Formulae* (New York: MacMillian, 1961).

A. Erdelyi, *Higher Transcendental Functions* (New York: Krieger, 1959).

D. J. Hand, *Discrimination and Classification* (New York: John Wiley, 1981), p.123.

D. L. Harnett, *Statistical Methods* (New York: Addison Wesley,1982).

C. Hastings, *Approximations for Digital Computers* (Princeton, NJ: Univerity Press, 1955)

D. V. Lindley, *Introduction to Probability and Statistics* (Cambridge, England: University Press, 1965).

I. Maindonald, *Statistical Computation* (New York: John Wiley, 1984).

L. Mann, Jr., *Applied Engineering Statistics for Practicing Engineers* (New York: Barnes and Noble, 1970).

W. Mendenhall and T. Sincich, *Statistcs for the Engineering and Computer Sciences* (San Francisco, CA: Dellen Press, 1984).

F. S. Merritt, *Applied Mathematics in Engineering Practice* (New York: McGraw-Hill, 1970).

D. B. Owen, *Handbook of Statistical Tables* (Reading, MA: Addison-Wesley, 1962).

Program Listing And Test Problem Output

(Listing begins next page.)

```
/*
calculator version of stat.c routines
routines for statistical functions and auxiliary functions used in their
computation

chisq() Chi-square
studt() Student's-t distribution
fdist() F distribution
Hot()   Hotelling's T-squared distribution ( generalized t dist)
prob() probability integral
cump() cummulative probability integral
icump() inverse cummulative prob. integral
erf()   error function (related simply to probability integral)
ierf()  inverse of the error function
loggam() logarithm of the absolute value of the gamma function
gamma()  gamma function
beta()    beta function
incbeta() incomplete beta function
incgam() incomplete gamma function
finv()   inverse of F distribution (F value given confidence,d.f.'s)
tinv()   inverse of student's t (t value given confidence,d.f.) two-sided.
chiinv() " of chi-sq
ks()    Kolmogorov-Smirnov distribution (1 sample)
wilcoxs() Wilcoxon Matched-Pair signed rank test
wilcoxon() Wilcoxon cummulative count (integer)
mannw()    Mann-Whitney confidence (calls wilcoxon)
invnr() auxilliary routine to use Newton-Raphson iteration for
     use with finv,tinv.
ncf() noncentral f distribution
ncc()       "      chi-sq
nct()       "      Student's t
incf()      "       f distribution inverse
inct()      "    t    "       "
incc()      "      chi-sq "        "

from More C tools for scientists and engineers by L. Baker
*/
#include <alloc.h>
```

```
#include <stdio.h>
#define DOFOR(i,to) for(i=0;i<to;i++)
#define abs(x) ((x)>0.? (x):-(x))
#define max(a,b) ((a)>(b)? (a):(b))
#define min(a,b) ((a)<(b)? (a):(b))
#define pi 3.14159265358979
#define errorcode -1.
#define D sizeof(double)
static double tolrel=1.e-7,tolabsg=1.e-5,tolabsb=1.e-5,
              conabs=1.e-5,conrel=1.e-3;
static int iterkti,iterkt,wilcox;

main(argc,argv) int argc;char **argv;
{int i,j,k,m,n,df1,df2;
float zz,rr,qq; long int lj,ln,lm,wilcoxs();
double x,Hot(),ierf(),erf(),y,z,q,r,exp(),loggam(),gamma(),ks(),mannw();
double prob(),chisq(),studt(),fdist(),incgam(),incbeta(),cump(),icump();
double finv(),tinv(),chiinv(),ncf(),ncc(),nct(),incf(),inct(),incc(),pow();
FILE *fileid,*in;
/*in=fopen("CON:","r");
if(!in)printf(" pblm opening for input\n");*/
/*BEGIN SPECIAL PLOTTING SECTION*/
/*fileid=fopen("PLOT.GAM","w");
fprintf(fileid,"1 \n");
for(i=0;i<100;i++)
   {
   x=(i-50)*.1+.05;
   fprintf(fileid," %f %e\n",x,gamma(x));
   }
fclose(fileid);
fileid=fopen("PLOT.FEW","w");
fprintf(fileid," 6 \n");
for(i=0;i<50;i++)
   {
   x=(i)*.1+.05;
   fprintf(fileid," %f %e %e %e %e %e\n"
,x,loggam(x),erf(x),ierf(x/5.1),prob(x),cump(x),icump(x));
   }
```

```
fclose(fileid);
*/
/*
fileid=fopen("PLOT.PRB","w");
fprintf(fileid,"6 \n");
for(i=0;i<50;i++)
   {
   x=(i)*.1+.05;
   y=i*.02;
   fprintf(fileid," %f %e %e %e %e %e %e\n",
x,chisq(x,10.),studt(x,10.),fdist(x,10.,5.),fdist(x,5.,10.)
,incbeta(.5,.5,y),incgam(2.,x));
   }
fclose(fileid);
fileid=fopen("PLOT.inv","w");
fprintf(fileid,"4 \n");
for(i=0;i<50;i++)
   {
   x=(i)*.01+.05;
   fprintf(fileid," %f %e %e %e %e\n"
,x,tinv(x,10.),finv(x,5.,10.),chiinv(x,10.),finv(x,10.,20.));
   }
fclose(fileid);
*/
/*END SPECIAL PLOTTING SECTION.*/
k=1;m=1;q=1.;x=1.;/*defaults*/
iterkt=iterkti=0;
while(1)
{
printf(" enter: 1 for F, 2 chi-sq, 3 Student's 4 Hotelling gen. t\n");
printf(" 5 z->p 6 p->z 7 gamma 8 erf 9 inverse erf 10 prob\n");
printf(" 11 inc beta 12 inc gamma 13 t-inv 14 F-inv 15 chi-sq inv\n");
printf(" 16 noncentral F 17 chi-sq 18 t 19 inv-F 20 inv-t 21 inv-chi\n");
printf(" 22 Kolmogorv-Smirnov 23 Mann Whitney 24 Wilcoxon 25conv param\n");
j=scanf("%d", &i);
if(j==-1)printf(" trouble\n");
if(i==2)
   {
```

```
      printf(" enter chi-sq value ");j=scanf("%f",&zz);
      z=zz;
      printf(" enter degrees of freedom(integer) ");j=scanf("%d",&k);
      if(k>0)x=k;
      y=chisq(z,x);q=1.-y;
      printf(" z=%f df=%f chisq(z,df)=%e %e\n",z,x,y,q);
      }
   else
      if(i==3)
      {
      printf(" enter student t value ");j=scanf("%f",&zz);z=zz;
      printf(" enter degrees of freedom(integer) ");j=scanf("%d",&k);
      if(k>0)x=k;
      y=studt(z,x); q=1.-y;r=q*.5;
      printf(" student's-t(z=%f,df=%f)=%e\n",z,x,y);
      printf("significance levels= %e[1-sided] %e[2-sided]\n" ,r,q);
      r=1.-r;
      printf(" cummulative t[1-sided]=%f %f[two-sided]\n",r,y);
      }
   else if(i==1)
      {
      printf(" enter F value ");j=scanf("%f",&zz);x=zz;
      if(j!=-1)printf(" echo F value=%f\n",x);
      else
         printf(" input error\n");
      printf(" enter degrees of freedom(2 integers) ");j=scanf("%d %d",&k,&m);
      if(k>0)z=k;
      if(m>0)q=m;
      y=fdist(x,z,q);
      printf(" F=%f fdist(F,%d,%d)=%e\n",x,k,m,y);
      }
   else if(i==4)
      {
         printf(" enter as integers degrees of freedom n and k\n");
         scanf("%d%d",&m,&k);
         if(m>0) n=m;
         printf(" enter value for T (NOT square)\n");
         scanf("%f",&zz);
```

```
    x=zz;
    printf(" echo n %d k %d T %f\n",n,k,z);
     y=Hot(x,n,k);
    printf(" generalized t dist=%e\n",y);
   }
else if (i==5)
   {
   printf(" enter z score\n");
   scanf("%f",&zz);
   x=zz;
   y=cump(x);/*.5*(1.+erf(.7071*x));*/
   printf(" z score=%e\n",y);
   }
else if (i==6)
   {
   printf(" enter p score\n");
   scanf("%f",&zz);
   x=zz;
   y=icump(x);/*1.4142*(ierf(2.*x-1.));*/
   printf(" p score=%e\n",y);
   }
else if (i==7)
   {
   printf(" enter x\n");scanf("%f",&zz);x=zz;
   printf(" gamma(%f)=%f\n", x,gamma(x));
   }
else if (i==8)
   {
   printf(" enter x\n");scanf("%f",&zz);x=zz;
   printf(" erf(%f)=%f\n", x,erf(x) );
   }
else if (i==9)
   {
   printf(" enter x\n");scanf("%f",&zz);x=zz;
   printf(" %f=erf(%f)\n", ierf(x),x );
   }
else if (i==10)
   {
```

```
    printf(" enter x\n");scanf("%f",&zz);x=zz;
    printf(" %f=prob(%f)\n", prob(x),x );
    }
else if (i==11)
    {
    printf(" enter x,a,b\n");scanf("%f%f%f",&zz,&rr,&qq);
    x=zz;r=rr;q=qq;
    printf(" %f=inc.beta(%f|%f,%f) %d\n", incbeta(r,q,x),x,r,q,iterkt );
    }
else if (i==12)
    {
    printf(" enter x,a\n");scanf("%f%f",&zz,&qq);
    x=zz;q=qq;
    printf(" %f=inc gamma(%f,%f)\n", incgam(q,x),q,x );
    }
else if (i==13)
    {
    printf(" enter 2-sided confid.,nu\n");scanf("%f%f",&zz,&qq);
    x=zz;q=qq;
    if(x<=0. || x>=1.)
        printf(" confidence must be between 0 and 1\n");
    else
        {
        printf(" %f=inverse t(%f,%f)\n", tinv(x,q),x,q);
        }
    }
else if (i==14)
    {
    printf(" enter confid,d.f.1,2\n");scanf("%f%f%f",&zz,&qq,&rr);
    x=zz;q=qq;r=rr;
    if(x<=0. || x>=1.)
        printf(" confidence must be between 0 and 1\n");
    else
        {
        printf(" %f=inv F(%f,%f,%f)\n", finv(x,q,r),x,q,r);
        }
    }
else if (i==15)
```

```
{
printf(" enter 1-sided confid.,nu\n");scanf("%f%f",&zz,&qq);
x=zz;q=qq;
if(x<=0. || x>=1.)
    printf(" confidence must be between 0 and 1\n");
else
    {
    printf(" %f=inverse chi-sq(%f,%f)\n", chiinv(x,q),x,q);
    }
}
else if (i==16)
{
printf(" enter  F, df1,df2, noncentrality.df integers\n");
scanf("%f%d%d%f",&zz,&df1,&df2,&qq);
x=zz;q=qq;
if(x<=0. )
    printf(" noncentrality must be positive");
else
    {
    printf(" noncentral F=%f\n", ncf(x,q,df1,df2) );
    }
}
else if (i==17)
{
printf(" enter  chisq, df,noncentrality.df integer\n");
scanf("%f%d%f",&zz,&df1,&qq);
x=zz;q=qq;
if(x<=0. )
    printf(" noncentrality must be positive");
else
    {
    printf(" noncentral chisq=%f\n", ncc(x,q,df1) );
    }
}
else if (i==18)
{
printf(" enter  t, df, noncentrality.df integer\n");
scanf("%f%d%f",&zz,&df1,&qq);
```

```
    x=zz;q=qq;
    if(x<=0. )
        printf(" noncentrality must be positive");
    else
        {
        printf(" noncentral t=%f\n", nct(x,q,df1) );
        }
    }
else if (i==19)
    {
    printf(" enter  confidence, df1,df2, noncentrality.df integers\n");
    scanf("%f%d%d%f",&zz,&df1,&df2,&qq);
    x=zz;q=qq;
    if(q<=0. )
        printf(" noncentrality must be positive");
    else
        {
        printf(" inverse noncentral F=%f\n", incf(x,df1,df2,q) );
        }
    }
else if (i==20)
    {
    printf(" enter  confidence, df, noncentrality.df integer\n");
    scanf("%f%d%f",&zz,&df1,&qq);
    x=zz;q=qq;
    if(q<=0. )
        printf(" noncentrality must be positive");
    else
        {
        printf(" inverse noncentral t=%f\n", inct(x,df1,q) );
        }
    }
else if (i==21)
    {
    printf(" enter  confidence, df, noncentrality.df integer\n");
    scanf("%f%d%f",&zz,&df1,&qq);
    x=zz;q=qq;
    if(q<=0. )
```

```
        printf(" noncentrality must be positive");
    else
        {
        printf(" inverse noncentral chisq=%f\n", incc(x,df1,q) );
        }
    }
else if(i==22)
    {
    printf(" enter d, n for kolmogorov smirnov\n");
    scanf("%e%d",&zz,&n);z=zz;
    q=ks(z,n);r= (1.-q);
    printf(" answer=%e siglevel=%e\n",q,r);
    }
else if(i==23)
    {
    printf(
    " enter n,m,u integers for Wilcoxon (Mann-Whitney) 2 sample statistic\n");
    scanf("%d%d%d",&n,&m,&k);
    i= m*n+(m*(m+1)>>1)-k;
    printf(" Wilcoxon=%d T=%d, mann-whitney= %e\n",wilcox,i,mannw(n,m,k));
    }
else if(i==24)
    {
    printf(" enter n,m integers for Wilcoxon matched pair signed rank\n");
    scanf("%ld%ld",&ln,&lm);
    lj=wilcoxs(ln,lm);
    printf(" count=%ld, prob.= %e\n",lj,lj/pow(2.,(double)ln));
    }
else if(i==25)
    {
    printf(" previous iteration count %d\n",iterkt);
    printf(" enter tolabsg=%e,tolabsb=%e,tolrel=%e nonzero to alter\n"
    ,tolabsg,tolabsb,tolrel);
    scanf("%e%e%e",&zz,&qq,&rr);
    if(zz!=0.) {tolabsg=zz;printf(" new tolabsg=%e\n",tolabsg);}
    if(qq!=0.) {tolabsb=qq;printf(" new tolabsb=%e\n",tolabsb);}
    if(rr!=0.) {tolrel=rr;printf(" new tolrel=%e\n",tolrel);}
    printf(" inverse funct. last iteration count=%d\n",iterkti);
```

```
    printf("conabs=%e,conrel=%e enter nonzero to alter\n"
    ,conabs,conrel);
    scanf(" %e %e",&zz,&qq);
    if(zz!=0.) {conabs=zz;printf(" new conabs=%e\n",conabs);}
    if(qq!=0.) {conrel=qq;printf(" new conrel=%e\n",conrel);}
    }
else
    {printf(" terminating j i %d %d\n",j,i);break;}
}
exit(0);
}
double arr(m,n)int m,n;
{/* m+n!/m!n! */
double product;
int i,nn,mm;
if(n>m){nn=n;mm=m;}
else{nn=m;mm=n;}
product=1.;
for(i=1;i<=mm;i++)
    {product*=(((double)(nn+i))/((double)i));
    }
return product;
}
long int wilcoxs(ni,mi) long int ni,mi;
{
long int n,m,x;
if(mi<0)return 0;
if(!mi)return 1;
x=(ni*(ni+1)) >>1;
if(mi>x) return wilcoxs(ni,x);
m=mi;n=ni;
if(n<0 || m<0 )printf(" warn n %d m%d\n",n,m);
return wilcoxs(n-1,m)+wilcoxs(n-1,m-n);
}

int wilcoxon(ni,mi,ui) int ni,mi,ui;
{
int n,m,u;
```

```
if(ui>ni*ni) return -1;
if(ui>=mi*ni) return (int)(arr(mi,ni) +.5);
if(ui<0)return 0;
if(!ui)return 1;
if(!mi)return 1;
u=ui;
if(mi>0 && ni>0 && ni<mi) {m=ni;n=mi;}else{m=mi;n=ni;}
if(n<0 || m<0 )printf(" warn n %d m%d\n",n,m);
return wilcoxon(n-1,m,u-m)+wilcoxon(n,m-1,u);
}


double mannw(n,m,u) int n,m,u;
{int a;double arr(),denom;
a=wilcoxon(n,m,u);
wilcox=a;
denom=arr(m,n);
return (double)a/denom;
}


double ks(d,n) double d;int n;
{
int ind,ndt,ndp,ndd,nddp,i,j,k,jmax,na=75;
double nd,*q,*f,sum,ft,fu,fv,fn,ci,pow(),sqrt(),exp(),mult;

if(n>na)
  {
  d*=sqrt((double)n);
/*  fv= d+1./(sqrt((double)n)*6.);
  ft= exp(-2.*fv*fv);
  fn=1.-2.*ft;
*/
  fu=exp(-2.*d*d)*(1.-d/sqrt((double)n)*.66666666);
  sum=1.-2.*fu;
/*  printf(" fn, sum %e %e\n",fn,sum);*/
  return sum;
  }
```

```
/* na chosen to avoid overflow problems for large n*/
if(n==1)return 2.*d-1.;/* pblms d<.5???*/
nd= n*d;
fn=(double)n;
ndt= 2.*nd;
if(ndt<1)return 0.;
ind=nd;
ndp=ind+1;
ndd= min(n,ind<<1);
f=malloc( D * (n+2) );
q=malloc( D * (n+2) );
nddp=ndd+1;
ci=1.;
f[0]=1.;
for(i=0;i<n;i++)
   {
   f[i+1]=f[i]*ci;
   ci++;
   }
mult=f[n]/pow(fn,fn);
/* might be efficient to invert the f[i] here*/
for(i=0;i<=n;i++) f[i]=1./f[i];
q[0]=1.;
if(ndd)
   {
   ci=1.;
   for(i=1;i<=ndd;i++)
      {
      q[i]=pow(ci,(double)i)*f[i];
      ci++;
      }

   if(ndp>n) goto r1;
   fv= ndp-nd;
   jmax= fv+1;
   for(i=ndp;i<=ndd;i++)
      {
      sum=0.;
```

```
    ft=nd;
    k=i;
    fu=fv;
    for(j=0;j<jmax;j++)
      {sum+=pow(ft,(double)j-1)*pow(fu,(double)k)*
        (f[j]*f[k]);
      ft++;fu--;k--;
      }
    q[i]-=2.*nd*sum;
    jmax++;
    fv++;
    }
  if(ndd==n)goto r1;
  }
for(i=nddp;i<=n;i++)
  {
  sum=0.;
  ci=1.;
  ft=2.*nd;
  for(j=1;j<=ndt;j++)
    {
    ft--;
    k=i-j;
    sum+= ci*pow(ft,(double)j)*q[k]*f[j];
    ci=-ci;
    }
  q[i]=sum;
  if(sum<0. || sum*mult>1.)
    {/*trouble*//*printf(" trouble k-s:  sum=%e\n",i,sum);
    for(j=1;j<=i;j++)printf(" q[%d]=%e f=%e\n",j,q[j],f[j]);*/
    return 1.;
    }
  }
r1:
free(f);free(q);
return q[n]*mult ;
}
```

```c
double gamma(x) double x;
{
double y,z,exp(),loggam();
y=exp(loggam(x));
if(x>=0.)return(y);
z=  2*(((int)(-x))%2) -1;
return(y*z);
}


double loggam(x) double x;
{
int i;
double z,tmp,ser,log(),sin(),*coeff;
static double logsr2pi=.918938533;
static double b[9]={.035868343,-.193527818,.482199394,-.756704078,
.918206857,-.897056937,.988205891,-.577191652,1.0};

/*if( x<0.&& x> -1. )
  {
  return((loggam(1.+x)-log(-x)));
  }
else requires two levels of recursion and  log call,not sin
*/
if (x<-0.) /*was x< -1. when above implemented */
    {/*transform to x>0. will blow up if x integer, as it should*/
    z=1.-x;/* z>2. */
    return(log(pi/abs(sin(pi*z)))-loggam(z) );
    }
else
  if (x<=1.)/* 0<=x<1 */
    {
    /*z=1.-x*/;/*  0<=z<1*/
    /*return( log(z*pi/sin(pi*z))-loggam(1.+z));*/
    /* Ab& Stegun-takes less than half the time*/
    if(x==0.)return 0.;
    tmp=b[0];
    coeff=&(b[1]);
```

```
    for(i=1;i<9;i++)tmp= tmp*x+ *(coeff++);
    return(log(tmp/x));
    }
/* use below for x>1.*/
else
  if(x<=2.)
    {
    tmp=b[0];
    coeff=&(b[1]);
    z=x-1.;
    for(i=1;i<9;i++)tmp= tmp*z+ *(coeff++);
    return(log(tmp));
    }
z=1./x;
tmp=z*z;
/*ser= (1./12.+tmp*(-1./360.+tmp*(1/1260.-tmp/1680.)   ))/x;*/
ser= (.08333333333333+tmp*(tmp*(0.000793650793-.000595238095*tmp)
  -.002777777777))*z;
return (logsr2pi-x+(x-.5)*log(x)+ser);
}
#define small 1.e-30

double incgam(a,x) double x,a;
{
int i,itmax=100;
double gln,exp(),log(),loggam(),sum,ap,del,fi,start,
old,tol=3.e-7,c0,d0,ana,offset,mult,delta;
/* error condition return -1 on invalid arguments*/
if( x< 0. || a<0. ) return(-1.);
if(x==0.)return(0.);
gln=loggam(a);
if (x< (a+1.))
  {
  /*series*/
  offset=0.;
  mult=1.;
  ap=a;
  sum=1./a;
```

```
  del=sum;
  DOFOR(i,itmax)
    {
    ap++;
    del*=x/ap;
    sum+=del;
    if( abs(del)<abs(sum)*tol) goto fini;
    }
    printf(" trouble incomplete gamma series\n");
  }
else
  {
  offset=1.;
  mult=-1.;
  old=0.;
  start=small;
  sum=start;
  d0=0.;c0=sum;
  DOFOR(i,itmax)
    {
    fi=i;
    if(i)ana=fi;
    else ana=1.;
    d0= (x+d0*ana);
    c0=(x+ana/c0);
    if(d0==0.)d0=small;
    if(c0==0.)c0=small;
    d0=1./d0;
    delta=d0*c0;sum*=delta;
    ana=fi+1.-a;
    d0= (1.+d0*ana);
    c0=(1.+ana/c0);
    if(d0==0.)d0=small;
    if(c0==0.)c0=small;
    d0=1./d0;
    delta=d0*c0;sum*=delta;
    if( abs(delta-1.)<tol)
      {sum-=start;goto fini;}
```

```
     }
   printf(" trouble incomplete gamma cont. fract\n");
   }
/*return(-1.);*/
fini:return(offset+mult*sum*exp(-x+a*log(x)-gln));
}


double chisq(csq,nu) double csq,nu;
{
double incgam();
return (incgam(.5*nu,.5*csq));
}



double incbeta(aa,bb,x) double aa,bb,x;
{
int itmax=25,m;
/* uses Abramowitz and Stegun 26.5.8 for Ix(a,b)
26.5.9 seems less reliable */
double offset,bmult,exp(),log(),loggam(),a,b,z,
 fm,twicefm,dc,aplusb,am1,ap1,tol=1.e-7,h,d,c,delta;
iterkt=0;
if(x<0. || x>1.) return(errorcode);
if(aa==0. )return(1.e10);
if (x==1.||x==0.) return x ;
bmult= exp(loggam(aa+bb)-loggam(aa)-loggam(bb)+aa*log(x)+bb*log(1.-x));
/*printf(" incbeta x,aa,bb=%e %e %e bt=%e\n",x,aa,bb,bt);*/
 if(x <((aa+1.)/(aa+bb+2.)) )
    {
    a=aa;
    b=bb;
    z=x;
    offset=0.;
    bmult/=aa;
    }
else
    {
    a=bb;
```

```
  b=aa;
  z=1.-x;
  bmult=-bmult/bb;
  offset=1.;
  };
aplusb=a+b;
am1=a-1.;
ap1=a+1.;
d=0.;h=small;c=h;
for(m=0;m<=itmax;m++)
  {
  fm=(double)(m);
  twicefm=(double)(m<<1);
  if(m)
    dc=fm*(b-fm)*z/((am1+twicefm)*(a+twicefm));/*d2m*/
  else
    dc=1.;
  d=1.+d*dc;
  c=1.+dc/c;
  if(d==0.)d=small;
  if(c==0.)c=small;
  d=1./d;
  delta=d*c;
  h*=delta;
  dc=-(a+fm)*(aplusb+fm)*z/((a+twicefm)*(ap1+twicefm));/*d2m+1*/
  d=1.+d*dc;
  c=1.+dc/c;
  if(d==0.)d=small;
  if(c==0.)c=small;
  d=1./d;
  delta=d*c;
  h*=delta;
  if(abs(delta-1.)<tol)return h*bmult+offset;
  iterkt++;
  };
/*printf(" inc. beta noconv.\n");*/
return (errorcode);/*or return best guess (offset+bmult*conv)*/
}
```

```
double beta(a,b) double a,b;
{
double exp(),loggam();
return  exp( loggam(a)+loggam(b)-loggam(a+b));
}

/*26.5.4 series expansion-
use only as a check on incbeta*/
/*
double IncBeta(a,b,x) double a,b,x;
{
int n,nmax=25;
double sum,term,log(),ap1,aplusb,pow,exp(),factor,beta(),fn;
ap1=a+1.;
aplusb=a+b;
factor= exp(a*log(x)+b*log(1.-x))/(beta(a,b)*a);
sum=1.;
pow=x;
iterkt=0;
for(n=1;n<nmax;n++)
   {
   fn=(double)n;
   term= pow*beta(ap1,fn)/beta(aplusb,fn);
   sum+=term;
   if( abs(term/sum)<tolrel || abs(term)<tolabsb)return(sum*factor);
   pow*=x;
   iterkt++;
   }
printf("IncBeta warn\n");
return(sum*factor);
}
*/

double studt(t,nu) double t,nu;
{
double incbeta();
return(1.-incbeta(nu*.5,.5, nu/(nu+t*t)) );
```

```
}

double Hot(t,n,k) double t;int n,k;
{
double incbeta(),nu;
nu=n-1;
return(1.-incbeta(nu*.5,.5*k,nu/(nu+t*t)) );
}

double fdist(f,nu1,nu2) double f,nu1,nu2;
{
double incbeta();
return(incbeta(.5*nu2,.5*nu1,nu2/(nu2+nu1*f)) );
}


int g__df1,g__df2;
double g_noncent;

double ncf(f,noncen,df1,df2)
double f,noncen; int df1,df2;
{
/* fdist returns Q want P=1-Q for P' then take 1-P' */
int i,itmax=10;
double nu1,nu2,exp(),fdist(),tol=1.e-3,term,sum,coef,arg1;
nu1=df1;nu2=df2;
arg1=noncen*.5;
coef=1.;
for (i=0,sum=0.;i<itmax;i++)
   {
   coef /= (double) max(i,1) ;
   term= coef*(1.- fdist(f, nu1+2.*i,nu2) );
   sum=sum+term;
   if( abs(term/sum) < tol)break;
   coef *= arg1;
   }
if(i>itmax)
   {
```

```
  printf(" no convergence in noncentral F\n");
  return(-1.);
  }
/*printf(" number of terms for noncentral F=%d\n",i+1);*/
return( 1.- exp(-arg1)*sum);
}


double nct(f,noncen,df1)
double f,noncen; int df1;
{
/* fdist returns Q want P=1-Q for P' then take 1-P' */
int i,itmax=10;
double nu1,nu2,exp(),incbeta(),tol=1.e-3,term,sum,coef,arg1;
nu1=df1;
arg1=noncen*noncen*.5;
nu2= nu1/(nu1+f*f);
coef=1.;
for (i=0,sum=0.;i<itmax;i++)
   {
   coef /= ((double) max(i*2-1,1) )*((double) max(i*2,1));
   term= coef*(incbeta(nu1*.5,.5+i,nu2) );
   sum=sum+term;
   if( abs(term/sum) < tol)break;
   coef *= arg1;
   }
if(i>itmax)
   {
   printf(" no convergence in noncentral t\n");
   return(-1.);
   }
/*printf(" number of terms for noncentral t=%d\n",i+1);*/
return( 1.- exp(-arg1)*sum);
}


double ncc(f,noncen,df1)
double f,noncen; int df1;
{
/* fdist returns Q want P=1-Q for P' then take 1-P' */
```

```
int i,itmax=10;
double nu1,y,exp(),chisq(),tol=1.e-3,term,sum,coef,arg1;
nu1=df1;
arg1=noncen*.5;
coef=1.;
for (i=0,sum=0.;i<itmax;i++)
  {
  coef /= (double) max(i,1) ;
  y=chisq(f, nu1+2.*i);
  term= coef*(y );
  sum=sum+term;
  if( abs(term/sum) < tol)break;
  coef *= arg1;
  }
if(i>itmax)
  {
  printf(" no convergence in noncentral chisq\n");
  return(-1.);
  }
/*printf(" number of terms for noncentral chisq=%d\n",i+1);*/
return( exp(-arg1)*sum);
}


double finv(f,nu1,nu2) double f,nu1,nu2;
{
double sqrt(),invnr(),fdist(),icump(),guess,exp(),h,y,l,w;
  /*guess for F dist*/
if(nu1==1. || nu2==1.)
  {
  if(f>.5)guess=.7;
  else
  guess= 1./sqrt(f);
  }
else
  {
  y=icump(1.-f);
  l=(y*y-3.)/6.;
  h=2./(1./(nu2-1.)+1./(nu1-1.));
```

```
  w= y*sqrt(h+l)/h-(l+5./6.-2./(3.*h))*(1./(nu1-1.)-1./(nu2-1.));
  guess=exp(w);
/*printf(" debug guess=%f\n");*/
  }
return (invnr(0,f,nu1,nu2,fdist,guess)) ;
}


double ncf3(f,nu1,nu2) double f,nu1,nu2;
{
return ncf(f,g_noncent,g_df1,g_df2);
}

double nct3(f,nu1) double f,nu1;
{
return nct(f,g_noncent,g_df1);
}
double ncc3(f,nu1) double f,nu1;
{
return ncc(f,g_noncent,g_df1);
}

double incf(f,df1,df2,noncen) double f,noncen;
int df1,df2;
{
double nu1,nu2,sqrt(),invnr(),ncf(),ncf3(),icump(),guess,exp(),h,y,l,w;
nu1=df1;nu2=df2;
g_df1=df1;g_df2=df2;g_noncent=noncen;
  /*guess for F dist*/
if(nu1==1. || nu2==1.)
  {
  if(f>.5)guess=.7;
  else
  guess= 1./sqrt(f);
  }
else
  {
  y=icump(1.-f);
```

```
    l=(y*y-3.)/6.;
    h=2./(1./(nu2-1.)+1./(nu1-1.));
    w= y*sqrt(h+l)/h-(l+5./6.-2./(3.*h))*(1./(nu1-1.)-1./(nu2-1.));
    guess=exp(w);
/*printf(" debug guess=%f\n");*/
    }
return (invnr(0,f,nu1,nu2,ncf3,guess)) ;
}


double tinv(a,nu) double a,nu;
{
double p,t,y,invnr(),studt(),iguess,icump(),term2,term3,term4,nui;
    /* guess for student's t*/
/*CAVEAT- INAACURATE FOR SMALL NU*/
nui=1./nu;
p=(1.-a)*.5;
t=icump(1.-p);
y=t*t;
term2=t/96.*(3.+y*(16.+5.*y));
term3=t/384.*(-15.+y*(17.+y*(19.+3.*y)));
term4=t/92160.*(-945.+y*(-1920.+y*(1482.+y*(776.+y*79.)))));
iguess= t*(1.+(.25*(1.+t*t)+(term2+(term3+term4*nui)*nui)*nui)*nui);
/*attempt itertive improvement*/
return (invnr(1,a,nu,0.0,studt,iguess)) ;
}


double chiinv(a,nu) double a,nu;
{
double p,t,x,sqrt(),invnr(),chisq(),iguess,icump();
/* approx. for large nu>30 */
x= icump(1.-a);
p=2./(9.*nu);
t= 1.-p+x*sqrt(p);
t=t*t*t;
iguess= nu*t;
return(invnr(1,a,nu,0.0,chisq,iguess));
}
```

```
double invnr(narg,x,nu1,nu2,value,iguess)
int narg;
double x,nu1,nu2,(*value)(),iguess;
{
double y,z,dz0=.005,dz,zp,v,deriv,delta,deltas,resid,rnew;
double sqrt();
int maxit=40,halvetop=10,i,j;
z=iguess;
iterkti=0;
j=0;
if(narg)
   { dz0=.05;
   }
for(i=0;i<maxit;i++)
   {
   iterkti++;
   dz= dz0+.001*z;
   zp=z+dz;
/*   v= (narg)? value(z,nu1):value(z,nu1,nu2);
   y= (narg)? value(zp,nu1):value(zp,nu1,nu2);
*/
   if(narg)
     {v=value(z,nu1);
      y=value(zp,nu1);
      }
   else
     {v=value(z,nu1,nu2);
      y=value(zp,nu1,nu2);
      }
/*if(narg)printf(" debug z=%f v=%f y=%f\n",z,v,y);*/
   deriv=(y-v)/dz;
   resid= v-x;
   delta= -resid/(deriv+.0001);
   resid*=resid;/*square residual as metric*/
   if(resid<conabs|| abs(delta/resid)< conrel) return(z);
/*if(narg)
printf(" debug deriv %f resid %f  delta=%f\n",deriv,resid,delta);*/
   z+=delta;
```

```
    deltas=delta;
    z= max(z,0.001);
    z=min(z,1.e4);/*no reasonable F should exceed this*/
    for(j=0;j<halvetop;j++)
        {
/*      v= (narg)? value(z,nu1):value(z,nu1,nu2);*/
        if(narg)
          {v=value(z,nu1);}
        else
          {v=value(z,nu1,nu2);
          }
        rnew=v-x;
        rnew*=rnew;
        if(rnew<resid)break;
/*if(narg)printf(" worse z=%f rn=%f old=%f v=%f %d\n",z,rnew,resid,v,j);*/
        delta*=.5;
        z-=delta;
        if(halvetop-j==1){/* no soap*/
                z-=deltas*.5;/* try other direction*/
                }
        }
    }

    printf(" iter=maxit trouble resid=%f z=%f narg=%d,iguess=%f x=%f\n"
    ,resid,z,narg,iguess,x);
    if(narg)printf(" nu1=%f\n",nu1);
    else
      printf(" nu1,nu2 %f %f\n",nu1,nu2);
return(z);
}


double erf(x) double x;
{
double exp(),t,z;
t= 1./(1.+x*.3275911);
z=((((t*1.061405429-1.453152027)*t+1.421413741)*t-.284496736)*t
  +.254829592)*t;
```

```
return (1.-exp(-x*x)*z);
}

double ierf(y) double y;
{
int i,maxi=20;
double test,sqrt(),pow(),log(),c,x,dx,f,df;
if(y==0.)return(0.);
if(y>=1.)return(1.e10);
if(y<0.) return(-ierf(-y));
c= 1./ sqrt(sqrt(1.-y));
c=sqrt(sqrt(c));/* for higher power version*/
/*guess*/
x=1.;
if(y<1.)x=y*.7;

for(i=0;i<=maxi;i++)
   {
   f=(((((.0000430638*x+.0002765672)*x+.0001520143)*x+
   .0092705272)*x+.0422820123)*x+.0705230784)*x+1.-c;
   df=((((((6.*.0000430638*x+5.*.0002765672)*x+4.*.0001520143)*x+
   3.*.0092705272)*x+2.*.0422820123)*x+.0705230784);


/*lower power version
   f= 1.-c+(((.078108*x+.000972)*x+.230389)*x+.278393)*x;
   df= (((4.*.078108*x+3.*.000972)*x+2.*.230389)*x+.278393);
   */
   dx= -f/df;
   x=x+dx;
   test=abs(dx);
/*low power
   if( test < 1.e-6 || test< .0001*x)break;
*/
   if( test < 1.e-8 || test< .0000001*x)break;
/*printf(" iter=%d x=%f dx=%f \n",i,x,dx);*/
   }
if(i==maxi)printf(" ierf max it=%d,x=%f,dx=%f,arg=%f\n",i,x,dx,y);
```

```
return (x);
}

double prob(x) double x;
{
double erf();
return(erf(x*.707106781));
}

double cump(x) double x;
{/* area under normal curve from -infinty to x*/
static double rt=.7071067812;
double erf();
return(.5*(1.+erf(x*rt)));
}

double icump(x) double x;
{
double ierf();
static double rti=1.414213562;
return(rti*(ierf(2.*x-1.)));
}

double inct(a,df1,noncen) double a,noncen;
int df1;
{
double nu1,nu2;
double invnr(),nct(),icump(),guess;
double nui,t,y,term2,term3,term4,p;
g_noncent=noncen;g__df1=df1;
nu1=df1;nu2=0.;
  /*guess for t dist*/
    /* guess for student's t*/
/*CAVEAT- INAACURATE FOR SMALL NU*/
nui=1./nu1;
p=(1.-a)*.5;
t=icump(1.-p);
y=t*t;
```

```
term2=t/96.*(3.+y*(16.+5.*y));
term3=t/384.*(-15.+y*(17.+y*(19.+3.*y)));
term4=t/92160.*(-945.+y*(-1920.+y*(1482.+y*(776.+y*79.))));
guess= t*(1.+(.25*(1.+t*t)+(term2+(term3+term4*nui)*nui)*nui)*nui);
return (invnr(1,a,nu1,nu2,nct3,guess)) ;
}


double incc(a,df1,noncen) double a,noncen;
int df1;
{
double nu1,nu2;
double sqrt(),invnr(),nct(),icump(),guess,exp(),p,t,x;
nu1=df1;nu2=0.;
g_noncent=noncen;g_df1=df1;
/* approx. for large nu>30 */
x= icump(1.-a);
p=2./(9.*nu1);
t= 1.-p+x*sqrt(p);
t=t*t*t;
guess= nu1*t;
return (invnr(1,a,nu1,nu2,ncc3,guess)) ;
}
```

statg

enter: 1 for F, 2 chi-sq, 3 Student's 4 Hotelling gen. t

5 z-p 6 p-z 7 gamma 8 erf 9 inverse erf 10 prob

11 inc beta 12 inc gamma 13 t-inv 14 F-inv 15 chi-sq inv

16 noncentral F 17 chi-sq 18 t 19 inv-F 20 inv-t 21 inv-chi

22 Kolmogorv-Smirnov 23 Mann Whitney 24 Wilcoxon 25conv

param

1

> **F Values for ANOVA.**

enter F value 4.19

echo F value=4.190000

enter degrees of freedom(2 integers) 2 6

F=4.190000 fdist(F,2,6)=7.26402e-02

1

enter F value 3.87

echo F value=3.870000

enter degrees of freedom(2 integers) 8 18

F=3.870000 fdist(F,8,18)=8.14881e-03

13

> **Inverse F for ANOVA.**

enter 2-sided confid.,nu

.95 18

2.109722=inverse t(0.950000,18.000000)

> **Erf Test.**

8

enter x

1

erf(1.000000)=0.842701

9

> **Inverse erf for comparison.**

enter x

.842701

1.00000=erf(0.842701)

> **Comparison of Student t and Hotelling T.**

3

enter student t value 2.

enter degrees of freedom(integer) 3

student's-t($z=2.000000$,$df=3.000000$)=8.60674e-01

significance levels= 6.96630e-02[1-sided] 1.39326e-01[2-sided]

cummulative t[1-sided]=0.930337 0.860674[two-sided]

4

enter as integers degrees of freedom n and k

4 1

enter value for T (NOT square)

2.

echo n 4 k 1 T 2.000000

generalized t dist=8.60674e-01

> **One-sided t is z for large degrees of freedom.**

3

enter student t value 2.

enter degrees of freedom(integer) 20000

student's-t($z=2.000000$,$df=20000.000000$)=9.54486e-01

significance levels= 2.27569e-02[1-sided] 4.55138e-02[2-sided]

cummulative t[1-sided]=0.977243 0.954486[two-sided]

6

enter p score

.977243

p, z scores.

p score=1.99988e+00

5

enter z score

2.

z score=9.77250e-01

6

enter p score

.977250

p score=2.00000e+00

Gamma -extrema.

7

enter x

-.504

gamma(-0.504000)=-3.544643

7

enter x

-1.573

gamma(-1.573000)=2.302410

7

enter x

-2.611

gamma(-2.611000)=-0.888137

7

enter x

| Gamma positive x. |

4

gamma(4.000000)=6.000000

| Probability integral. |

10

enter x

1

0.682689=prob(1.000000)

| Relationship between F and t. |

3

enter student t value 2

enter degrees of freedom(integer) 2

student's-t(z=2.000000,df=2.000000)=8.16497e-01

significance levels= 9.17517e-02[1-sided] 1.83503e-01[2-sided]

cummulative t[1-sided]=0.908248 0.816497[two-sided]

1

enter F value 4

echo F value=4.000000

enter degrees of freedom(2 integers) 1 2

F=4.000000 fdist(F,1,2)=1.83503e-01

| z vs. tabular value. |

5

enter z score

2

z score=9.77250e-01

| F vs. tabular value. |

1

enter F value 5.05

echo F value=5.050000

enter degrees of freedom(2 integers) 5 5

F=5.050000 fdist(F,5,5)=5.00063e-02

enter: 1 for F, 2 chi-sq, 3 Student's 4 Hotelling gen. t

> **Kolmogorov-Smirnov statistic.**

22

enter d, n for kolmogorov smirnov

.16796 51

answer=9.00014e-01 siglevel=9.99863e-02

> **Wilcoxon/Mann-Whitney statistic.**

23

enter n,m,u integers for Wilcoxon (Mann-Whitney) 2 sample statistic

4 3 1

Wilcoxon=2 T=17, mann-whitney= 5.71429e-02

> **Wilcoxon matche-pair signed rank test.**

24

enter n,m integers for Wilcoxon matched pair signed rank

19 136

count=499250, prob.= 9.52244e-01

enter: 1 for F, 2 chi-sq, 3 Student's 4 Hotelling gen. t

5 z-p 6 p-z 7 gamma 8 erf 9 inverse erf 10 prob

11 inc beta 12 inc gamma 13 t-inv 14 F-inv 15 chi-sq inv

16 noncentral F 17 chi-sq 18 t 19 inv-F 20 inv-t 21 inv-chi

22 Kolmogorv-Smirnov 23 Mann Whitney 24 Wilcoxon 25conv param

44

terminating j i 1 44

CHAPTER 7

Multivariate Statistics: The SVD Revisited

Chapter Objectives

This chapter is unique among those of this book in that it does not include C programs. Rather, it continues the discussion begun in Chapter 6 of applications of the Singular Value Decomposition (SVD) to statistical problems. In particular, we will concentrate on discriminant analysis, regression analysis (multiple and stepwise), and canonical correlation.

Regression: Multiple, Weighted, Stepwise

The basic regression problem is fitting a function by the least-squares method to data. The program of Chapter 5 of *C Tools* suffices to perform this for a linear function of an arbitrary number of independent variables, i.e., perform multiple regression. If the function to be fit is a nonlinear function, we require the methods discussed in Chapter 6 of *C Tools* to minimize the least-square error of approximation in an iterative manner. We will confine our attention here to the linear problem.

Once one has obtained the least squares best fit, there are many questions of interest. For example, does an independent variable contribute significantly to the variability of the observed result? The null hypothesis in this case is that its coefficient in the functional fit should really be zero. For a discussion of these aspects to the regression problem, see Chapter 6 under the use of the t statistic.

Weighted Least Squares: Heteroscedasticity

We did not consider weighted least squares in Chapter 5 of *C Tools*. Each error residual, i.e., each equation, is given a multiplier weight $w[i]$ which measures the importance attached to that equation. The larger the weight, the better that equation will be fit, at the cost of a poorer fit to the others. This might be simply the number of observations made with that result, or some estimate allowing for better or poorer observations, or the importance of minimizing some particular residual due to its cost or likelihood. We can easily modify the methods of Chapter 5 of *C Tools* for the weighted least squares problem by introducing a vector W which contains the square roots $\sqrt{(w[i])}$, $i = 0,...m -1$ associated with each constraint equation. Defining the vector $\mathbf{b'} = \mathbf{Wb}$, and a matrix $\mathbf{A'}$ in which each row of the matrix $\mathbf{A}$ has been multiplied by the corresponding sqrt(w[i]), we solve the least squares problem of minimizing $|\mathbf{A'} \ x - \mathbf{b'} \ |$ for x. Note that the solution vector x is not rescaled.

Heteroscedasticity is a term used primarily, it seems, by economists. It describes the situation in which the variance of the independent variables (the observations) in a regression fit are different. In the statistical analysis of the results of a regression fit discussed in Chapter 6, it is tacitly assumed that all the variances are equal. This is often false; in economics, variables with larger means often have larger variances as well. Weighted least squares is the way to address this difficulty.

Note that if you wish to remove column means (means over each value of x) from the matrix first, which is a good idea from the numerical conditioning viewpoint, they must be weighted, i.e., each column mean (including $\mathbf{b'}$) must be defined as $\Sigma \ w[i]c[i] / \Sigma \ w[i]$. This mean is the subtracted from each corresponding column, and then the multiplication of the row (including the corresponding element of b) by $\sqrt{(w[i])}$ should be performed. Note that the residual vector directly computed is in actuality a vector of scaled residuals, the ith scaled by $\sqrt{(w[i])}$.

The SVD can be used to perform stepwise multiple regression. This is illustrated in Lawson and Hanson (see Chapter 5 of *C Tools*). Stepwise regression typically begins with the program fitting using only one of the independent variables at a time, and then printing the result of the variable that was the optimal choice (in terms of accounting for more of the variance than the others could singly). Next, the two-variable fits in which the variable already selected is used as one and the others tried out in sequence are considered and the optimal chosen. Some programs will now hold the second variable fixed and check back to see if a better fit may be obtained by selecting the first variable differently. The process continues until the program or the user or the variables are exhausted. The standard reference for stepwise multiple regression is the article by M. A. Efroymson as Chapter 17 of *Mathematical Methods for Digital Computers*, edited by A. Ralston and H. S. Wilf (NY: John Wiley, 1960). An algorithm is presented there which employs ·nodified Gaussian elimination. It should be possible, depending upon hardware and patience, to do exhaustive stepwise regression for up to perhaps 20 independent variables by means of the SVD (1023 selections). For n variables, the SVD may be performed with all $2^n -1$ possible choices of variables to participate in the fit. This is expensive, but if the problem is ill-conditioned, it may be worth it (so long as it is still affordable). If stepwise regression is done by programs that check all the previous choices of variables, the costs will be similar; some versions only check on the order of n^2, making the process far more economical and practical for large n, but less rigorous. The SVD cannot directly measure the importance of individual variables in one full calculation, as the singular values measure the importance of the principal components, which are linear combinations of the variables. Still, the SVD used once with all the dependent variables can give a good indication of the relative importance of each variable, since the principal components (columns of V) may be examined one at a time to gauge the contribution of each variable.

Before leaving the subject of linear regression we wish to note its close association with analysis of variance. This will be discussed in Chapter 8.

Total And Generalized Least Squares

the Total Least Squares Problems Allows There To Be Random Errors in the coefficients as well as the observations. Thus, we have the residual vector $r = y - (A + E)x$, where E is a matrix of unknown errors, and we wish to minimize the sum of the squares of all of the elements of r and E. Define the matrix F as the matrix whose first columns are those of E and whose last column is r, and similarly define the matrix Z whose leading columns are those of A and whose last is $- y$, and define a vector z whose first elements are the (unknown) x and whose last element is 1. Then we must minimize the squares of the elements of r subject to the equation $(Z + F)z = 0$. Find the SVD of Z as $USV^\wedge$. Then the matrix F may be found as $US'V^\wedge$ where S' is a diagonal matrix in which $s'[i] = 0$ for the first n elements (i=0,...,n −1) and the remainder $s'[i] = - s[i]$. If the last column of V is denoted by $(q[0],q[1],....q[n - 1],p)$ then $x = q/p$ gives the coefficients which solve the regression problem. See Hammarling and Golub and van Loan (reference in Chapter 1).

The generalized least-squares problem provides us with additional information about the error. Thus, $y = Ax + w$ where w is a "noise" vector with zero mean and a related symmetric positive definite covariance matrix W, which is m x m (see Golub and van Loan for definitions and more details). Due to the properties of W it may be factored according to the Cholesky decomposition (see Chapter 3 of *C Tools*), i.e., as, $BB^\wedge$ (Hammarling initially uses the notation F_a and then switches without explanation to B on the next page). We still wish to determine the vector of coefficients x that minimize the square of the residual |r| in $y = Ax + Br$ (for transformed A,y, this is equivalent to minimizing $|B^{-1} (y - AX)|$, but as we have said many times before, one does not want to perform the inversion of B and the multiplication if it can be avoided). For details, see the book by Golub and van Loan. The SVD (or just a QR factoring) is found for A, say $USV^\wedge$. The full m x m U matrix is needed!

Canonical Correlation

One way to define the canonical correlation problem (see Wilks, Section 18.9) is to obtain the highest possible correlation between two linear functions (one of whose coefficients are the unknowns to be determined) of two sets of variables, given a set of observations as functions of the variables of those sets. One set may be viewed as observables used to predict the other set. In this case, the coefficients of the first set are to be found while those of the latter are given.. This may be expressed more mathematically as: determine the vector a defining the linear combination of the columns of a matrix Y, i.e., $y = Ya$, such that we have a best predictor for regression on a matrix X, i.e., which minimizes $|y - Xb|/|y|$, the vector b defining the linear combination to be predicted. Or, one may ask to minimize $|Xb|/|y|=|Xb|/|Ya|$ for all choices of a and b. We will assume that the two data matrices, X and Y are defined as in Chapter 5 of *C Tools* with zero means. More generally, Hammarling defines a transformation matrix A such that the matrix $Z = YA$ is orthogonal and such that the regression of a column of Z on X maximizes the multiple correlation coefficient. In each case, the SVD of the X and Y matrices is determined, $Y = USV^\wedge$ and $X = U'\ S'\ V'^\wedge$. In the more restrictive problem (as defined in Chambers) form the matrix $W = U'^\wedge U$, find its SVD as $U''S''V''^\wedge$. The canonical correlations are the singular values $s''[i]$ and the linear combinations of Y and X are given by solving $S'V'\ ^\wedge B = U''$ and $SV^\wedge A = V''$. Here A and B are matrices whose columns are a and b vectors. A given b may then be constructed from a linear combination of the columns of the B matrix. As usual, if any $s[i]$ are zero we "invert" S by setting the corresponding element of the inverse of S to zero.

Discriminant Analysis Revisited

We had previously discussed one form of discriminant analysis in Chapter 4 of *C Tools*, as a generalized eigenvalue problem. In fact, it may be treated as a form of the canonical correlation problem and the SVD brought to bear (see Chambers). Here, X is a data matrix for dummy variates the ith of which is 1 if the observation is in the ith group and zero otherwise. The W matrix is a matrix of group means, $W[i][j] = \sqrt{(n[i])}\ y[i][j]$ where $y[i][j]$ is the mean of the jth column of the data matrix Y for the ith group. See Chambers for more details.

We had not touched upon the question: "given an individual's measurements, into which of two groups should he be assigned as most likely being a member?" The SVD can be used to robustly determine this as well. Given an individual specified by the vector of measurements v, we need to determine whether he is closer to the centroid of group 1 or group 2 (say). Let $C = X^\wedge X/(n-1)$ be the sample covariance matrix (zero mean) as defined in Chapter 5 and Hammarling. The conventional procedure, as discussed in Koch and Link or Cooley and Lohnes (see Chapter 4), is to invert C (call this inverse D). Call the vector of the observation means of the groups v[i]. For discrimination between the jth and kth group, form $v' = v[j] - v[k]$, and form the coefficient vector $c = Cv'$. The discriminant function is then the scalar $d = cv$. If the d associated with the observation d is closer to that for v[j] than v[k], the individual should be classified in the jth group, otherwise the kth group. The scalar $d^2 = v' {}^\wedge Dv'$, which is positive because C and hence D are positive definite, gives the distance between the two groups and may be used with the individual distance to estimate the confidence of the assignment.

The use of the SVD enables us to perform this operation more robustly. Rather than invert C to form D, apply the SVD to the normalized data matrix $A = X/\sqrt{(n-1)}$, getting $USV^\wedge$. The inverse of C is then $VS^{-2}V^\wedge$. Furthermore, the distance d^2 between groups may be written as $v'[i]s[i]^{-2}v'[i]$ and evaluated more simply than otherwise.

For a discussion of confidence estimation with regard to discriminant analysis, see Chapter 6 where Hotelling's T squared statistic is discussed.

Multivariate statistics are covered further below in Chapter 8, Analysis of Variance, where MANOVA and ANCOVAR, among other things, are discussed.

Cryptography

C. Moler and D. Morrison (unpublished) have found a method for applying the SVD to the (probable) determination of vowels and consonants in a cryptogram. See the paper by B. R. Schatz.

References

J. M. Chambers, *Computational Methods for Data Analysis* (New York: J. Wiley, 1977).

B. R. Schatz, *Cryptologia*, Vol. **1**, 2, April 1977.

S. Hammarling, *SIGNUM* **20**, 2, July 1985.

CHAPTER 8

Analysis of Variance

Chapter Objectives

In this chapter we will develop tools to:

– perform a general analysis of variance (ANOVA)

We will discuss the theoretical basis of this method, covering such topics as orthogonal contrasts, analysis of covariance, and multivariate statistical tests.

Analysis Of Variance

Analysis of variance (ANOVA) is the general term for a family of statistical methods. The general idea is to compare a number of observations for differing values of parameters called "factors" for a number of different values called "levels" (or "treatments") and to attempt to determine whether some factors are or are not having a significant effect on the observations. There is a close kinship between ANOVA and regression analysis (see Chapter 5 of *C Tools*), which will be discussed below. The orthogonal matrices and quadratic forms discussed in Chapters 4 and 5 will, perhaps surprisingly, be useful here. Finally, we will discuss multivariate extensions, MANOVA and ANCOVAR, of ANOVA.

ANOVA

The most intuitive discussion of ANOVA I have found is in E. Bright Wilson, Jr.'s *Introduction to Scientific Research*. Suppose for simplicity that an experiment is done with two factors, each of which has two levels, so there are a total of 4 measurements. For concreteness, say we were testing the effect of temperature (the first factor) and catalyst (second factor) in the yield of a chemical process, the levels being high and low for the first factor and present or absent for the second. Then we set up a 2 x 2 array of measurements:

(high, catalyst present) (high, catalyst absent)

(low, catalyst present) (low, catalyst absent)

We wish to determine if the catalyst has a significant effect, and if the temperature does, and if there is an interaction effect (perhaps the catalyst requires high temperatures to be effective). If there is replication (i.e., we do not perform just four measurements but redo each measurement a number of times), we can estimate the random error, and with this estimate determine if the interaction effect is significant.

One "heuristic" method discussed by Wilson would be to take selected means. First take the mean of all observations. Then the mean of the two high temperature measurements, from which we subtract the mean of the two low temperature measurements, would tell us (qualitatively) if there were a significant temperature effect. We could similarly gauge the effect of catalyst and of interaction. How do we formalize such a process to draw quantitative conclusions? The key is using Fisher's F statistic. To do this, we need to deal with the ratios of chi-square variables (see Chapter 6), so we need to deal with squares and sums of squares.

We form squares of linear combinations of the observations, as in the means and differences of means discussed above. Particularly useful are linear combinations which are orthogonal. Thus, consider the sum $y[i] = \sum a[i][j]X[j]$ where the vector $X[j]$ is a composite vector (see Chapters 4 and 5 of *C Tools*) of the columns of the observations. The matrix **A** is assumed orthonormal. One of rows of **A** is used to form the (normalized) mean, e.g., $a[0][i]= 1/\sqrt{n}$ where there are n observations (4 in our example). Of special interest are rows in which the sum of the coefficients is zero. Such vectors are called contrasts (contrasts in general need not be normalized). The most obvious (normalized) contrasts for our example might be $(1,1, -1, -1)/2$ which would difference the observations with catalyst from those without, or $(1, -1,1, -1)/2$ which would similarly "contrast" the high and low temperature cases. By the orthonormality of **A**, it may be shown that sum $\sum y_i^2 = \sum X_i^2$. In addition to the normalized mean row $(1,1,1,1)/2$ (actually twice the mean due to the normalization) we have the row $(1, -1, -1,1)$ which measures the interaction (which is not seperable from random errors unless we have an estimate of those, as multiple observations would provide). If we wanted to test the hypothesis that temperature was the dominant variable, and that the variances due to the catalyst and the interaction between temperature and catalyst were merely random errors, we would want to use the F test on the ratio of $X^{\wedge}(1, -1,1, -1)X$ to half the sum of the other two contrasts used in a similar manner,

$(X^\wedge(1,1, - 1, - 1,)X + X^\wedge(1, - 1, - 1,1)X)/2$. (If the mean were zero, we could use a denominator $X^\wedge(1,1,1,1)X$ instead.) The test for the role of catalyst would be similar, with the the $(1,1, - 1, - 1)$ vector in the numerator and $(1, - 1,1, - 1)$ in the denominator. In these F tests, there would be one degree of freedom for the numerator and two for the denominator. Notice (see Chapter 6) that the F statistic becomes the Student's t statistic for this simple case. This is of significance when we compare ANOVA and multiple regression methods, as we have seen in Chapter 6 the role of Student's t in the latter. If we wished to test the significance of the interaction term, we could use a test involving the interaction sum of squares $X^\wedge(1, - 1, - 1,1)X$ in the denominator and one of the other contrasts (which we believed significant) in the numerator. The F statistic would have a $v_1 = 1$ $v_2 = 1$ in this case. As Wilson notes, very large F values are needed to establish significance for such small numbers of degrees of freedom; one solution is to reduce the role of random variances by replicating measurements.

For problems larger than our 2 x 2 example, it would be nice to have a computer generate the orthonormal matrices involving the (normalized) mean and the contrasts. This can be done by a method invented by Helmert. For the case of a 3 x 3 orthogonal matrix, this produces the transpose of the matrix of eigenvalues from the example problem of Chapter 4!

Ian Oliver has implemented an ANOVA analysis by means of orthogonal matrices in an ALGOL and presented in the Collected Algorithms from the CACM, number 330, which serves as the basis of our program. It produces the necessary sums of squares. We still need to form ratios of the type

$$F = SS(1)/df(1) / SS(2)/ df(2) = MS(1)/MS(2)$$

where F is an F statistic with degrees of freedom $df(1)$ and $df(2)$, $SS(i)$ is a sum of squares with associated degrees of freedom $df(i)$, and MS is a "mean square" in the conventional notation. If F is larger than the critical F value at the desired confidence level, we reject the null hypothesis. In general, $MS(2)$ is the MSE or mean square of the error (which may include interaction effects), while $MS(1)$ corresponds to a treatment or treatments of interest. For example, the simplest one factor treatment model would have:

	SS	d.f.	MS	F-test
treatments	SSt	n − 1	MSt	MSt/MSE
error	SSE	m − n	MSE	
total	SST	m − 1		

Here there are m observations and n levels, $m = m$ where r is the replication factor of each observation, $SST = \Sigma (y - \bar{y})^2$ and SSt, which measures the differences in means of different treatment levels, is $SSt = r \Sigma (\overline{y[i]} - \overline{y})^2$, with $\overline{y}$ the mean of all the y observations and $\overline{y[i]}$ the mean of the observations at the ith treatment level. And, $SSE = \Sigma \Sigma (y - \overline{y[i]})^2$, measures random errors and interactions. Note that SST = SSt + SSE, and df(T) = df(t) + df(E). In general the total degrees of freedom and sum of squares should equal the total of the problem degrees of freedom and all of the individual contributions to the sum of squares. The total degrees of freedom is n − 1 because the mean is computed from the data.

We may form orthogonal contrasts and test, using $SSc = \Sigma (c^{\wedge}y[i])^2$, the significance of the contrast tested (e.g., the contrasts discussed above would test the significance of the difference of two means, or of the interaction term). In the cases discussed, the F statistic would have 1 degree of freedom in the numerator, and m − n in the denominator—again an example of a student t statistic. See Montgomery for more information, such as the use of nonorthogonal contrasts, or unbalanched designs (see below for the definition of balanced).

In a two factor ANOVA analysis, such as our first example, with factors a and b each with a and b levels, respectively, the table becomes

	SS	d.f.	MS	F-test
a treatment	SSa	a −1	MSa	MSa/MSE
b treatment	SSb	b −1	MSb	MSb/MSE
interaction	SSab	(a −1)(b −1)	MSab	MSab/MSE
error	SSE	ab(r −1)	MSE	
total	SST	abr −1		

Here there are r replications of each measurement. The interaction may be separated from the random errors and its significance tested. (Oliver's algorithm does not directly provide for replications but this can be circumvented with only slight difficulty-see below).

Types Of ANOVA

There are two classes of ANOVA applications: Model I, which deals with situations as above in which the treatments are variable parameters, and Model II, in which they are random variables. In each case, we wish to determine whether the treatments have significant effects and if so, significant iterations. The difference between Model I and Model II is more in interpretation than practice. See Crow et al. for a discussion.

Our discussion will concentrate on the Model I interpretation. In this case, ANOVA is probably being used to interpret an experiment. It is therefore wedded to the topic of experimental design. The simple 2 x 2 experiment we have used as our example is a simple case of a "balanced factorial" design, in which each of the treatment levels has the same number of observations. This case is the simplest to analyze. It also has the property that the results of the ANOVA analysis are insensitive to differences in the variances for different treatment levels. An assumption of the ANOVA model is that these variances are equal, and is used in the test of the null hypothesis. If the samples are balanced, the F statistic is insensitive to deviations from this condition. Also, the "power" of the test (likelihood that a false null hypothesis is rejected) is maximized for equal samples (see Montgomery's book).

It is of interest sometimes to group multiple observations for the same sets of levels in blocks. For example, if one is studying various factors in worker productivity, it might be useful to group together observations made on Monday, those made on Tuesday, etc., in case there were an effect on productivity due to the day of the week. The use of blocks amounts to introducing a new set of factors, the block "number," and the analysis goes over into that of the factorial design with this change. For example, in using student's t to given confidence intervals for the difference between a pair of treatment (or block) means, the number of degrees of freedom to be used is $n - (f - 1 + b)$ where n is the total number of observations, b the number of blocks, and f the number of levels (treatments). A blocked design would have a table something like:

	SS	d.f.	MS	F-test
treatments	SSt	$n - 1$	MSt	MSt/MSE
blocks	SSB	$b - 1$	MSB	
error	SSE	$(n -1)(b -1)$	MSE	
total	SST	$m -1$		

(In our example below, we treat the blocking as another variable.)

Another popular **design** involves nested sampling. See Mendenhall and Sincich for details. As with blocking, nesting does not require a significant change of method. Confounding refers to using blocks which are smaller than the total number of treatment combinations. Tables are available for designing such experiments for block sizes a power of 2 or 3. Various other experimental designs to minimize the number of observations exist, such as Latin squares, Youder incomplete Latin squares, etc. See the books by John and Montgomery. The latter has a rather complete discussion of the application of ANOVA and regression to such experiments, while for former concentrates more on the design than the analysis.

Relationship With Multiple Regression

Because ANOVA and multiple linear least-squares regression developed independently, the disparate terminologies of the methods serves to exaggerate the differences between the two methods. The F test of ANOVA is often the equivalent of the Student's t test for significance of regression analysis (see Chapter 6).

ANOVA and multiple regression have a mutual relation similar to that of thermodynamics and statistical mechanics. The former is more general but somewhat weaker in the information it can provide. This is because of the linearity assumption of multiple regression. ANOVA can provide information about the interaction term which is absent in linear regression. It is also useful when the observation is not a quantitative observation which is assumed to be linearly related to some functions, but is perhaps a qualitative observations (e.g., 1 = present and 0 if absent, or any similar model). On the other hand, it is trivial to handle unbalanced designs with a multiple regression analysis, it is merely another row in the matrix (the costs may not be trivial however). Regression analysis provides the coefficients which quantitatively characterize the dependence of the observable on the factors. More information has to be put into the regression model, but more detailed information comes out.

In multiple linear regression, we minimize the residual error term. This term may be viewed as the sum of the squares of the error (and nonlinear interaction) term. If the regression model is $y = Ax$, then $R = y^{\wedge}Ax$ represents the reduction in sum of squares due to the model fit ("treatments"). Then the error sum of squares may be written as $SSE = \Sigma y^2 - R$. If the regression coefficients were all zero, i.e., the data was uncorrelated, then $R = 0$. We can test the significance of the regression by an F test on $\{R/(f - 1)\} / \{SSE/(n - f)\}$ where the degrees of freedom are $f - 1$ and $n - f$ for n observations and f factors (variables). This is essentially the ANOVA result, the only difference being that in ANOVA we generally separately treat the mean of all the observed y's (it is not a factor), while in regression it might be one of the variables. For a regression with the means removed (see Chapter 5 of *C Tools*) the results would be identical. This example should bring out the close connection between ANOVA and regression.

MANOVA

The multivariate version of ANOVA is called MANOVA. In this case, we have more than one dependent variable (set of observations). It is simplest to view MANOVA as a regression problem, for which instead of solving (in a least-squares sense) $y = Ax$ (the univariate problem) we solve $Y = AX$ where now Y is a matrix with, say, r columns, as is now X. Alternatively, Y and X may be viewed as composite vectors (see Chapter 6). Note that the columns of the X matrix may be found as the x vectors by solving r separate univariate regressions. See books by Maindonald and Bibby and Toutenburg for disucussions from this point of view. The QR (or SVD or Cholesky) factorizations may then be used to calculate a generalized ANOVA table of sum of squares as the Helmert matrices were used. See Maindonald, section 6.3. Table 8.1 shows typical MANOVA test criteria. Their computation can generally be done with the programs of Chapters 4 and 5 of *C Tools* for eigenvalue and singular value determination.

TABLE 8.1

MANOVA Criteria

F-Test	maximum eigenvalue of $(T - W)W^{-1}$
Wilk's Lambda	$|W|/|T|$
Lawley-Hotelling Trace	Sum of eigenvalues$((T - W)W^{-1})$

(T is the total and W the "within group" variance matrices. See Chapter 4 of *C Tools* for complete definitions). Note that the trace is the sum of the diagonal elements of the matrix. As the trace is an "invariant" of the matrix under rotation, the eigenvalues need not be explicitly calculated.

Analysis Of Covariance (ANCOVAR)

Montgomery (op. cit.) describes analysis of covariance as a fusion of ANOVA and multiple linear regression. Suppose that in addition to the factors x[i](independent variables) that affect the observable y, another variable linearly related to y, the *covariate* z, influences the value of y. This covariate cannot be controlled but it can be observed and its influence corrected for. A model of the form $y = Ax + bz$ is then appropriate, where b is a regression coefficient for y on z which must be solved for. This may be treated as a regression problem with one additional variable (b) or as a simultaneous regression ANOVA problem. In practice, additional variables, such as the product of the covariate z with the treatment, are introduced into the model to permit testing for interaction effects between the covariate(s) and the treatments (see, e.g., Edwards).

I have encountered the term analysis of covariance in a different context. In J. C. R. Li's book, analysis of covariance (ANCOVAR) is discussed as the extension of linear regression as discussed above to multiple samples, i.e. a matrix Y, but now we no longer permit the independent variables X to be independently regressed to each sample. For example, we might want to fit the same model of, say, the rates of growth of children, to data obtained in different countries. The y values would be height, say, while the x might be age. The samples might be America, Europe, etc. Note that this version of an ANCOVAR problem would reduce to the other version if the covariate z were, say, 0 in America, 1 in Europe, etc. A more typical example of ANCOVAR in which the covariate is a discrete variable would be in a study of the weight gain with a number of different feed grains on a number of different breeds of cattle, in which the covariate would be the initial weight of each cow (see Mann). Assuming that the weight gain varied linearly with the cow's weight at the start of the experiment, we could use ANCOVAR to control for this variable and measure its effect. Note the need to assume that the covariate's effect is linear. If, in the discrete problem, we assigned Asia a value of $z = 2$, we would be implicitly assuming that the "continent" effect was twice as big as the difference between America and Europe.

What is of most interest in ANCOVAR is testing the null hypothesis that the *regression coefficients are the same* among samples This can be done by an F test on a ratio like MSd/MSt, where MSd = (SS2 − SS1)/(k − 1) and MSt = (SS1)/(k(n − 2)), k is the number of treatments, n the number of levels, SS1 the total residual sum of squares and SS2 is the sum of squares for a common regession coefficient for all treatments (see Edwards). These mean squares may be rewritten in terms of the total sum of squares and the regression coefficients.

By contrast, in MANOVA the homogeneity of the *sample means* is of most interest. The MANOVA problem is therefore related to Hotelling's T test for the distances between groups (see Chapter 6 as well as the discussions of discriminant analysis in Chapter 4 of *C Tools*). ANCOVAR may similarly be done by testing the significance of the differences between regression means.

Cooley and Lohnes in their chapter on "multivariate analysis of variance and covariance" describe a covariance adjustment method applied to the matrices of discriminant analysis.

Program And Test Problems

The three test problems contained in the driver main() program are all adapted from the text of Mendenhall and Sincich. The first is for the randomized block design of their example 13.5. In all of the printouts, ss refers to the sum of squares appropriate to that factor. Our global sum of squares is referred to in their text as CM, while the sum of squares for the two factors is their SST and SSB (for treatment and block, respectively).

As discussed above, the "interaction" and "error" effects cannot be distinguished unless there are multiple observations to enable us to determine the error variances. In this model, the text calls SSE, the "error" sum of squares what is called the interaction term in the printout. Note that we treat the block merely as another factor, giving us a two factor ANOVA instead of a blocked single factor ANOVA. The problems are equivalent. The F test for the significance of the treatment of the ratio of the sum of squares for factor 1, divided by the number of treatments $f - 1$ (in this case, 2) is divided by the sum of squares for the interaction, listed in the printout as .186667 (SSE in the text's notation), which is divided by $(n - b - f - 1)$, in this case 6 $(.26/2)/(.18666/6) = 4.19$. The appropriate number of degrees of freedom for the numerator and denominator are 2 and 6 respectively. See Chapter 6 for the significance level of 7.26%.

The next problem, example 13.7, is a two factor model. Because the text of Mendenhall and Sincich has a replication factor of three for each observation while we use merely the sum of the three observations, our sums of squares must be divided by three for comparison with theirs. The appropriate F for a test of the null hypothesis that all of the treatment means are equal can be formed from the ratio of

$$\frac{ss(factor\ 1) + ss(factor\ 2) + ss(\ interaction)}{n - 1}$$

where $n(=9$ for this example) is the total number of level pairs (the product of $f=3$ for each factor) and

$$\frac{ss(total) - \{\ sum\ of\ sums\ of\ squares\ in\ numerator\}}{degrees\ of\ freedom(total) - degrees\ of\ freedom\ (sums)}$$

The total number of degrees of freedom is $nm - 1(= 26)$, where $m(= 3)$ is the multiplicity of each measurement. The total degrees of freedom from the two factor means and the interaction term is $(f - 1)\ (= 2)$ for each of the two factors, and the product of these for the interaction term $2+2+4=8$. Thus the degrees of freedom for the "error" term denominator is $26-8=18$. The "calculator" example of Chapter 6 determines the confidence level for an F test with $F = 3.87$ and 8,18 degrees of freedom. Also presented there is the determination of t for a 95% confidence in the difference of the factor means. This must be calculated iteratively using the calculator, as the confidence level and not the t is the given. See Mendenhall and Sincich for details of the application of the student's t in this case. Finally, the last example is that for the two-stage nested sample ANOVA, example 14.1 of Mendenhall and Sincich.

	Subroutines and Functions of Chapter 8
anova()	perform ANOVA analysis (see listing for details of required arguments)
indx()	determines the location in a linear array of a multi-dimensional vector. See listing for details of the required argument. Note that the FORTRAN convention (storage by columns, first index changing first) is used.
orthog()	generate Helmert matrices.
panova()	prints ANOVA results in convenient form

References

J. Bibby and H. Toutenburg, *Prediction and Improved Estimation in Linear Models* (New York: Wiley Interscience, 1977)

W. R. Cooley and P. R. Lohnes, *Multivariate Procedures for the Behavioral Sciences* (New York: John Wiley, 1962).

A. L. Edwards, *Multiple Regression and the Analysis of Variance and Covariance* (New York: W. H. Freeman, 1985).

G. S. Koch and R. F. Link, *Statistical Analysis of Geological Data* (New York: Dover, 1970).

J. C. R. Li, *Statistical Inference* (Ann Arbor, Mich: Edwards Bros.,1964, 2 volumes).

P. W. M. John, *Statistical Design and Analysis of Experiments* (New York: MacMillian, 1971).

J. H. Maindonald, *Statistical Computations* (New York: John Wiley, 1984).

H. B. Mann, *Analysis and Design of Experiments* (New York: Dover, 1949).

W. Mendenhall and T. Sinich, *Statistics for the Engineering and Computer Sciences* (San Francisco: Dellen Press, 1984).

D. C. Montgomery, *Design and Analysis of Experiments* (New York: John Wiley, 1976).

E. B. Wilson, Jr., *Introduction to Scientific Research* (New York: McGraw-Hill,1952).

Program Listing And Test Problem Output

(Listing begins next page.)

```
/* analysis of variance ANOVA package

from More C tools for Scientists and Engineers by L. Baker

DEPENDENCIES: none
*/

/*#include "libc.h"
#include "math.h"
*/

#define DOFOR(i,to) for(i=0;i<to;i++)
#define INDEX(i,j) [j+(i)*coln]
#define failsafe 1000

anova(x,n,levels,t,i,ti,tlimit,q,a,b)
double x[],t[],q[],a[],b[];int n,levels[],i[],ti[],tlimit[];
{
/* CACM 330*/
int k1,k2,j,factor,coln,j1,indx(),kount;
kount=0;
DOFOR(factor,n)
  {
  coln=levels[factor];
  orthog(q,coln);
  DOFOR(j,n) i[j]=0;
  loop1:
    DOFOR(i[factor],coln)
      a[i[factor]]=x[indx(i,levels,n)];
  DOFOR(k1,coln)
    {
    b[k1]=0.;
    DOFOR(k2,coln)b[k1]+=a[k2]*q INDEX(k2,k1);
    }

  DOFOR(i[factor],coln)
    x[indx(i,levels,n)]=b[i[factor]];
```

```
DOFOR(j,n)
  {
  if(j!=factor)
    {
    i[j]++;
    if (i[j]<=levels[j]-1) goto loop1;
    else
       i[j]=0;
    }
  }


  }
DOFOR(j,n)
  {
  ti[j]=0;
  tlimit[j]=2;
  }
loop2:
  DOFOR(j,n) i[j]=ti[j];
k1=indx(ti,tlimit,n);
t[k1]=0.;
loop3:
  k2=indx(i,levels,n);
x[k2]*=x[k2];
t[k1]+=x[k2];
DOFOR(j,n)
  {
  if(ti[j]!=0)
    {
    i[j]++;
    if(i[j]<=levels[j]-1) goto loop3;
    else
       i[j]=1;
    }
  }
DOFOR(j,n)
  {
  ti[j]++;
```

```
    if(ti[j]<=1)goto loop2;
    else
       ti[j]=0;
    }
 return;
 }


 int indx(subscript,limit,n)
 int subscript[],limit[],n;
 {
 int j,temp;
 temp=0;
 for(j=n-1;j>=0;j--)
    {
    temp=limit[j]*temp+subscript[j];/*ftn-1*/
    }
 return(temp);/*ftn+1*/
 }


 orthog(q,coln) int coln; double q[];
 {
 double rsize,fj,fj1,sqrt();
 int i,j;
 rsize=coln;
 DOFOR(i,coln) q INDEX(i,0) = 1./sqrt(rsize);
 for(j=1;j<coln;j++)
    {fj=(double)j;fj1=fj+1.0;
    DOFOR(i,j)
       q INDEX(i,j)=-1./sqrt( fj*fj1  );
    q INDEX(j,j)= sqrt( fj/fj1 );
    for(i=j+1;i<coln;i++) q INDEX(i,j)=0.;
    }
 return;
 }



 panova(t,n) int n;
 double t[];
```

```
{
int i,j,k,l,k1,j1;
printf("\n analysis of variance %d factors\n",n);
printf(" global ss=%f\n",t[0]);
k=1;
DOFOR(j,n)
  {
  printf(" ss for factor %d is %f (index %d)\n",j,t[k],k);
  k=k<<1;
  }
j1=1;
DOFOR(j,n)
  {k1=1<<(j+1);
  for(k=j+1;k<n;k++)
    {
    l= k1+j1;
    printf(" ss for interaction %d %d is %f %d\n",j,k,t[l],l);
    k1=k1<<1;
    }
  j1<<1;
  }

return;
}


main(argc,argv) int argc;char **argv;
{
static double x[9]={64.,61.,58.,61.,71.,61.,52.,64.,66.};
static double y[12]=
   {4.6,4.9,4.4,6.2,6.3,5.9,5.0,5.4,5.4,6.6,6.8,6.3};
static double z[30]=
   {5.01,4.61,5.22,4.93,5.37,4.74,4.41,4.98,4.26,4.80,
   4.99,4.55,4.87,4.19,4.77,5.64,5.02,4.89,5.51,5.17,
   5.07,4.93,4.81,5.19,5.48,5.90,5.27,5.65,4.96,5.39};
double q[36],a[36],b[36],t[36],sst,ss2,ss3,ms1,ms2;
int levels[6],ti[36],i[36],tlimit[36];
int n,j,k,l,j1,k1;
/*ex 13.7 p. 576ff  simple 2 way anova*/
```

```
n=2;
levels[0]= 3;
levels[1]= 4;
anova(y,n,levels,t,i,ti,tlimit,q,a,b);
panova(t,n);

printf("another problem\n");
/* ex13.5 p.565 two factor anova*/
n=2;
DOFOR(j,n)levels[j]=3;
anova(x,n,levels,t,i,ti,tlimit,q,a,b);
panova(t,n);
printf(" yet another problem\n");
/* example 14.1 p.624 nested sample TYPE II MODEL */
n=2;
levels[0]=5;
levels[1]=6;
sst=0.0;
l=1; DOFOR(k,n) l*=levels[k];/* count of observations*/
printf(" %d observations \n",l);
DOFOR(k,l) sst+= z[k]*z[k];
anova(z,n,levels,t,i,ti,tlimit,q,a,b);
panova(t,n);
ss2= sst-t[0];
ss3=ss2-t[2];
ms1= t[2]/(levels[1]-1);
ms2= ss3/(levels[1]*(levels[0]-1));
printf(" sst=%f, ss2=%f ss3=%f\n ms1=%f ms2=%f\n",sst,ss2,ss3,ms1,ms2);
exit(0);
}
```

analysis of variance 2 factors
global ss=383.070000
ss for factor 0 is 0.260000 (index 1)
ss for factor 1 is 6.763333 (index 2)
ss for interaction 0 1 is 0.186667 3
another problem

analysis of variance 2 factors
global ss=34596.000000
ss for factor 0 is 60.666667 (index 1)
ss for factor 1 is 24.666667 (index 2)
ss for interaction 0 1 is 138.666667 3
yet another problem
30 observations

analysis of variance 2 factors
global ss=755.811213
ss for factor 0 is 0.879620 (index 1)
ss for factor 1 is 2.469747 (index 2)
ss for interaction 0 1 is 1.396620 3
sst=760.557200, ss2=4.745987 ss3=2.276240
ms1=0.493949 ms2=0.094843

CHAPTER 9

Random Numbers And Variables

Chapter Objectives

In this chapter we will present code to:

– generate random numbers and test such generators

– use those random numbers to generate common statistical distributions

Introduction

In this chapter we will discuss the generation and testing of random numbers and their uses as random distributions. Actually, to be precise, we are finding pseudorandom numbers, since the numbers are generated by a regular algorithm and could be generated in an identical manner the next day if desired. This can be an advantage in many circumstances as we shall see. We want these pseudorandom numbers to have the statistical properties of true random numbers.

A great deal of effort has gone into the problem of generating such pseudorandom numbers, and we will use what is generally accepted as a state-of-the-art random number generator.

(Pseudo)Random Numbers

From this point on, we will use the term random even when it is more correct to speak of pseudorandom numbers. This is in conformity with customary usage. Random numbers are of value in "simulation" problems. These are generally, but not exclusively, problems in which non-deterministic or stochastic processes, which have built-in randomness, are to be studied. An example would be a queuing problem as discussed in Chapter 12. If we owned a supermarket and wanted to determine what the optimal number of checkout positions to staff at a given time was, we might obtain data on the statistics of customer arrival rates at the checkout counter, and statistics on the number of groceries purchased and the duration of service at the checkout counter. We might also develop some statistics on customer dissatisfaction, i.e., at what point a long wait either loses a sale (a "balk" or "reneg" in the terminology of queuing theory–see Chapter 12), or causes the customer to shop elsewhere next time. We can then run a number of simulations with these statistics. None will reproduce the exact situation observed, but we can compute results based on observed statistics more economically and more rapidly than observing for that equivalent number of days. We can then decide upon the optimal staffing.

Deterministic problems can be treated through simulation with random numbers. Such techniques are often referred to as "Monte Carlo" methods. One simple example might be to compute the multiple integral of a function over a known volume. We could randomly select points within the volume, obtain the function values at these points, compute an average based upon that sampling, and thereby obtain the integral as the product of the volume and the average. More typically, Monte Carlo methods are applied to transport problems (see Chapters 3 and 4). We follow a set of "test" particles that are taken as representative of what is being transported (neutrons, photons, whatever) and follow their flights. Random numbers are used to determine if the particle has a collision, and if so at what angle it is scattered. Monte Carlo methods are used in such transport problems when the geometry of the material and/or the scattering behavior is complicated and difficult to treat with a deterministic model.

There are ways to generate truly random numbers, e.g., using noise sources. Pseudorandom numbers often have advantages. A case can be re-run with the same "random" numbers but with other changes to isolate the significance of those other changes without the confusion caused by different random numbers. This is employed as a variance reduction technique, called "common random numbers," and enables some conclusions to be drawn with fewer computations.

Random Variables: Distributions

Probability distributions can be either continuous or discrete. An example of the latter would be the Poisson distribution. If we ask, say, how many decays occur in a radioactive sample over a given time interval, the answer must be a whole number. However, it is a random number, as such decays are not predictable. If the nuclei decay independently, and have a single decay rate, then the Poisson distribution for that rate can be used to generate random numbers characteristic of the process.

Continuous random distributions can take on any value within an allowed interval. For example, in the queuing problem, the time interval until the arrival of the next customer is a continuous random variable. If we assume independent customer arrivals, then the arrival distribution is the exponential distribution. As you might expect, the Poisson and exponential distributions are closely related. In fact, the usual method for generating the former requires the latter. For simulation problems, the continuous distributions are of most value, and we will concentrate on those.

Random variables, discrete or continuous, can be characterized by the distribution function F(x), which is the probability that the random variable will be less than x upon measurement. F is the integral from $-\infty$ to x of the probability density function f(y).

Once we have a random floating point number which is equally likely to be anywhere in the range 0 $-$ 1, we can generate other random distributions. The uniform random distribution is often used because of its simplicity. When almost nothing is known about the correct distribution, it may be used. Also, in "debugging" a model it may be of interest.

The most useful probability distribution is probably the exponential distribution. It is simple and often the appropriate distribution. The probability density is of the form (for x > 0) of f = exp($-$ x/b)/b. It is a memoryless distribution, i.e., it has the Markov property that the future history is independent of the past. If it is used to model time to failure, for example, the device modeled will fail according to the same distribution no matter how long it has gone without failure. (Almost certainly one would not use the exponential distribution for predicting the failure of, say, tires or light bulbs.) The exponential distribution is in fact the only continuous distribution with this property.

There are many other distributions which can be generated. The k–erlang distribution is a sum of exponential distributions. The gamma distribution has a probability density which has a power of x multiplying an exponential factor. It is often used in modeling serving time in queues. The Weibull distribution has two parameters, and generalizes the gamma distribution by having an arbitrary power of x in the exponent. It is widely used in reliability models where its extra freedom allows observed failure rates to be modeled. The Gaussian or normal distribution is often used to model errors. By the central limit theorem, quantities which are the sum of a large number of random numbers are normally distributed.

Random numbers from these distributions may all be generated by first generating uniform random numbers and then massaging them. The exponential distribution may be generated by generating U, a uniform random variable in the interval 0 $-$ 1, and setting X = $-$ b log(U). The k–erlang distribution is generated similarly. The normal distribution may be generated in a number of ways, the most usual in practice being the polar or Box-Muller method. Two uniform random numbers, U[0] and U[1] are generated.

Form V[i] = 2U[i] − 1, and W = V[0]^2 + V[1]^2 . If W1, reject this step and try again. Otherwise, form $Y = \sqrt{-2 \log W}$). Then S[i] = V[i]Y provides us with two normally distributed random numbers, with zero mean and variance of 1. For general means and variances, see the C program at the end of the chapter. Note that there is a slight inconvenience in that we generate two random numbers per call. Generally, we can only use one at a time. In the simple code below, we merely return one of them. It might be more efficient to have a flag in the function normal(), which is initially 0. When it is called with the flag zero, it sets the flag to 1 and generates S[0] and S[1], returning the former and saving the latter (as a static or global variable). When called and the flag is one, it resets the flag to zero and returns the saved value.

For details on generating and applying other distributions, both discrete and continuous, see **Law and** Kelton's Simulation Modeling and Analysis, Chapter 7.

Testing Randomness

Testing the randomness of a random number generator is a bit awkward. The generator might fail the test, but in general no test establishes the converse, namely, that no more testing is needed, as the generator is truly random.

One of the more popular tests is the "poker test." View the output of the generator as a sequence of digits-say decimal digits. Then, if it is random, the digits 0–9 **should appear** with equal frequency, i.e., each appears one tenth of the time. Check this. The chi-squared test of Chapter 6 can be used to test the hypothesis that the distribution of digits is sufficiently random, at some confidence level, given the frequencies of the digits for some test run. If so far so good, look at the pairs of digits 00–99. Each should occur 1/100 of the time. Test this. Repeat until exhaustion sets in.

Program And Test Problems

The C program of this chapter contains a number of functions. The random number generators are rand(), the "minimal" generator discussed by Park and Miller, and u16() and u32() due to L'Ecuyer , which are designed for machines with 16 and 32 bits of precision, respectively. These are more sophisticated but also more costly. See the appropriate articles of details on how to appropriately "seed" the generators. All three are members of the class of the usual "linear congruential" random number generators, and produce the next random number y[n] from the previous y[n − 1] by means of a formula of the form: y[n] = ay[n − 1] + b (mod c). Here b is typically 0, and the more sophisticated generators combine the results of two or more such calculations to obtain increased randomness. The random numbers are generated as integers and then converted to floating point numbers in the range of 0 to 1. The least significant binary digits of the integer may be less random than the others, but this is of no consequence if we use the floating point number. These programs represent untold cummulative effort expended in the development of reliable random number generators.

We also include implementations of the fast methods developed by Ahrens and Dieter for the exponential, Cauchy, and normal distributions. Depending upon your machine, these are typically somewhat faster. If many random numbers are needed, even small gains can result in getting answers much sooner.

A #define statement is used to define the function urand() as a generic generator of random numbers from 0 to 1. In the code below, it is assigned to the minmial generator random, but this may easily be changed to u32(), for example.

TABLE 9.1

Programs of Chapter 9

erlang()	erlang distribution
expon()	exponential distribution
cauchy()	cauchy distribution
logistic()	logistic distribution
randi()	random integer between 1 and nvalue
uniform()	uniformly distributed random number between a and b
normal()	two normally distributed random numbers
norm()	uses normal to supply one normal random number at a time
u32()	uniform 0–1 random number generator for 32 bit machines
u16()	uniform 0–1 random number generator for 32 bit machines
random()	uniform 0–1 "minimal" random number generator
ex()	fast exponential distribution
ca()	fast cauchy distribution
na()	fast normal distribution

A variety of random distributions are obtainable from this random number source. The Box–Muller method is used to generate normally distributed random deviates, for example. The normality of these deviates is tested by forming the first four moments of the distributions: mean, variance, skewness, kurtosis. As defined here (there are various definitions for kurtosis), these should be 0,1,0,0 for an ideal normal distribution. In general, of course, such a test would not prove randomness. For example, the "random" numbers could be 0, .01,.02,.03,....,.99,1.,0,.01 and would satisfy these conditions on the moments of the distribution! However, as the random number generator we are using is not a newcomer, we have confidence in it.

The distributions supplied are the erlang, exponential, logistic, normally distributed random numbers, a random integer between 1 and nvalue, and a uniform random number in the interval a to b.

References

J. H. Ahrens and U. Dieter, *Comm. ACM*, **31,** 1330, Nov. 1988.

P. L'Ecuyer, *Comm. ACM,* 31, 742, June 1988.

S. K. Park and K. W. Miller, *Comm. ACM*, **31**, 1192, Oct. 1988.

A. M. Law and W. D. Kelton, *Simulation Modeling and Analysis* (New York: McGraw-Hill, 1982).

Program Listing And Test Problem Output

(Listing begins next page.)

```
/*
package of routines to generate and apply random numbers

from More C Tools for Scientists and Engineers by L. Baker

*/
/* You may change stmt below, replacing random() with u16() or u32() */

#define urand()  random()

long int seed;
int naflag,nflag;
long int s1,s2;
int s16,s26,s36;
double u32(),u16(),random();
double ex(),ca(),na();

double erlang(k,mean) int k; double mean;
{
double exp(),expon(),emult,sum;
int i;
emult= mean/k;
sum=0.;
for (i=0;i<k;i++) sum+=exp(expon(emult));
return(sum);
}

double expon(mean) double mean;
{/* assumes rand has been seeded with proper iy*/
double log(),urand();
return(-mean*log(urand()) );
}

double cauchy()
{
double tan(),pi=3.141592653589793,random();
return  tan((pi-random())*.5);
}
```

```
double logistic(a,k) double a,k;
{
/* logistic distribution F= 1/{1+exp-(x-a)/k }
   mean a, variance b^2= (k*pi)^2/3  */
double random(),log(),x;
x=random();
return a+k*log(x/(1.-x));
}


int randi(nvalue,probd) int nvalue;float probd[];
/* random integer betwen 1-nvalue in accord with probd distrib.*/
{
int i,n1;
double u;
u=rand();/* u(0,1) uniform random */
n1=nvalue-1;
for (i=0;i<n1;i++) if(u<probd[i])return(i);
return(nvalue);
}


double uniform(a,b) double a,b;
{
double urand();
return(a+(b-a)*urand());
}


double normal(mean,sd,s1,s2) double mean,sd,*s1,*s2;
{
double log(),urand(),sqrt(),r1,r2,v1,v2,s,ss;
int iter;
iter=0;
while(1)
  {
  r1=urand();r2=urand();
  v1=2.*r1-1.;v2=2.*r2-1.;
  s=v1*v1+v2*v2;
  if (s<1.)
```

```
    {
    ss=sqrt(-2.*log(s)/s)*sd;
    *s1=v1*ss+mean;
    *s2=v2*ss+mean;
    return(*s1);
    };
/*  iter++;
  if(iter>10)
    {
    printf(" trouble in normal %f %f %f\n",r1,r2,s);
    break;
    }
*/
  };/*end while*/
  return(0.);/* Keep DeSmet happy*/
}


double snorm1,snorm2;

double norm(mean,sd) double mean,sd;
{
/* nflag must be initialized to 1 before first call*/
nflag^=1;
if(nflag)return snorm2;
return normal(mean,sd,&snorm1,&snorm2);
}
/* TEST CODE BELOW
*/
main(argc,argv) int argc; char **argv;
{
int i,j,k;
double urand(),normal(),mean,sd,z,y,x,xs,ys,rk,meant,m2,var,mu3,mu4,skew,kurt;
double sum1,sum2,sum3,sum4;
double u,random();
long int outseed;
seed=1;
naflag=1;
nflag=1;
```

```
s1=12345;s2=67890;
s16=12;s26=23;s36=34;
for(i=0;i<=10000;i++)
  {outseed=seed;
  u=random();
  }
printf(" u=%f seed = %ld \n",u,outseed);
printf(" results of u16:\n");
for(i=0;i<=1000;i++)
  {u=u16();
  if(i%100 ==0)printf(" u=%f \n",u);
  }
printf(" results of u32:\n");
for(i=0;i<=1000;i++)
  {u=u32();
  if(i%100 ==0)printf(" u=%f \n",u);
  }
/* now test distributions */
mean=0.;sd=1.;
while(1)
{printf(" enter count");scanf("%d",&k);
if(k<=0)break;
printf(" kount=%d\n",k);
sum1=sum2=sum3=sum4=0.;
for (i=0;i<k;i++)
  {
  u=normal(mean,sd,&x,&y);
/*  printf(" return normal %f %f\n",x,y);*/
  sum1=sum1+x+y;
  xs=x*x;ys=y*y;
  sum2=sum2+xs+ys;
  sum3=sum3+xs*x+ys*y;
  sum4=sum4+xs*xs+ys*ys;
  }
printf(" tabulating\n");
rk=.5/k;
meant=sum1*rk;
m2=meant*meant;
```

```
var=sum2*rk-m2;
mu3=(sum3-3.*sum1*sum2*rk)*rk+2.*meant*m2;
mu4=sum4*rk-3.*m2*m2+6.*m2*sum2*rk-4.*sum3*sum1*rk*rk;
skew=mu3/(var*sqrt(var));
kurt=(mu4/(var*var)-3.)*.5;
/* mean should equal 0. approximately.
   var    "    " 1.    "        (variance=sd*sd)
  skewness         0.
kurtosis           0.             as defined here, which is
CRC Basic Stat. tables definition.  Others define kurtosis without
the fact of .5 and/or without the -3.
*/

printf(" mean=%f,var=%f,skew=%f,kurt=%f\n",meant,var,skew,kurt);
}/* end while*/
mean=0.;sd=1.;
printf(" now fast normal dist mean=0 var=1\n");
while(1)
{printf(" enter count");scanf("%d",&k);
if(k<=0)break;
printf(" kount=%d\n",k);
sum1=sum2=sum3=sum4=0.;
for (i=0;i<k;i++)
   {
   x=na();y=na();
   sum1=sum1+x+y;
   xs=x*x;ys=y*y;
   sum2=sum2+xs+ys;
   sum3=sum3+xs*x+ys*y;
   sum4=sum4+xs*xs+ys*ys;
   }
printf(" tabulating\n");
rk=.5/k;
meant=sum1*rk;
m2=meant*meant;
var=sum2*rk-m2;
mu3=(sum3-3.*sum1*sum2*rk)*rk+2.*meant*m2;
mu4=sum4*rk-3.*m2*m2+6.*m2*sum2*rk-4.*sum3*sum1*rk*rk;
```

```
skew=mu3/(var*sqrt(var));
kurt=(mu4/(var*var)-3.)*.5;
/* mean should equal 0. approximately.
   var    "    "  1.    "        (variance=sd*sd)
   skewness          0.
kurtosis             0.              as defined here, which is
CRC Basic Stat. tables definition.  Others define kurtosis without
the fact of .5 and/or without the -3.
*/
printf(" mean=%f,var=%f,skew=%f,kurt=%f\n",meant,var,skew,kurt);
}/* end while*/
printf(" now exponential dist\n");
mean=0.;sd=1.;
while(1)
{printf(" enter count");scanf("%d",&k);
if(k<=0)break;
printf(" kount=%d\n",k);
sum1=sum2=sum3=sum4=0.;
for (i=0;i<k;i++)
  {
  x=ex();y=ex();
/*  printf(" return normal %f %f\n",x,y);*/
  sum1=sum1+x+y;
  xs=x*x;ys=y*y;
  sum2=sum2+xs+ys;
  sum3=sum3+xs*x+ys*y;
  sum4=sum4+xs*xs+ys*ys;
  }
printf(" tabulating\n");
rk=.5/k;
meant=sum1*rk;
m2=meant*meant;
var=sum2*rk-m2;
mu3=(sum3-3.*sum1*sum2*rk)*rk+2.*meant*m2;
mu4=sum4*rk-3.*m2*m2+6.*m2*sum2*rk-4.*sum3*sum1*rk*rk;
skew=mu3/(var*sqrt(var));
kurt=(mu4/(var*var));
/* mean should equal 0. approximately.
```

```
  var    "    "  1.    "          (variance=sd*sd)
   skewness           0.
kurtosis               0.              as defined here, which is
CRC Basic Stat. tables definition.  Others define kurtosis without
the fact of .5 and/or without the -3.
*/

printf(" mean=%f,var=%f,skew=%f,kurt=%f\n",meant,var,skew,kurt);
}/* end while*/
mean=0.;sd=1.;
printf(" now cauchy\n");
while(1)
{printf(" enter count");scanf("%d",&k);
if(k<=0)break;
printf(" kount=%d\n",k);
sum1=sum2=sum3=sum4=0.;
for (i=0;i<k;i++)
   {
   x=ca();y=ca();
/*   printf(" return normal %f %f\n",x,y);*/
   sum1=sum1+x+y;
   xs=x*x;ys=y*y;
   sum2=sum2+xs+ys;
   sum3=sum3+xs*x+ys*y;
   sum4=sum4+xs*xs+ys*ys;
   }
printf(" tabulating\n");
rk=.5/k;
meant=sum1*rk;
m2=meant*meant;
var=sum2*rk-m2;
mu3=(sum3-3.*sum1*sum2*rk)*rk+2.*meant*m2;
mu4=sum4*rk-3.*m2*m2+6.*m2*sum2*rk-4.*sum3*sum1*rk*rk;
skew=mu3/(var*sqrt(var));
kurt=(mu4/(var*var));
/* mean should equal 0. approximately.
   var    "    "  1.    "          (variance=sd*sd)
   skewness           0.
```

kurtosis   0.   as defined here, which is
CRC Basic Stat. tables definition. Others define kurtosis without
the fact of .5 and/or without the -3.
```
*/
```

```
printf(" mean=%f,var=%f,skew=%f,kurt=%f\n",meant,var,skew,kurt);
}/* end while*/

exit(0);
}


double u32()
{/*32 bit*/
long int z,k;
k= s1/ 53668;
s1= 40014*(s1-k*53668)-k*12211;
if(s1<0) s1+=2147483563;
k= s2/52774;
s2=40692*(s2-k*52774)-k*3791;
if(s2<0)s2+=2147483399;
z=s1-s2;
if(z<1)z+=2147483562;
return z*4.665613e-10;
}


double u16()
{/*16 bit*/
int z,k;
k= s16/ 206;
s16= 157*(s16-k*206)-k*21;
if(s16<0) s16+=32363;
k= s26/217;
s26=146*(s26-k*217)-k*45;
if(s26<0)s26+=317227;
k= s36/222;
s36=142*(s36-k*222)-k*133;
```

```
if(s36<0)s36+=31657;
z=s16-s26;
if(z>706)z-=32362;
z+=s36;
if(z<1)z+=32363;
return z*3.0899e-5;
}

double random()
{
long int a=16807,m=2147483647,q=127773,r=2836;
long int lo,hi,test;
hi= seed / q;
lo= seed % q;
test= a*lo-r*hi;
seed=(test>0)?test: test+m;
return (double) seed/m;
}

double ex()
{
static double ln2=.6931471805599453,a=5.7133631526454228,
b=3.4142135623730950,c=-1.6734053240284925,p=.9802581434685472,
q=5.6005707569738080,r=3.3468106480569850,h=.0026106723602095,
d=.08576764376269050;
double g,aux,u,up,y,random(),exp(),aux2,aux1,H=2.28421e-4;
/*H=h*d/p;*/
u=random();
g=c;
dbl: u=u+u;
if(u<1.)
   {
   g+=ln2;
   goto dbl;
   }
u--;
if(u<p) return (g+q/(r-u));
while(1)
```

```
  {
  u=random();
  aux=b-u;
  y= a/aux;
  up=random();
  aux1=(up*H+d)*aux*aux;     aux2=exp(-(y+c));
  if( aux1 <= aux2 )return (g+y);
  }
return(0.);/*for DeSmet*/
}


double ca()
{
static double a=.6380631366077803,b=.5959486060529070,
q=.93399629257603656,w=.2488703380083841,c=.6366197723675813,
d=.5972997593539963,h=.0214949094570452,p=4.9125013953033204;
double u,random(),t,s,up,x;
u=random();
t=u-.5;
s=w-t*t;
if(s>0.0)return t*(c/s+d);
while(1)
   {
   u=random();
   t=u-.5;
   s=.25-t*t;
   up=random();
   x=t*(a/s+b);
   if( s*s*((1+x*x)*(h*up+p)-q)+s<=.5)return x;
   }
return(0.);
}
static double y;

double na()
{
int b;
double ex(),random(),t,up,u,e,s,ca,x,r;
```

```
static double a=.6380631366077803,g=.5959486060529070,
q=.93399629257603656,w=.2488703380083841,c=.6366197723675813,
d=.5972997593539963,h=.0214949094570452,p=4.9125013953033204;
/* initialize naflag=1*/
naflag ^= 1;
if(naflag) return y;
u=random();
b=(u<.5)? 0:1;
e=ex();
r=e+e;
/* ca= cauchy dist*/
u= (b)? u+u-1. : u+u;
t=u-.5;
s=w-t*t;
if(s>0.0) ca=t*(c/s+d);
else while(1)
   {
   u=random();
   t=u-.5;
   s=.25-t*t;
   up=random();
   ca=t*(a/s+g);
   if( s*s*((1+ca*ca)*(h*up+p)-q)+s<=.5)break;
   }
x=sqrt(r/(1.+ca*ca));
y=ca*x;
if(!b) return x;
else return -x;
return 0.;
}
```

random

u=0.740342 seed = 1043618065
results of u16:
u=0.103635
u=0.007076
u=0.310350
u=0.118467
u=0.017952
u=0.994515
u=0.055989
u=0.841905
u=0.665194
u=0.192593
u=0.951102
results of u32:
u=0.945421
u=0.478123
u=0.284571
u=0.558089
u=0.089258
u=0.820092
u=0.155831
u=0.669209
u=0.283712
u=0.886159
u=0.998433
enter count100
kount=100
tabulating
mean=-0.063685,var=0.981206,skew=0.135472,kurt=-0.096051
enter count100
kount=100
tabulating
mean=0.100033,var=0.850644,skew=-0.006753,kurt=-0.137631
enter count0
now fast normal dist mean=0 var=1
enter count100

```
kount=100
tabulating
mean=-0.000247,var=0.974484,skew=-0.205231,kurt=-0.014965
enter count100
kount=100
tabulating
mean=-0.016908,var=1.227272,skew=-0.140209,kurt=-0.013809
enter count0
now exponential dist
enter count100
kount=100
tabulating
mean=1.077606,var=1.228961,skew=1.851852,kurt=6.701594
enter count0
now cauchy
enter count100
kount=100
tabulating
mean=-1.751826,var=604.957403,skew=-3.766170,kurt=58.740733
enter count100
kount=100
tabulating
mean=-4.912820,var=4363.738861,skew=-13.639850,kurt=190.298027
enter count100
kount=100
tabulating
mean=0.206630,var=49.725317,skew=-0.880653,kurt=35.191939
enter count100
kount=100
tabulating
mean=2.768414,var=3073.295676,skew=13.644866,kurt=190.959889
enter count0

C:\TC>mcapture
```

Chapter 10

Bresenham's Line-Drawing Algorithm

Chapter Objectives

In this chapter we present a tool for:

– rapidly drawing straight lines on raster graphics devices

Introduction

The preceding chapter concerned a plotting program which drew points, not lines. Often, however, this is not sufficient and two points must be connected with a (straight) line. This chapter concerns the classic method for doing so: Bresenham's algorithm. First published in 1965 (*IBM System Journal*, **4**, p. 25, 1965), it has been rediscovered a number of times (see e.g., *Dr. Dobb's Journal,* Dec. 1982, pp. 58ff).

We discuss this algorithm here for a number of reasons. We will use it in the next chapter when we discuss a contour plotting package. The algorithm is interesting in its own right, as an illustration of how floating-point computations may be changed into integer calculations. It also leads to a discussion of optimization of C programs.

Many new machines have graphics chips which implement line-drawing primitives in silicon, probably with Bresenham's algorithm (an example would be the "Blitter" in the Commodore Amiga). Such chips generally service the screen only, however, and unless memory-mapping is used and available for direct output to some hardcopy device, the user will probably find himself having to draw straight lines without the services of such a chip, at least if he wants something less ephemeral than a screen image. The methods we discuss are applicable to drawing circles, ellipses, and other curves as well (see below), so it is of some interest to understand these methods. Perhaps some reader may find himself called upon to implement these algorithms in silicon.

In what follows, we will assume that the purpose is to draw a line as a series of adjacent pixels on a specified two-dimensional lattice. This lattice is called the raster of the device (screen, etc.). A primitive called plot (x,y) is assumed which will "turn on" or plot a point at location x,y of the raster. The program is to draw the line from the point x[min],y[min] to the point x[max],y[max].

A formal, rigorous derivation of Bresenham's algorithm may be found, for example, in Foley and van Dam. Actually, they present only the case for lines with slopes between 0 and 1 in detail, leaving the general case as an exercise for the reader. We present below an heuristic derivation, using "stepwise refinement" to go from a simple, obvious implementation which requires floating point calculations, to the more complicated, final algorithm. While our presentation in the next section only covers slopes in the range 0-1, we don't feel any guilt about this as the implementations in C we present are fully general, and we discuss how these generalizations are realized below. We present a variety of implementations with different tradeoffs for speed and size. The most compact implementation of Bresenham's algorithm I've seen is by Will Baden, in *Dr. Dobb's Journal,* Nov. 1983, p.86. However, this code (which is in Pascal) achieves conciseness at the cost of requiring statements of the form y+=dy instead of the more "verbose" code which utilizes y++ and y-- as needed. The latter version is (perhaps) faster, as it should not require any memory accesses on machines which implement increment and decrement instructions, but this assumes a compiler smart enough to realize this. Other presentations of the method with different philosophies may be found in an implementation by N. Barkakati in *Dr. Dobb's Journal*, May, 1986 with corrections by J. Mente in the September, 1986 issue, and by J. R. Van Aken and C. R. Killebrew, Jr. in *BYTE,* March, 1988.

Heuristic Derivation Of Bresenham's Algorithm

Consider first drawing a line with positive slope in the direction of increasing x (we will consider the other cases later). This case further subdivides into two cases, lines with slopes greater than and less than or equal to one. If the slope is less than one, we will want to step in the x-direction, occasionally incrementing the y-value of the point as well. If the slope is greater than one, we will want to step in the y direction, occasionally incrementing the x value of the point. If the slope is one, then we of course want to increment the x and y values each step until the line has been fully drawn. We need only discuss the case with slope less than one, since the other case obtains when we exchange the variables x and y.

If we were using floating point arithmetic, we could use the following algorithm to plot the desired line, starting at the point (x0,y0):

```
x = x0;y = y0;
plot (x0,y0);
while(x < xmax)
    {
    x = x +  dx;
    y = y +  (dy/dx) dx;
    plot (x,y);
    }
```

We may take dx as 1 pixel, so long as the subroutine plot() understands this. We want to avoid the use of floating point arithmetic for maximum speed.   As (dy/dx) < 1 and dx = 1 are assumed, y will only occasionally increase to the next integer. We can achieve this effect by a loop which counts, using an auxiliary variable d, until y should be incremented:

```
d= d0;
while (x < xmax)
    {
    x++;
    d = d + dy;
    if (d == 0) { d = - dx; y++;}
    plot (x,y);
    }
```

Note that if dx = m*dy, where m is an integer, then this loop will increment y once for every m times that x is incremented. In general, we may define m, the inverse slope (hence m>1), as, in C terminology

(int)dx/dy

that is, the greatest integer not greater than (dx/dy), which is evaluated using floating point arithmetic. We can avoid the use of floating point by taking dx as the x[max]-x[min] and similarly dy =y [max] − y[min]. Notice that what we are doing, in effect, is performing division by repeated subtraction. This "regression" to first grade arithmetic is needed as we didn't learn floating point numbers (fractions) until second or third grade (except for you child prodigies out there).

What value should be taken for d0? A first guess might be d0 = − dx. This would increment y after m steps, for m defined as above. However, it is clear that we would prefer y to be incremented half way into the interval. Thus, we should take $d0 = -dx/2$. We have still not gotten away from non-integral arithmetic. This can easily be fixed, however, by dealing with doubled values

```
d = - dx;
while  (x < xmax)
      {
      x++;
      d = d + 2dy;
      if (d == 0) { d = -2dx; y++;}
      plot (x,y);
      }
```

We have written 2dy and 2dx rather than 2*dy or 2*dx because in practice one will assign these values to variables outside the loop, rather than perform multiplications (or left shifts) within the loop.

There is one further change we can make for slightly greater efficiency. We can avoid the incrementing of d twice in some of the timesteps. If the inverse slope m is very large, this will not help much, but if it is close to one this will save some arithmetic:

```
d = 2dy - dx;
while (x < xmax)
      {
      x++;
      if (d == 0) { d = d + 2dy - 2dx; y++;}
      else
            { d = d + 2dy;}
      plot (x,y);
      }
```

We have for clarity not written $d = d + 2dy$ as $d += dy$ here, although we have done so in the C code that implements these algorithms. It is plausible that the latter form is implemented more efficiently by some compilers on some machines, but this cannot be taken for granted. It is also plausible that one should use register variables for x,y, and d if possible. Again, how many register variables are available and just how much good this will do will vary greatly. It is also probable, but not guaranteed, that statements like x++ or x-- will be faster than x=x+deltax or x-=deltax.

This is because most microprocessors have instructions which increment (or decrement) registers by one. This is worth bearing in mind when algorithms are written not just for positive slopes. While it would be possible to simplify some of the algorithms presented by using statements like y += deltay, where deltay is set (outside the loop) to 1 for positive slopes and -1 for negative slopes, we have chosen to treat these cases separately in order to allow the use of statements such as y++ or y– –. This will always cost some memory space and may or may not result in faster codes. We illustrate the various possibilities below.

As a final efficiency consideration, we believe that, for the most part, the shift dy<<1 will be faster than the multiplication 2*dy. This will also vary from machine to machine and compiler to compiler. The shift might indeed be slower on some. Since this doubling is only performed a few times per line segment, it is not as important a consideration as those operations which are inside the while loop and executed many times. However, even this doubling operation could become a cost item to be considered if many line segments are to be drawn.

By obvious symmetry, the case of slopes greater than one can be treated by interchanging the role of the variables x and y, as mentioned above. The negative slope cases can similarly be treated by replacing the statement y++ with y– –, assuming dx is taken as positive and dy as negative, taking dy = abs(dy), and treating the small and large slope cases as for the positive slope cases.

In the above, it was implicitly assumed that x[min] < [max], so that we could use positive increments of x via the statement x++. If this is not the case, there are two possibilities. The simplest is to exchange x[min] for x[max] and y[min] for y[max], thereby having converted the problem to the case with positive x increments. This may be undesirable in some applications, in which case x— will have to be used, again with appropriate sign changes in the above code.

Our version is not the most compact or simplest form of Bresenham's method, because it has been optimized for speed. The innnermost loops have been made as simple (and therefore as fast) as possible. The operators ++ and -- are used to permit machines which can take advantage of these operators to perform rapid register increments. The program pauses after a graph has been plotted to allow you to inspect the output. Just hit any key to proceed to the next plot).

In the test problems, we have tried to cover all possible inputs. This includes making sure that lines with slopes of 1, zero, or infinity are all correctly plotted, as well as lines with slopes of magnitude between 0 and

1, or greater than one, positive or negative. A test raster of 20 x 20 pixels is used. Program main() invokes subroutine test() each test problem. Test clears the "screen" raster and requests that the line be drawn. Subroutine draw() implements the Bresenham algorithm, and show() plots the test raster on the screen.

Drawing Circles And Other Conics

The fundamental ideas behind Bresenham's algorithm for straight lines has been extended by him to circles, and to other curves by other authors.

Consider first a circular arc. The equation for a circle centered at the origin is $x^2 + y^2 = r^2$. With a bit of differential calculus, this becomes x dx + y dx = 0. If we start of at one end of the arc to be plotted, the relation above gives us the relation of dx to dy. We can use the line drawing algorithm one step at a time to walk round the circle. Details may be found in Foley and van Dam, **Berger**, or "Curve Drawing Algorithms for Raster Displays," by J. van Aken and M. Novak, *ACM Trans. Graphics,* **4**, 147, 1985. This article presents a variety of methods for plotting lines, circles, and ellipses with other possible curves discussed. A discussion of drawing circles akin to our heuristic derivation of Bresenham's algorithm may be found in Mike Higgins column in *Computer Language*, May 1986, p. 13 (volume 3, number 5). That same issue contains, by the way, an article by Mark White and Richard Reppert, beginning on p. 45, which presents C code for clipping and filling polygons, two fundamental graphics operations. (Clipping refers to limiting the extent of an area within a specified window, while filling refers to turning on pixels within an area whose boundaries are specified). The two texts cited each contain discussions of these topics.

TABLE 10.1

Programs of Chapter 10

plot	places point on raster display
show	sends finished output to display
test	invokes cleara, draw, show
cleara	clears the dispaly area
draw	draw straight line between given endpoints on raster device

References

M. Berger, *Computer Graphics with Pascal* (New York: Benjamin/Cummings, 1986).

J. D. Foley and A. van Dam, *Fundamentals of Interactive Computer Graphics* (New York: Addison Wesley,1983)

Program Listing And Test Program Output

(Listing begins next page.)

```
/* version of Bresenham's line-drawing algorithm
          optimized for speed

from More C tools for scientists and engineers by L. Baker

*/

/*
#include "libc.h"
*/

#define abs(x) ((x)>=0 ? (x) : -(x) )

#define XSIZE 50
#define YSIZE 50

int xsize= XSIZE, ysize=YSIZE, diagnose=0;
char screen[ XSIZE ][ YSIZE ];

plot(x,y,z) int x,y;char z;
{
if( x< xsize  && y < ysize && x>=0 && y>=0)screen[x][y]=z;
if(diagnose) printf(" x %d y %d plotted\n",x,y);
return;
}

show()
{
int i,j;
for(j=0;j< xsize;j++)
{ printf("\n");
for(i=0;i< ysize ;i++)printf("%c",screen[i][j]);}
printf("\n");
}


cleara()
{int i,j;
```

```
for (i=0;i< xsize ;i++)
   {for(j=0;j< ysize;j++) screen[i][j]=' ';}
}

draw (x1,y1,x2,y2,symbol)
int x1,y1,x2,y2;char symbol;
{/*Bresenham line draw consult Foley & van Dam for algorithm
 this version based on code by N. Barkakati, corrected by
  J. Mente, and improved by pulling an if test out of
  the while loops (at the cost of 4 not 2 while loops in code
  additional optimization attempted through the use of
  register and static variables and shifts instead of multiplies as
  in the first version of this method*/
static int dx,dy,incr1,incr2,incr3,end;
register x,y,d;
dx=abs(x2-x1);
dy=abs(y2-y1);
if (dx>dy)
{/* slope abs value less than 1 march in x */
if (x1>x2)
   {
   x=x2;
   y=y2;
   end=x1;
   dy=y1-y2;
   }
else
   {
   x=x1;
   y=y1;
   end=x2;
   dy=y2-y1;
   };

incr1=dy<<1;
incr2=(dy-dx)<<1;
incr3=(dy+dx)<<1;
d= (dy>=0)?incr1-dx:incr1+dx;
```

```
plot(x,y,symbol);

if(dy>=0)
{

while (x< end)
   {
   x++;
   if (d<0)
      {
      d+=incr1;
      }
   else /*d>=0*/
      {
         y++;
         d+=incr2;/*was dy>0*/
      };
   plot(x,y,symbol);
   }

}/*dy>=0*/
else
{/*dy<0*/

while (x< end)
   {
   x++;
   if (d<0)
      {
         y--;
         d+=incr3;
      }
   else /*d>=0*/
      {
      d+=incr1;/*was dy<0 */
      };
   plot(x,y,symbol);
```

```
   }

}/*dy<0*/

}/*dx>=dy*/
else
{/*dx<dy*/
/* slope greater than 1 interchange role of x&y*/
if (y1>y2)
   {
   x=x2;
   y=y2;
   end=y1;
   dx=x1-x2;
   }
else
   {
   x=x1;
   y=y1;
   end=y2;
   dx=x2-x1;
   };

incr1=dx<<1;
incr2=(dx-dy)<<1;
incr3=(dx+dy)<<1;
d=(dx>=0)? incr1-dy:incr1+dy;
plot(x,y,symbol);


if(dx<0)
{
while (y< end)
   {
   y++;
   if (d<0)
      {/* WAS dx<=0*/
        x--;
```

```
            d+=incr3;
        }
    else /* d>=0 */
        {
            d+=incr1;
        };
    plot(x,y,symbol);
    }
}/*dx<0*/
else
{/*dx>=0*/

while (y< end)
    {
    y++;
    if (d<0)
        {
        d+=incr1;
        }
    else /* d>=0 */
        {/*was dx>0*/
            x++;
            d+=incr2;
        };
    plot(x,y,symbol);
    }

}/* else dx>=0*/
}/* dx<dy end else*/
return;
}
```

```
/* version of Bresenham's line-drawing algorithm
            optimized for speed

from More C tools for scientists and engineers by L. Baker

*/
#include <stdio.h>
#define abs(x) ((x)>=0 ? (x) : -(x) )
extern xsize,ysize,diagnose;

main(argc,argv) int argc;char **argv;
{
/*test Breese*/
int c;
xsize=20;ysize=20;diagnose=1;
test(10,0,10,20);/*vertical*/
c=getchar();
test(0,10,20,10);/*horizontal*/
c=getchar();
test(0,0,20,20);/* 45 degree*/
c=getchar();
test(0,20,20,0);/*-45*/
c=getchar();
test(0,20,4,0);
c=getchar();
test(0,20,20,4);
c=getchar();
test(20,20,0,0);
c=getchar();
test(0,0,20,4);/* slope<1*/
c=getchar();
test(0,0,4,20);/* slope>1*/
}


test(x1,y1,x2,y2) int x1,y1,x2,y2;
{cleara();
draw(x1,y1,x2,y2,'X');
```

```
show();
}
```

```
x 10 y 0 plotted
x 10 y 1 plotted
x 10 y 2 plotted
x 10 y 3 plotted
x 10 y 4 plotted
x 10 y 5 plotted
x 10 y 6 plotted
x 10 y 7 plotted
x 10 y 8 plotted
x 10 y 9 plotted
x 10 y 10 plotted
x 10 y 11 plotted
x 10 y 12 plotted
x 10 y 13 plotted
x 10 y 14 plotted
x 10 y 15 plotted
x 10 y 16 plotted
x 10 y 17 plotted
x 10 y 18 plotted
x 10 y 19 plotted
x 10 y 20 plotted
            X
            X
            X
            X
            X
            X
            X
            X
            X
            X
            X
            X
            X
            X
            X
            X
```

```
        X
        X
        X
        X
x 0 y 10 plotted
x 1 y 10 plotted
x 2 y 10 plotted
x 3 y 10 plotted
x 4 y 10 plotted
x 5 y 10 plotted
x 6 y 10 plotted
x 7 y 10 plotted
x 8 y 10 plotted
x 9 y 10 plotted
x 10 y 10 plotted
x 11 y 10 plotted
x 12 y 10 plotted
x 13 y 10 plotted
x 14 y 10 plotted
x 15 y 10 plotted
x 16 y 10 plotted
x 17 y 10 plotted
x 18 y 10 plotted
x 19 y 10 plotted
x 20 y 10 plotted
```

XXXXXXXXXXXXXXXXXXXXX

```
x 0 y 0 plotted
x 1 y 1 plotted
x 2 y 2 plotted
x 3 y 3 plotted
x 4 y 4 plotted
x 5 y 5 plotted
x 6 y 6 plotted
x 7 y 7 plotted
x 8 y 8 plotted
x 9 y 9 plotted
x 10 y 10 plotted
x 11 y 11 plotted
x 12 y 12 plotted
x 13 y 13 plotted
x 14 y 14 plotted
x 15 y 15 plotted
x 16 y 16 plotted
x 17 y 17 plotted
x 18 y 18 plotted
x 19 y 19 plotted
x 20 y 20 plotted


X
 X
  X
   X
    X
     X
      X
       X
```

```
X
 X
  X
   X
    X
     X
      X
       X
        X
         X
          X
```
x 20 y 0 plotted
x 19 y 1 plotted
x 18 y 2 plotted
x 17 y 3 plotted
x 16 y 4 plotted
x 15 y 5 plotted
x 14 y 6 plotted
x 13 y 7 plotted
x 12 y 8 plotted
x 11 y 9 plotted
x 10 y 10 plotted
x 9 y 11 plotted
x 8 y 12 plotted
x 7 y 13 plotted
x 6 y 14 plotted
x 5 y 15 plotted
x 4 y 16 plotted
x 3 y 17 plotted
x 2 y 18 plotted
x 1 y 19 plotted
x 0 y 20 plotted

```
          X
          X
          X
```

```
        X
        X
        X
        X
        X
       X
       X
      X
      X
     X
     X
    X
    X
   X
  X
 X
```

x 4 y 0 plotted
x 4 y 1 plotted
x 4 y 2 plotted
x 3 y 3 plotted
x 3 y 4 plotted
x 3 y 5 plotted
x 3 y 6 plotted
x 3 y 7 plotted
x 2 y 8 plotted
x 2 y 9 plotted
x 2 y 10 plotted
x 2 y 11 plotted
x 2 y 12 plotted
x 1 y 13 plotted
x 1 y 14 plotted
x 1 y 15 plotted
x 1 y 16 plotted
x 1 y 17 plotted
x 0 y 18 plotted
x 0 y 19 plotted
x 0 y 20 plotted

```
X
X
X
X
X
X
X
X
X
X
X
X
X
X
X
X
X
X
X
X
x 0 y 20 plotted
x 1 y 19 plotted
x 2 y 18 plotted
x 3 y 18 plotted
x 4 y 17 plotted
x 5 y 16 plotted
x 6 y 15 plotted
x 7 y 14 plotted
x 8 y 14 plotted
x 9 y 13 plotted
x 10 y 12 plotted
x 11 y 11 plotted
x 12 y 10 plotted
x 13 y 10 plotted
x 14 y 9 plotted
x 15 y 8 plotted
x 16 y 7 plotted
x 17 y 6 plotted
```

x 18 y 6 plotted
x 19 y 5 plotted
x 20 y 4 plotted

```
        X
        XX
         X
         X
         X
        XX
        X
        X
        X
       XX
       X
      X
      X
     XX
    X
```

x 0 y 0 plotted
x 1 y 1 plotted
x 2 y 2 plotted
x 3 y 3 plotted
x 4 y 4 plotted
x 5 y 5 plotted
x 6 y 6 plotted
x 7 y 7 plotted
x 8 y 8 plotted
x 9 y 9 plotted
x 10 y 10 plotted
x 11 y 11 plotted
x 12 y 12 plotted
x 13 y 13 plotted

```
x 14 y 14 plotted
x 15 y 15 plotted
x 16 y 16 plotted
x 17 y 17 plotted
x 18 y 18 plotted
x 19 y 19 plotted
x 20 y 20 plotted

X
X
 X
  X
   X
    X
     X
      X
       X
        X
         X
          X
           X
            X
             X
              X
               X
                X
                 X
                  X
x 0 y 0 plotted
x 1 y 0 plotted
x 2 y 0 plotted
x 3 y 1 plotted
x 4 y 1 plotted
x 5 y 1 plotted
x 6 y 1 plotted
x 7 y 1 plotted
x 8 y 2 plotted
x 9 y 2 plotted
```

```
x 10 y 2 plotted
x 11 y 2 plotted
x 12 y 2 plotted
x 13 y 3 plotted
x 14 y 3 plotted
x 15 y 3 plotted
x 16 y 3 plotted
x 17 y 3 plotted
x 18 y 4 plotted
x 19 y 4 plotted
x 20 y 4 plotted
```

```
XXX
   XXXXX
      XXXXX
         XXXXX
          XX
```

```
x 0 y 0 plotted
x 0 y 1 plotted
x 0 y 2 plotted
x 1 y 3 plotted
x 1 y 4 plotted
x 1 y 5 plotted
```

x 1 y 6 plotted
x 1 y 7 plotted
x 2 y 8 plotted
x 2 y 9 plotted
x 2 y 10 plotted
x 2 y 11 plotted
x 2 y 12 plotted
x 3 y 13 plotted
x 3 y 14 plotted
x 3 y 15 plotted
x 3 y 16 plotted
x 3 y 17 plotted
x 4 y 18 plotted
x 4 y 19 plotted
x 4 y 20 plotted

```
X
X
X
 X
 X
 X
 X
 X
  X
  X
  X
  X
  X
   X
   X
   X
   X
   X
    X
    X
```

CHAPTER 11

Contour Plotting

Chapter Objectives

In this chapter, we will:

– produce two-dimensional contour plots of functions

– apply the Bresenham line drawing method of the previous chapter

Introduction

After plots of simple functions versus a single variable, as discussed in chapter 15, plotting contours, i.e., the value of a function vs. two variables, is of most interest. Such plots are of value whenever two-dimensional arrays of data exist. Chapter 9 has already used contour plots to present the results of a field solver. In this chapter we draw upon the results of the preceding chapter to draw lines.

The method of this chapter will be based on the discussion and FORTRAN code of J. S. Wagner's, "Simple, Portable Contour Routines," Report SAND85-2244 of Sandia National Laboratories, Nov. 1985. This report contains a number of contouring routines, including ones for uniformly spaced grids and methods with a more sophisticated (and costly) interpolation method for smoother contours.

It is more striking to produce three-dimensional plots of a function z(x,y). Such a plot is complicated by a number of factors: 1) from what direction should the viewpoint of the plot be viewed, 2) should hidden lines be removed, 3) where should the perspective plane be located? Programs that implement such plots are very much larger and consume much more time than that given here. A contour plot is probably superior in conveying the information when nothing is previously known of the function; once you have the contour plot, you can decide on appropriate view angles, etc.

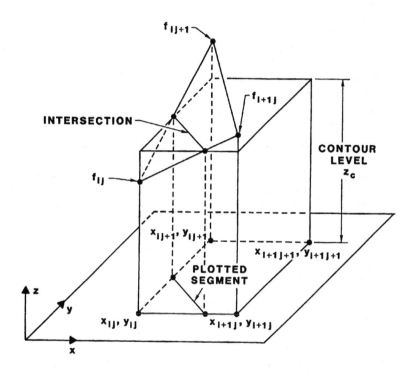

Figure 11.1. Interpolation to Find Contour

The Method

The subroutine cxy3() examines each grid "cell," defined by its lower-left hand point x[i],y[j], to determine if one of the contour lines crosses the z(x,y) curve in that cell. If so, it draws a straight line through the cell, from one boarder to another (see figure). The function to be plotted is interpolated as a plane determined by its value at the three points,

(x[i][j],y[i][j]), (x[i+1][j],y[i+1][j]), and (x[i][j+1],y[i][j+1])

to determine if the contour value falls within the range. If so, the line is plotted as shown in the figure. This algorithm is rapid because the endpoints of the segment to be plotted may quickly be found by linear interpolation between the two function values along that side.

A more sophisticated method (see the reference by Wagner) uses the four points at all of the corners of the cell. Clearly, a plane cannot in general be fit through these points. Wagner defines a central point, with the value of the average of the four corner points, thus forming a set of four triangles. The contour drawn is then, in general, two line segments which meet within the cell. The contours produced by this method are somewhat smoother.

The Program and Test Case

Subroutine cxy() organizes the tests for contour crossings and line drawings, which are actually done by c3(). Subroutine p2() controls the plotting of the line, selecting the identifying character to plot the line. A variety of choices are possible, depending upon how the contour line should be identified. If we are using a high resolution output medium, the contour will instead have to be labeled periodically with a printed, readable string of some form. Subroutine drawf(), which actually plots the line segments, does so via a call to draw(). Draw implements Bresenham's algorithm. The routine is taken from the previous chapter with the minor change that the plotting symbol is passed in as an argument. Subroutine plot() "draws" the points by filling an array, which was previously blanked out by subroutine cleara(). This array is sent to the screen by subroutine show(). Subroutine setup() scales the x,y values to the bounds of the array to be plotted. main() supplies the problem, i.e., the arrays defining the grid x[],y[], and the function to be contoured z(x,y). In the version to plot the results of the multigrid Poisson solver of Chapter 3, it reads these arrays from the data file PLOT.DAT.

References

In addition to the references in Chapter 10, and Wagner's report cited above, I would recommend Ian Angell's book, *A Practical Introduction to Computer Graphics* (New York: Halsted Press (John Wiley),1981). This book contains a variety of FORTRAN routines, including programs for three-dimensional plots and hidden line removals. See also Algorithm 475, "Visible Surface Plotting," in the *Collected Algorithms of the ACM*, by Thomas Wright. This is a package of three FORTRAN programs that can plot three-dimensional arrays of data, including hidden line removal.

There is at least one typographical error in Wagner's report. On p. 27, the argument list for the call to subroutine c3 is inconsistent with that required by the subroutine on page 22. Care should therefore be exercised in adapting any of this code, as it was obviously not offset directly from working routines.

TABLE 11.1

Programs of Chapter 11

cxy	invoke c3 to find contour lines for each grid cell
p2	invoke draw of contour line with appropriate symbol
drawf	invoke draw (see Chapter 15) on scaled raster surface
c3	locate countour lines

routines from Chapter 10 (draw, cleara, etc.) used to draw coutour plots

---

Program Listing and Test Problem Output

(Listing begins next page.)

```
/*
contour plotting program designed to plot
2d data in file PLOT.DAT

from More C tools for scientists and engineers by L. Baker

*/

#define DOFOR(i,to) for(i=0;i<to;i++)
#define INDEX(i,j) [(j)+(i)*coln]
#define abs(x) ((x)>=0 ? (x) : -(x) )
#define sgn(x) ((x)>=0 ? 1 : -1 )
#define max(a,b) ( (a)>(b)? (a):(b))
#define min(a,b) ((a)<(b) ? (a):(b))
#define BLANK 32
#define NULL '\000'
/* =' ' didn't seen to work?*/
/*globals*/
char screen[50][50];
char contr[10]={'0','1','2','3','4','5','6','7','8','9'};
float xmin,xmax,ymin,ymax,xscale,yscale,xoff,yoff;

cxy(x,y,f,nx,ny,coln,zc,nc)
int nx,ny,nc,coln;float *x,*y,*zc,*f;
{/* contour f grid x(nx,ny),y(nx,ny)*/
float xp[4],yp[4],xd[3],yd[3],fd[3];
int i,j,k,np,nx1,ny1;
nx1=nx-1;ny1=ny-1;

DOFOR(i,nx1)
  {
  DOFOR(j,ny1)
    {
/*k= j+i*ny ;printf(" i%d,j%d,k %d\n",i,j,k);*/
    xd[0]=x INDEX(i,j);
    xd[1]=x INDEX(i,j+1);
    xd[2]=x INDEX(i+1,j);
    yd[0]=y INDEX(i,j);
```

```
    yd[1]=y INDEX(i,j+1);
    yd[2]=y INDEX(i+1,j);
    fd[0]=f INDEX(i,j);
    fd[1]=f INDEX(i,j+1);
    fd[2]=f INDEX(i+1,j);
/*printf(" xd %f %f %f yd %f %f %f fd %f %f %f\n",
xd[0],xd[1],xd[2],yd[0],yd[1],yd[2],fd[0],fd[1],fd[2]);
*/
    DOFOR(k,nc)
      {
      c3((xd),(yd),(fd),xp,yp,&np,zc[k]);
      p2(xp,(yp),np,(zc[k]),k);
      };
    xd[0]=x INDEX(i+1,j);
    xd[1]=x INDEX(i,j+1);
    xd[2]=x INDEX(i+1,j+1);
    yd[0]=y INDEX(i+1,j);
    yd[1]=y INDEX(i,j+1);
    yd[2]=y INDEX(i+1,j+1);
    fd[0]=f INDEX(i+1,j);
    fd[1]=f INDEX(i,j+1);
    fd[2]=f INDEX(i+1,j+1);
/*printf(" xd %f %f %f yd %f %f %f fd %f %f %f\n",
xd[0],xd[1],xd[2],yd[0],yd[1],yd[2],fd[0],fd[1],fd[2]);
*/
    DOFOR(k,nc)
      {
      c3((xd),(yd),(fd),xp,yp,&np,zc[k]);
      p2(xp,(yp),np,(zc[k]),k);
      };
    }
  }
return;
}


p2(xp,yp,np,zc,k) float zc,*xp,*yp;int np,k;
{int i;
```

```
char tick;
if (np<0) return;
/*DOFOR(i,np)printf("p2 x=%f y=%f\n",xp[i],yp[i]);*/
/*if (zc==0.) tick='0';
else if (zc<0.) tick='-';
else
   tick='+';   */
tick=contr[k];

DOFOR(i,np)
   {
   drawf(xp[i],yp[i],xp[i+1],yp[i+1],tick);
   };
return;
}


drawf (x1,y1,x2,y2,symbol) char symbol; float x1,x2,y1,y2;
{int xfrom,xto,yfrom,yto;
xfrom= (x1-xoff)*xscale;
xto=(x2-xoff)*xscale;
yfrom=(y1-yoff)*yscale;
yto=(y2-yoff)*yscale;
/*printf(" x %d %d y %d %d\n",xfrom,xto,yfrom,yto);*/
draw(xfrom,yfrom,xto,yto,symbol);/* bresenham line plotter*/
return;
}


c3(xd,yd,fd,xp,yp,np,zc)
float xd[],yd[],fd[],xp[],yp[],zc; int *np;
{
int itl[3],itu[3],it,indexu,indexl;
float d,alpha,eps;
eps=1.e-28;
itl[0]=0;itl[1]=1;itl[2]=2;
itu[0]=1;itu[1]=2;itu[2]=0;
*np=-1;
/*printf(" xd %f %f %f yd %f %f %f fd %f %f %f\n",
xd[0],xd[1],xd[2],yd[0],yd[1],yd[2],fd[0],fd[1],fd[2]);
```

```
*/
DOFOR(it,3)
   {
   indexu=itu[it];
   indexl=itl[it];
   d= fd[indexu]-fd[indexl];
   if (abs(d) < eps) continue;
   alpha=(zc-fd[indexl])/d;
   if( alpha < 0. || alpha > 1.)continue;
   *np=(*np)+1;
   xp[*np]=xd[indexl]+alpha*(xd[indexu]-xd[indexl]);
   yp[*np]=yd[indexl]+alpha*(yd[indexu]-yd[indexl]);
/*printf(" np %d xp,yp %f %f %f %f %f\n",
*np,xp[*np],yp[*np],zc,fd[indexu],fd[indexl]);*/
   }
return;
}
setup()
{
xscale=(49.)/(xmax-xmin);
xoff=xmin;
yoff=ymin;
yscale=(49.)/(ymax-ymin);
cleara();
return;
}

main(argc,argv) int argc;char *argv[];
{float fmax,fmin;
int nx,ny,nc,k,i,j;
float x[50][50],y[50][50],r[50],z[50],f[50][50],zc[11];
int fin;
fin=fopen("plot.dat","r");
if(fin==-1)printf(" input pblm\n");
fscanf(fin,"%d %d",&nx,&ny);
printf(" nx,ny= %d %d\n",nx,ny);
fscanf(fin," %f ",&fmin);/* throw away first boundary point*/
DOFOR(i,nx-1) {fscanf(fin,"%f ",&(r[i]));/*printf(" r=%f\n",r[i]);*/}
```

```
fscanf(fin," %f ",&fmin);/* throw away first bounadry point*/
DOFOR(i,ny-1) {fscanf(fin,"%f ",&(z[i]));/*printf(" z=%f\n",z[i]);*/}

nc=5;
fmax=-1.e10;fmin=1.e10;
DOFOR(i,nx){
  DOFOR(j,ny)
    {
    x [i][j]=r[i];
    y [i][j]=z[j];
    fscanf(fin," %e ",&(f[i][j]));

      fmax= max(fmax,f[i][j]);
      fmin=min(fmin,f[i][j]);
    };
    };
nx--;ny--;
printf(" fmin,fmax= %f %f\n",fmin,fmax);

xmax=1.;
xmin=0.;
ymax=1.;
ymin=0.;
DOFOR(i,nc)zc[i]= ((float) (i+1) )*(fmax-fmin)/((float)(nc+1))+fmin;
DOFOR(i,nc){printf("contour %f symbol %c\n", zc[i],contr[i]);};
setup();
printf(" xoff %e xscale %e yoff %e yscale %e \n",xoff,xscale,yoff,yscale);
cxy(x,y,f,nx,ny,50,zc,nc);
show();
exit(0);
}
```

```
nx,ny= 17 17
fmin,fmax= 1.000000 2.000000
contour 1.166667 symbol 0
contour 1.333333 symbol 1
contour 1.500000 symbol 2
contour 1.666667 symbol 3
contour 1.833333 symbol 4
 xoff 0.00000e+00 xscale 4.90000e+01 yoff 0.00000e+00 yscale 4.90000e+
begin contour plot:
```

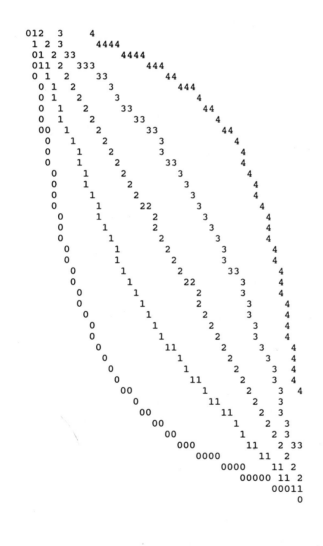

Chapter 12

Sorting: Priority Queues And Heapsort

Chapter Objectives

In this chapter, we will present tools to:

– implement priority queues

– sort in O(n log n) time n items, even for worst cases

This will be done with the heap data structure. Usually, treatments of heaps use arrays to contain the elements to be sorted. This is very inflexible, as it requires the number of items to be processed to be known ahead of time. It also requires the key value to be the data to be sorted itself, rather than one part of the data. By using an array of pointers, the latter constraint can be removed. This is alluded to briefly in Sedgewick's book. Here, we will use a tree structure to hold the heap. As storage allocation will be dynamic, heaps of any size which can fit in memory can be processed.

Sorting

Entire books have been written on sorting, and justifiably so. Data must be organized if specific information is to be retrieved when needed. In general, data cannot be relied upon to be received in the desired order, and so effort must be devoted to sorting it to meet our specifications (an amusing exception to this rule, often cited, is to have a number of post office boxes, with different categories of customers or correspondents directed to use different box numbers. At the cost of multiple box rentals, one receives the data sorted into categories by the postal service. This merely shifts the burden, of course, and it is not free, although this might be the most economical way to do it).

There are great variations in the efficiency of sorting methods, so the penalty for using a poor sort can be large. This has resulted in a great deal of effort expended on developing the "best" sort. This naturally leads to conflicting claims as to just what sort that optimal sort is. This (as you might suspect) has no unique answer. It depends upon various issues including: how many data items have to be sorted, will they all fit into the computer's memory during the sorting process (internal sort) or do they have to buffered in and out onto disks or other storage media (external sort), what is known about the data (are the keys on which the ordering is based completely random or are they structured in some way?).

We shall consider only internal sorts here; external sorting is a very specialized field and we refer the reader with a large amount of data requiring an external sort to consult one of the references listed below. If a very small number of items (i.e., about a dozen) need to be sorted, it hardly matters how the sorting is done In this case a very simple and short sort can be used, especially if the keys upon which the data is to be sorted are all the data there is. An example of this might be a small floppy disk directory to be alphabetized.

In general, however, the key is merely part of the data recorded to be sorted. It might be desired to print that sorted directory with the file size and creation date, along with its name, for example. We want to sort the complete data records, not just the keys. But this could require a lot of moving around of data if we're not careful. A simple solution to this dilemma is to associate with each key a pointer to the data record. The ordering of the keys is coupled with the ordering of the pointers. The only data moved around in memory are the pointers. The sort we are to discuss will use this approach. It is therefore more useful than many of the sorts the reader may encounter which merely produce sorted keys.

It can be proved that sorting N numbers (keys) will generally require order N log N comparison operations. Therefore, a variety of sorts which require order N^2 comparisons may be expected to be inferior to the best available sorts. This rules out many popular sorts (bubble, insertion, selection) unless the number items to be sorted is very small.

You may have heard of so-called "linear" sorts (e.g., radix sort), that require order N operations. Doesn't this violate what the theorem referred to above? No. A radix sort on a key of b bits requires order Nb operations. In order to accommodate N keys, as b bits will allow integer keys in the range from 0 to 2^b, b is of order log N, and we have recovered the N log N behavior. For a full discussion of radix sorts, see the references below. The various tradeoffs in its use should only be considered for special applications. (For example, the "worst case" performance of the radix sort can be poor indeed if the keys are not randomly distributed, e.g., if many records have the same key.) This leaves us with a variety of N log N sorts, including Heapsort and Quicksort. We will not consider the latter for two reasons. First, it is often available as a system subroutine, for example on UNIX systems.   It is a popular sort which can be found in many references.   Instead, we consider here the Heapsort.   Our reason is that while considering the Heapsort we will   develop   the machinery for processing the data structure known as a "heap." This data structure can be of great value in applications removed from sorting, for example, priority queues. Quicksort, on the other hand, would not lead us into such interesting spinoffs.   According to Knuth, its average time is about twice that of Quicksort.   Quicksort can have terrible worst case sorting times.   If the data is already sorted, some versions of Quicksort can require order N^2 comparisons.   Because one often sorts data which is already partially sorted, this can be disastrous.

Heaps And Priority Queues

One way to go about sorting data is to build up an ordered list. Whenever new data arrives, it is inserted into its proper place. If other data has to be moved to permit this, those moves are made. This method clearly costs the most initially, but once the effort is expended to build up the sorted list, recovering the sorted data is inexpensive.   Alternatively, one could keep the data in an unsorted manner, and search through each time we need a particular element (e.g., the record corresponding to the maximum value of the key).   This costs us basically nothing to build up the list, but lots to find what we want each time we need something from the list.   The heap is a compromise; it maintains the data in a partially ordered list.   Moderate effort is expended both in placing new records into the list as well as extracting data from the list.   The heap is therefore an ideal means of storing a data list which is dynamically changing, that is, having records added to and deleted from itself in the course of the calculation. The heap structure can be used for an efficient sort of data which is read in or already present, but it shows itself at its best in dynamic problems such as priority queues.

In common usage, a queue is a line of customers waiting for service, such as customers waiting at a supermarket checkout counter, cars waiting for gas, etc. The principle of "first come, first served" is generally assumed in such a case. In operations research, the meaning of queue is broadened with the concept of "queue discipline." Instead of "first in, first out" (FIFO) as in the supermarket, we might have "last in, first out" (LIFO).   This might cause riots at Safeway, but is a common data structure, known as a "stack," in computer science. A priority queue is a queue in which each customer has a priority or weight assigned. The next customer taken from the queue will be the one with the highest priority.   Examples might be computer jobs on a large multi-user system, in which the user can "bid" to pay more for time in order to get his results sooner, or a hospital emergency room where a more urgent case might receive treatment before an earlier arrival. Priority queues arise often in computer simulations of such customer-server systems. Such simulations form a large part of the computer effort expended on operations research (surveys have shown simulation to account for 25% of the operations research techniques used, in second place behind statistical analysis (29%) and ahead of linear programming (19%).

Programs For Heap Manipulation

A heap may be defined as a binary tree in which each node has higher priority than **either of its** children. A tree is a data structure consisting of a collection of items containing data called nodes and links between nodes called branches. In a tree there is one "root" node, which sends branches out to its children, which in turn send out branches to their children, etc. No node has more than one parent node, however. Consequently, there are no closed loops in trees. There is at most one way to get to a given node from any other node, and always one way to get from the

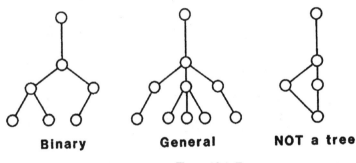

Binary **General** **NOT a tree**

Figure 12.1. Trees

root to any node. In a binary tree, each node may have at most two children. The figure sketches typical trees. Generally, trees are drawn with the root at the top and the branches growing downward. A heap then will look something like this (the elements are sequentially numbered):

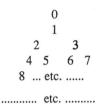

The astute reader will have noticed that the numbers on the left-hand side of the heap are the powers of two: 1,2,4,8, etc. This property of heap structure simplifies determining the index of a child, for example, and is often made use of in the programs that deal with heaps.

From the definition of a heap, we see that the highest priority item in the heap will always be easy to find, because it must be at the root node. The next highest priority item, however, can be in two places, and after that the next highest priority item can be in a number of places. (Exercise: how many?) The heap is therefore a great way to store the data if we want the highest priority item at hand when needed, but a bad idea if we want at any time, say, the top three priority items. Fortunately, in the queues discussed above, and many other applications (such as sorts) all we need is the data one at time.

The basic operations needed to deal with heaps are:

1) to create a new heap
2) to insert data into a heap
3) to remove the highest priority item (and maintain the structure as a heap thereafter, i.e., bring the next highest priority item to the root node.)

These are all implemented with two auxiliary routines designed to insure that the data is organized so as to obey the heap definition after items have been removed or added. These routines are pqupheap and pqdownheap and move elements that may not be in the proper position up or down the heap. These can be implemented recursively, as a portion of the heap is a heap.

There are a number of heap manipulations that are simple and of interest, but not as important as those listed above:

1) to replace the highest priority element in the queue and then extract the highest priority item in the new heap.
2) to delete an arbitrary element from the heap.

The deletion operation can be useful in modeling renegs in queues. A reneg in queueing theory occurs when a customer leaves the queue without receiving service if he has waited too long.

We will illustrate our procedures by sorting the characters in the string ASORTINGEXAMPLE (Sedgewick's example—see references below). We will take the ordering in general such that A is the lowest priority, while X is the highest priority and moves to the top root of the heap. With this convention, the heapsort will produce a result sorted in alphabetical order. We also illustrate the opposite ordering in some of the programmed examples below.

To briefly illustrate how a heap works, it may help to show how a heap is built from the sample input with a diagram of the heap (the results from the computer run will show this in detail but not as picturesquely). We will assume the data enters one at a time, as it would in most priority queue applications (but see the heapsort discussion below, in which the data is entered into the array at one time and then the heap condition is enforced). (The sentinel will not be shown. Also, recall that for our implementation the heap actually contains pointers to the data rather than the data itself.) First, A enters at the top of the heap:

> A

Then S enters in the next available location:

> A
>
> S

However, the heap condition is violated. The auxiliary routine upheap() detects this by comparing the parent A with the child S and fixes the problem by exchanging them:

> S
>
> A

Then O enters:

> S
>
> A   O

Procedure upheap() is again invoked, but as the heap condition is satisfied, does nothing. By now, you should have the idea.

Typically, programming texts and articles illustrate heaps by sorting the keys in an array. Rarely is the key the entire datum of interest. A slightly more useful representation is to use an array of pointers to the data records and sort these by the order of the key. The use of the array, a static data structure, means we must know the maximum number of heap elements beforehand. We will implement heaps with a dynamic data structure, the tree, enabling arbitrary size heaps limited only by computer memory. There are additional overhead costs and some changes in the algorithm required. See the references for discussions of simpler heap implementations using arrays.

The data structure is defined by:

struct element {

int key; /* the key upon which we sort */

struct element *left,*right,*father;

DATA *data; /*pointer to any data associated with key*/

}

The pointer **father** points to the element of which the current element is a child; it will be NULL for the root. The other pointers are to the left and right children (if any) of the current element. The algorithms for heap manipulation are similar for trees and arrays, except that it is not as easy with the tree representation to find an element's location. A special function called father() is supplied to locate the kth element's father (and hence the element itself) in the tree. It is used most often to find where to insert the last element in the tree. It is also used to delete an arbitrary element from the heap.

Heapsort

By generating a heap by inserting the elements one by one, and then extracting the elements in the same way, always maintaining a heap structure, we can sort a list. Because a heap is a binary tree, it can be implemented as a simple array or list. The root node will be in the first position, it will have up to two children, the next lower row will have up to 4 nodes, etc. The heap grows by filling one row at a time before proceeding to add nodes to the next lower depth.

We have introduced the functions compare() and comparee() which are controlled by the global integer variable order. If order=0, the priority rule is largest key value corresponds to highest priority. With this ordering, the largest key element is at the root (top) of the heap, and the heapsort produces alphabetical ordering, i.e. smallest first (in ASCII coding, the letter A is smaller than the letter Z). With order=1, this is reversed. This reversed order could be of use in simulating FIFO queues, in which the key becomes the time of arrival and the lowest key (earliest arrival time) corresponds to the next customer to be served. The computer code to do this, along with subroutines to do all of the operations listed above, is given below. The output of the test driver is also shown. The output is full of the grisly details of what is happening as items are added to or deleted from the heap. This is not only to allow a thorough check on the program, but to allow the reader to see exactly how a heap data structure works.

The main program merely invokes the various tests. First, the global integer variable order is set equal to zero, to set for heaps with the largest at the top. This is the order for a heapsort in ascending or alphabetical order (see below). After most of the test examples, order is set to one for a test of smallest first ordering. This latter ordering would be of interest in a priority queue in which the key were the time of arrival of a customer, and which had a first-come, first-served policy.

Construct inserts the elements into the heap and moves them downward as necessary using pqdownheap to maintain heap order. We need only start at the next-to-lowest level of the heap for the comparisons, so the initial index passed to pqdownheap for a heap of m elements is m/2, or m>1 using a binary shift.

Comparee() and Compare() do the comparisons of two keys, returning the appropriate answer based on the value of order. The former compares for "greater than or equal", the latter just for inequality. For order=0, the largest key has the highest priority and goes to the root. For order=1, the smallest key gets priority (alphabetic order). Compare() returns 1 for a < b, otherwise 0, if order is 0; for order = 1, it will return 0 for a < b and 1 otherwise. Use of these routines to isolate the comparisons makes it trivial to change queue discipline merely by setting the global parameter order.

Pqdownheap moves an element away from the root, if necessary. It compares an element with its children in the heap, exchanging it with the appropriate child if necessary, to maintain the heap condition. Note that because of the simple binary tree heap structure, the index of the children of the jth element in the heap are simply 2j and 2j+1. Pqinsert adds an element to the heap by putting into the last place and propagating it upward, if necessary, to maintain a heap.

Pqupheap is the "inverse" of pqdownheap, comparing a child with its father (only one this time, with an index one-half that f its offspring). If necessary, parent and child are exchanged.

Pqremove removes the first element from the heap and returns it. It then takes last element in the heap and puts it at the root. Then the size of the heap is decremented by one to account for the lost element. Pqdownheap is then used to restore the heap condition, which is probably violated by the new first element.

Pqheaps does a heapsort. After it is finished, the heap of pointers has become a linear list of pointers sorted by key. The order of sort is opposite to the priority queue discipline. If we want alphabetical order, or smallest key first, we use a heap with the largest element at the root. First we construct the heap. We then remove the the first element, putting it into the last position in the heap storage. This element is no longer considered part of the heap. The heap size is decremented by one.

We do this to the next root, putting it in the position before the element we just removed. We continue this process until the heap has only one element at its root. If the order were largest first (order = 0), this element corresponds to the smallest key. The keys increase until the largest element, in last place in the new linear array which has replaced the heap. Note that there are two very different ways to obtain data sorted in ascending order with our heap-manipulating routines. If we want that data one at a time for processing, as in a priority queue simulation, we can use a heap with the smallest item first, and just keep removing it from the heap. To produce a sorted array via Heapsort, we use the opposite ordering, putting the largest items first. Pqreplace is a complicated operation. We attempt to enter a new item at the root of the priority queue heap and remove the resultant root. If we are using order = 0, so the largest-key item is at the root, if we attempt to enter a larger key, that element merely "bounces off" the queue. This operation can be useful in some queue simulations with preemption (an important customer arrives and gets immediate service, even if that means interrupting another customer).

Pqdelete removes an item from the priority queue or heap. That item is specified by its location in the data array. The auxiliary array inv[], which has been used to keep track of such things, is employed to find its pointer in the heap. We then remove the item, replacing its pointer with that of the last item in the heap and decrementing the size of the heap. We finally restore the heap condition caused by this motion. This is the only heap operation in which we have used the data in inv[]. If you will not need pqdelete, you can save overhead in time and storage by omitting the operations on inv[].

References

Jon Bentley,"How to Sort," *Communications ACM*, **27**, 287-291, April 1984.

Jon Bentley, "Thanks, Heaps," *Commications ACM*, **28**, 245-250, March 1985.

D. E. Knuth, *Sorting and Searching,Vol III in the Art of Computer Programming* (Reading, Mass: Addison Wesley, 1973).

Ledbetter & Cox, *Industrial Engineering*, **9**, 19-21, 1977.

Robert Sedgewick, *Algorithms* (Reading, Mass: Addison Wesley, 1983).

Roger Wainwright, *Communications ACM*, **28**, 396-402,April 1985; (comments and author's response Volume **29**, 331-335. Wainwright's method (and others) preserves the O(N log N) scaling of time with count of sorted objects for sorted lists. Due to a typographical error, he appeared to claim that his method never behaved as poorly as N^2. Several people wrote in to present counterexamples to such a claim. Any variant of Quicksort must have a worst case performance of order N^2. The trick is to make the cases that perform this poorly unlikely.)

TABLE 12.1

Functions

pqconstruct	build a heap
pqinsert	insert an element into a heap (add an element)
pqremove	remove first element in priority queue
pqreplace	change first element
pqheaps	do heapsort (assumes pqconstruct called)
pqdelete	remove arbitrary element from queue
pqupheap	move element toward root, maintaining heap condition
pqdownheap	move element away from root, maintaining heap
father	find father of kth element
compare	<> comparisons
comparee	<= or >= comparisons

Program Listing and Test Problem Output

(Listing begins next page.)

```
/*
indirect heap routines for priority queue, heapsort
modified from heap.c to use a binary tree rep. instead
of arrays for greater flexibility in storage allocation.

from More C Tools for Scientists and Engineers by L. Baker

*/

#include "stdio.h"
#include "stdlib.h"
#include "alloc.h"

/*#include "libc.h"
  */
/*
main-various tests
pqconstruct-build a heap initial data
pqinsert-insert an element
pqremove-remove FIRST element
pqreplace-change first element
pqheaps-heapsort
pqdelete-remove arbitrary element

auxiliary routines-
pqupheap move element toward root to maintain heap condition
pqdownheap move element away from root to maintain heap
compare <> comparisons
comparee <= and >= comparisons
*/

int order,heapsizenow;
/* order= 0 largest first (top) highest priority first
  1 smallest first- alphabetic ordering
*/

#define MAX(x,y)  ((x)>(y)?(x):(y))
#define MIN(x,y)  ((x)<(y)?(x):(y))
```

```
/* in reality, data might not be merely int*/
#define DATA int
#define NULL 0
struct element
   {
   int key;
   struct element *left,*right,*father;
   /* pointer to other data*/
   DATA *data;
   };

struct element *root;

#define ESIZE sizeof( *root)

static char keyvector[]="ASORTINGEXAMPLEZB"; /* or char *a? */

main(argc,argv) int argc; char *argv[];
{
/*test above on sedgewick example*/
int i,j,heapsize;
struct element *k,*itself(),*pqremove(),*pqreplace(),*l;
char list[20];
order=0;/* establish heap convention */
heapsize=15;
printf(" Esize = %d\n", ESIZE );
pqconstruct(heapsize);/*establish heap */
printf(" after construct %d %d\n",heapsizenow,heapsize);
for(j=0;j<15;j++)list[j]=(itself(j)->key);
printf(" now print heap:\n");
for(j=0;j<15;j++)printf("%c",list[j]);
printf(" now test pqinsert\n");
heapsizenow=0;
root=NULL;
for (i=0;i<15;i++)
  {
  k=malloc( ESIZE );
```

```
  k->key=keyvector[i];
  k->father=NULL;
  k->data=NULL;
  k->left=NULL;
  k->right=NULL;
  pqinsert(k);
  }
for(j=0;j<15;j++)list[j]=itself(j)->key;
for(j=0;j<15;j++)printf("%c",list[j]);
printf("\n now test pqheaps %d %d\n",heapsizenow,heapsize);
pqheaps(list);
for (i=0;i<15;i++) printf("%c",list[i]);putchar('\n');
/*nw test remove*/
pqconstruct(heapsize);
printf(" after construct for removetest %d %d\n",heapsizenow,heapsize);
j=0;
for (i=14;i>=0;i--)
  {
  k=pqremove();
  /*      for(j=0;j<i;j++)printf("%c",itself(j)->key);*/
  /*printf("removed %c\n",k->key);*/
  list[j++]=k->key;
    };
for(j=0;j<15;j++)printf("%c",list[j]);putchar('\n');
/* now test replace-build up first */
pqconstruct(heapsize);/*establish heap */
printf(" testing replace %d\n",heapsizenow);
for (i=0;i<heapsizenow;i++)
    list[i]=itself(i)->key;
for(i=0;i<heapsizenow;i++)putchar(list[i]);putchar('\n');
/*replace with Z attempted- should bounce back at us*/
  k=malloc( ESIZE );
  k->key=keyvector[15];
  k->father=NULL;
  k->data=NULL;
  k->left=NULL;
  k->right=NULL;
l=pqreplace(k); printf(" place %c returns %d %c\n",k->key,
```

```
    i,l->key);
/* replace with B attempted- should get X extracted */
k->key=keyvector[16];
l=pqreplace(k);printf(" place %c returns %d %c\n",keyvector[16],i,
l->key);


order=1;/* 'alphabetic'ordering in fact, pqheaps REVERSE order*/
/*heapsort test*/
pqconstruct(heapsize);
for(i=0;i<15;i++)printf(" heaped %d %c\n",i,itself(i)->key);
pqheaps(list);
for (i=0;i<15;i++) printf(" sorted %c\n",list[i]);
/*now test delete*/
printf(" now test delete\n");
pqconstruct(heapsize);
for (i=0;i<15;i++)
    printf(" %d %c\n",i,itself(i)->key);
for (j=0;j<heapsizenow;j++)
{
printf(" deleting %c \n",itself(j)->key);
pqdelete(itself(j));/*delete ith element*/
for (i=0;i<(14-j);i++)
    printf(" %d %c\n",i,itself(i)->key);
}
/* test pqupheap*/
order=0;
pqconstruct(heapsize);
for (i=0;i<15;i++)
    printf(" %d %c\n",i,itself(i)->key);
for (j=0;j<heapsizenow;j++)
{
printf(" deleting element %d, heapsizenow=%d\n",j,heapsizenow);
k=itself(j);
if(!k)exit(0);
printf(" deleting %c \n",k->key);
pqdelete(k);/*delete ith element*/
for (i=0;i<(14-j);i++)
  {
```

```
  k=itself(i);
  if(!k)break;
  printf(" %d %d %c\n",i,k->key,k->key);
  }
printf(" j=%d,heapsizenow=%d\n",j,heapsizenow);
if(j==heapsizenow)break;
}
printf(" end of tests");
/*exit(0);*/
}

pqconstruct(heapsize) int heapsize;
{
struct element *newelmnt;
for(heapsizenow=1;heapsizenow<=heapsize;heapsizenow++)
  {
  newelmnt=malloc( ESIZE );
  newelmnt->left=NULL;
  newelmnt->right=NULL;
  newelmnt->father=NULL;
  newelmnt->data=NULL;
  newelmnt->key=keyvector[heapsizenow-1];
  if(heapsizenow==1)
    {
    root=newelmnt;
    }
  else
    walkdown(newelmnt);
  }
heapsizenow--;
}

struct element *dad;/*inserting new element, dad will be its father*/

walkdown(newelement)
struct element *newelement;
/* starting from root, walk down toward  empty last element in heap
  adding the new element into heap in proper fashion*/
```

```
{
int pow2,halfpow,id,kp,leftson,sonid,temporary;
struct element *son,*toinsert,*temp;
DATA *tempdata;
/*printf(" walkdown heapsizenow=%d\n",heapsizenow);*/
kp=heapsizenow;
toinsert=newelement;
id=kp;
leftson=-1;/*undefined*/
dad=NULL;/*dad should initially be NULL as we start at root*/
for(pow2=1;(id>>=1)>0;pow2<<=1) ;
/*printf(" initially pow2=%d\n",pow2);*/
id=kp-pow2;
/*sonid for debugging purposes */
sonid=1;/*root*/
halfpow=1;
son=root;
for(;halfpow>0;pow2>>=1)
   {
   if(!son)break;
/*   printf(" son=%c toinsert=%c\n",son->key,toinsert->key);*/
   if(comparee( son->key,toinsert->key))
      {
      /* exchange son and toinsert, placing toinsert into tree and
         removing son*/
      temporary= son->key;
      son->key=toinsert->key;
      toinsert->key=temporary;
      tempdata= son->data;/* a pointer is a pointer*/
      son->data=toinsert->data;
      toinsert->data=tempdata;
      }
/*   printf(" son=%c toinsert=%c\n",son->key,toinsert->key);*/
   halfpow=pow2>>1;
/*printf(" debug father %d %d %d %d %c\n",id,pow2,sonid,leftson,son->key);*/
   if( id>=halfpow)
      /*go to right*/
      {
```

```
        dad=son;
        leftson=0;
        son=son->right;
        id-=halfpow;
        sonid=(sonid<<1)+1;
        }
      else
        /*to left*/
        {
        dad=son;
        leftson=1;
        son=son->left;
        sonid<<=1;
        }
/*printf(" debug2 father %d %d %d %d\n",id,pow2,sonid,leftson);*/
      }/* end loop*/
toinsert->father=dad;
if(leftson)
    {
    dad->left=toinsert;
    }
else
    dad->right=toinsert;
toinsert->father=dad;
/*printf(" adding at sonid=%d lefson=%d kp=%d %c\n"
    ,sonid,leftson,kp,toinsert->key);*/
}

struct element *father(k,leftson,startat)
int k,*leftson;
struct element *startat;
/*determine father of kth element, and if this element is left/rt child*/
/* goes down from root- is there a better way? */
/* k of root is zero (not 1) */
{
int pow2,halfpow,id,kp,sonid;
struct element *son;
if(!k)
```

```
  {
  *leftson=0;/*doesn't matter*/
  return 0;/* its root */
  }
kp=k+1;
id=kp;
for(pow2=1;(id>>=1)>0;pow2<<=1) ;
id=kp-pow2;
/*sonid for debugging purposes */
sonid=1;/*root*/
halfpow=1;
for(son=startat;halfpow>0;pow2>>=1)
  {
  halfpow=pow2>>1;
/*printf(" debug father %d %d %d %d %c\n",id,pow2,sonid,*leftson,dad->key);*
  if(!halfpow)
    {
    return dad;
    }
  if( id>=halfpow)
    /*go to right*/
    {
    dad=son;
    *leftson=0;
    son=son->right;
    id-=halfpow;
    sonid=(sonid<<1)+1;
    }
  else
 ·  /*to left*/
    {
    dad=son;
    *leftson=1;
    son=son->left;
    sonid<<=1;
    }
/*
printf(" debug2 father %d %d %d %d dad=%c\n",id,pow2,sonid,*leftson,dad->ke
```

```
if(!son)printf(" returning as dad\n ");
*/
  if(!son)return dad;/*dad,leftson/rightson set*/
  }

/*never get here */
printf(" bad exit father sonid=%d lefson=%d kp=%d\n",sonid,*leftson,kp);
exit(0);
}

struct element *itself(k) int k;
{
/* k of root is assumed to be 0 not 1 */
struct element *dad;
int leftson;
dad=father(k,&leftson,root);
/*printf(" itself k=%d leftson=%d\n",k,leftson);*/
if(!dad)
  return root;
else if(leftson) return dad->left;
else return dad->right;
}


comparee(a,b) int a,b;
{/* for order =0 returns 1 if a<=b else 0
          1   "   0 if a<=b else 1
 order=0 for largest at top (sedgewick)
     1 for priority queue with key time (FCFS) */

return ( ((a<=b) ? 1-order : order) );
}

compare(a,b) int a,b;
{/* for order =0 returns 1 if a<b else 0
          1   "   0 if a<b else 1
 order=0 for largest at top
     1 for priority queue with key time (FCFS) */
```

```
return ( ((a<b) ? 1-order : order ) );
}

pqdownheap(ei) struct element *ei;
/* move e down the heap as necessary */
{
int childkey,ekey,temporary;
struct element *left,*right,*child,*temp,*e;
DATA *dataptr,*tdata;
e=ei;
while(1)
  {
  ekey=e->key;
  left=e->left;
  right=e->right;
  if (left && right)
    {
    if(comparee(left->key,right->key) )
          child=right;
    else
          child=left;
    }
  else if (left) child=left;
  else if(right) child=right;
  else return;
  childkey= child->key;
  if(comparee(ekey,childkey) ) /*exchange*/
      {
      tdata=child->data;
      child->data=e->data;
      e->data=tdata;
      temporary=child->key;
      child->key=e->key;
      e->key=temporary;
      e=child;/* move down*/
      }
  else return;/*done- no more exch nece*/
```

```
   }
}

pqinsert(e) struct element *e;
{
if(!heapsizenow)
   {
   root=e;
   heapsizenow++;
   return;
   }
/*else*/
heapsizenow++;
walkdown(e);
}

pqupheap(e) struct element *e;
{
/* this is only operation to use father pointer*/
/* it in turn is only used in the delete op*/
struct element *left,*right,*dad,*temp;
DATA *d;
int v,j,temporary;
while(1)
   {
   if(!(e))return;
   v=e->key;
   dad=e->father;
   if(!dad)return;
   if(comparee( dad->key , v))
      {/*swap e with dad*/
      d=dad->data;
      dad->data=e->data;
      e->data=d;
      temporary=dad->key;
      dad->key=e->key;
      e->key=temporary;
      }
```

```
  e=e->father;/*move up*/
    }
}

struct element *pqremove()          /*remove first element*/
{
struct element *remove,*oldlast,*dad;
int leftson;
remove= root;
--heapsizenow;
if(!heapsizenow)
   {
   remove=root;
   root=NULL;
   return(remove);
   }
   dad=father(heapsizenow,&leftson,root);
   if(leftson)
      {
      oldlast=dad->left;
      dad->left=NULL;
      }
   else
      {
      oldlast=dad->right;
      dad->right=NULL;
      }
/*make oldlast new root*/
if(dad!=root)
   {
   oldlast->right=root->right;
   oldlast->left=root->left;
   oldlast->father=NULL;
   (root->left)->father=oldlast;
   (root->right)->father=oldlast;
   }
else if(heapsizenow==1)
   {/*were only two elements*/
```

```
      oldlast->father=NULL;
      root=oldlast;
      return (remove);
      }
else
   {
   oldlast->left=root->left;
   oldlast->father=NULL;
   root=oldlast;
   return(remove);
   }
root=oldlast;
pqdownheap(root);
return (remove);
}


pqheaps(list)
char list[];                /*heapsort*/
/* for tree heap, better to output or construct linked list*/

{
struct element *b,*c,*temp;
int key,index,leftson;
DATA d;
index=0;
/* construct heap from initially unordered array */
/*pqconstruct(); */ /* assume pqconstruct has been called already*/
/*printf("\n");*/
do   {/*exchange first, last */
   list[index++]=root->key;
   dad=father(--heapsizenow,&leftson,root);
   if(leftson)
      {
      b=dad->left;
      dad->left=NULL;
      }
   else
      {
```

```
      b=dad->right;
      dad->right=NULL;
      }
  /* in-place sort makes no sense now, as heapsize decreases and
     elements d from heap */
      root->data=b->data;
      root->key=b->key;          1   ARRAH
      pqdownheap(root);
      } while (heapsizenow>0); /* n=1 will exchange 1 with itself-no need*/
  list[index]=root->key;
  }


struct element *pqreplace(ev) struct element *ev;
{
/* ev is placed into the priority queue, and then the root element removed-
if the new item is highest priority, the heap is unchanged and the
new item's index in the data array is return
 NOTE THAT EV MAY BE ALTERED!*/
ev->left=root;/* note that root is unchanged*/
ev->right=NULL;
pqdownheap(ev);
return (ev);
}


pqdelete(item) struct element *item;
{
/*delete   item
*/
int oldkey,newkey,leftson,remove;
struct element *last,*dad,*father(),*child,*itself();
if(item==root)
   { last=pqremove();
     return;
   }
oldkey=item->key;
/*delete the item, replacing it with
 last element in heap*/
   dad=father(--heapsizenow,&leftson,root);
```

```
       if(!dad)
    {
               printf(" warning- deleting  fatherless element\n");
               exit(0);        return;
    }
   if(leftson)
     {
     last=dad->left;
     dad->left=NULL;
     }
   else
     {
     last=dad->right;
     dad->right=NULL;
     }
if(item==last)
   {return;}
/*reuse dad as father of item*/
dad=item->father;
if(item== (dad->left) )
             {
                 dad->left=last;
             }
else
             {
             dad->right=last;
             }
last->left=item->left;
last->right=item->right;
last->father=dad;
child=item->left;
if(child)
   child->father=last;
child=item->right;
if(child)
   child->father=last;
newkey=last->key; if(newkey==oldkey)return;
/* if key unchanged, finished*/
```

```
/*otherwise, move new element up or down heap as needed.*/
/* order 0 max on top- compare(a,b) true a,b-
if newkey is smaller (usual heap convention) want downheap*/
if (compare(newkey,oldkey))pqdownheap(last);
else pqupheap(last);
return;
}
```

Esize = 18
after construct 15 15
now print heap:
XTPGSONAERAIMLE now test pqinsert
XTPGSONAERAIMLE
now test pqheaps 15 15
XTSRPONMLIGEEAA
after construct for removetest 15 15
XTSRPONMLIGEEAA
testing replace 15
XTPGSONAERAIMLE
place Z returns 15 Z
place B returns 15 X
heaped 0 A
heaped 1 A
heaped 2 E
heaped 3 G
heaped 4 E
heaped 5 M
heaped 6 I
heaped 7 S
heaped 8 R
heaped 9 X
heaped 10 T
heaped 11 O
heaped 12 P
heaped 13 N
heaped 14 L
sorted A
sorted A
sorted E
sorted E
sorted G
sorted I
sorted L
sorted M
sorted N
sorted O

sorted P
sorted R
sorted S
sorted T
sorted X
now test delete
0 A
1 A
2 E
3 G
4 E
5 M
6 I
7 S
8 R
9 X
10 T
11 O
12 P
13 N
14 L
deleting A
0 A
1 E
2 E
3 G
4 L
5 M
6 I
7 S
8 R
9 X
10 T
11 O
12 P
13 N
deleting E
0 A

```
1 G
2 E
3 N
4 L
5 M
6 I
7 S
8 R
9 X
10 T
11 O
12 P
deleting E
0 A
1 G
2 I
3 N
4 L
5 M
6 P
7 S
8 R
9 X
10 T
11 O
deleting N
0 A
1 G
2 I
3 O
4 L
5 M
6 P
7 S
8 R
9 X
10 T
deleting L
```

0 A
1 G
2 I
3 O
4 T
5 M
6 P
7 S
8 R
9 X
deleting M
0 A
1 G
2 I
3 O
4 T
5 X
6 P
7 S
8 R
deleting P
0 A
1 G
2 I
3 O
4 T
5 X
6 R
7 S
deleting S
0 A
1 G
2 I
3 O
4 T
5 X
6 R
0 X

```
1 T
2 P
3 G
4 S
5 O
6 N
7 A
8 E
9 R
10 A
11 I
12 M
13 L
14 E
```
deleting element 0, heapsizenow=15
deleting X
```
0 84 T
1 83 S
2 80 P
3 71 G
4 82 R
5 79 O
6 78 N
7 65 A
8 69 E
9 69 E
10 65 A
11 73 I
12 77 M
13 76 L
```
j=0,heapsizenow=14
deleting element 1, heapsizenow=14
deleting S
```
0 84 T
1 82 R
2 80 P
3 71 G
4 76 L
```

5 79 O
6 78 N
7 65 A
8 69 E
9 69 E
10 65 A
11 73 I
12 77 M
j=1,heapsizenow=13
deleting element 2, heapsizenow=13
deleting P
0 84 T
1 82 R
2 79 O
3 71 G
4 76 L
5 77 M
6 78 N
7 65 A
8 69 E
9 69 E
10 65 A
11 73 I
j=2,heapsizenow=12
deleting element 3, heapsizenow=12
deleting G
0 84 T
1 82 R
2 79 O
3 73 I
4 76 L
5 77 M
6 78 N
7 65 A
8 69 E
9 69 E
10 65 A
j=3,heapsizenow=11

deleting element 4, heapsizenow=11
deleting L
0 84 T
1 82 R
2 79 O
3 73 I
4 69 E
5 77 M
6 78 N
7 65 A
8 69 E
9 65 A
j=4,heapsizenow=10
deleting element 5, heapsizenow=10
deleting M
0 84 T
1 82 R
2 79 O
3 73 I
4 69 E
5 65 A
6 78 N
7 65 A
8 69 E
j=5,heapsizenow=9
deleting element 6, heapsizenow=9
deleting N
0 84 T
1 82 R
2 79 O
3 73 I
4 69 E
5 65 A
6 69 E
7 65 A
j=6,heapsizenow=8
deleting element 7, heapsizenow=8
deleting A

0 84 T
1 82 R
2 79 O
3 73 I
4 69 E
5 65 A
6 69 E
j=7,heapsizenow=7
end of tests

Chapter 13

The Real-World Interface: Typewriter Emulators and Printer Controllers

Introduction

This chapter is a potpurri (and I hope not in the literal meaning of "rotten pot") of programs that illustrate useful programs for dealing with printers, etc., and other "real-world" grimy details.

The major program in this section is a typewriter emulator. It is useful for situations in which a word processor is overkill. In particular, when one is filling out forms which require answers on certain lines and/or in certain columns, it is not practical to use a full word processor. What is needed is a typewriter. This program provides one, to the limit of your printer's abilities. You can, using this program, easily get to exactly the chosen line of the form, which is nontrivial with most word processors. The smarter printers buffer the line rather than printing character by character, and unless yours can be forced into incremental mode, you will have some guesswork as to finding the correct column. This can be done with a scratch sheet if necessary. Even those dot matrix printers that allow incremental printing tend to print "on the fly," so the print head is not positioned where it will next print. Once the desired column has been found, the column number can be used as a tab set, as on a typewriter. The typewriter emulator permits an incremental mode (printing character by character as they are typed) which is useful for determining columns, etc., and a buffered mode in which you can correct errors, print overstruck characters (printer permitting).

We include two programs for setting printer parameters. The trivial one sets the parameters of a NEC 8023A or C. Itoh 8510 in terms of elite, pica, or condensed characters, etc. The other program is similar, but is for an Hewlett-Packard LaserJet printer. It is designed to accept the name of a file to be printed, either on the command line when the program name is typed to invoke the program, or (if one is not present on the command line) to read in the name from the console. If you do give it a name, it types that file according to the specifications that follow. Then it resets the printer to default values and quits. If you do not provide any filename, it assumes you wish to set the printer to new (non-default) values, and does so. The margins are set and type fonts are selected. The program generally allows a return carriage on entry to force resort to defaults defined within the program.

Typewriter Program-Features

The typewriter operates one line at a time. Only this line is displayed. The line can either be treated in a buffered mode, allowing you to backspace and correct typing errors, or in incremental mode, sending one character at a time. The latter is most useful in finding the proper column for a tab setting, which is necessary in filling out forms. Just hit the space bar as necessary to get over to the correct column. This assumes that your printer can be set to an incremental mode. Printers with internal buffers often allow you to toggle their mode setting to and from buffered, and this feature is provided for in this program.

Tabs can be expanded in a set number of spaces (as on some computer software), or set and cleared by spacing over to the column and hitting the appropriate control codes, "exactly" as a typewriter operates. The margins are also set in a manner analogous to a typewriter, by moving the cursor to the desired column and sending the appropriate control code. The menu of control codes is always part of the screen display, as is the "ruler" and a column indicator.

You can toggle between serial and parallel output ports, and read or write using files. You can overstrike previous characters on printers which allow backspacing. Usually this cannot be done with buffered printers unless an incremental mode can be selected. You can also choose to reset the configuration at any time. There are two printer configurations, for the serial and parallel ports.

Details on using the program are found in the documentation file which follows the program listings. The on-screen information should be enough to get you through. If the program seems to be "hung," check the printer to be sure that it is on, selected, and connected. Remember that control-Z is the code to quit!

Typewriter Program-Programming Notes

This program comes in two versions: one for the IBM-PC and associated clones, and the orginal version, which was implemented for CP/M (Z80 microprocessor) machines. The principal difference is in the screen handling. For the former, we use operating system calls. Specifically, we use the routines in PCIO.A file supplied with DeSmet C. Subroutine cursor uses function scr_rowcol() from PCIO.A to move the cursor to a specified row and column. Subroutine clearh() uses scr_clr() from PCIO.A to clear the screen (and home the cursor). Function get() uses scr_csts() from PCIO.A to obtain an input character. It assumes that if there has been no character input, the function returns a NULL code (0). It loops until a character has been typed. Finally, the intialization routine scr_setup() in PCIO.A is called from main() to insure that all housekeeping chores related to the use of the other routines in the package are performed. With this information, it should be easy to convert the program for use with another C compiler on an IBM-PC or clone. It should be noted that these library routines are not in the default library, but must be explicitly assembled and bound with the user's program by the user. These routines, in turn, use the interrupt call designed to handle video operations (with hexidecimal code 10 in the AH register). The CP/M operating system version instead assumes that the various operations needed to position the cursor, write characters to or clear the screen, are accessed by sending appropriate control codes to the console. For example, on the Kaypro II, whose screen emulates an ADM-3A terminal (approximately), sending the code 26 clears the screen and "homes" the cursor to the upper left location on the screen. This configuration is saved in a disk file. The program checks for this file. If it is not present, it demands that you create it by entering the necessary configuration information. The default information in the sample program is appropriate for the Kaypro or any other machine whose video terminal emulates the ADM-3A.

It is interesting to note that later versions of MSDOS support the use of the ANSI.SYS file, which enables a similar terminal operation to that discussed above (instead of the 10H interrupt). Through the use of "escape sequences," that is, sending a string of characters beginning with the character 27 decimal (the escape code), the console can be sent instructions rather than text to be displayed. For example, the clear screen/ home cursor command as defined by ANSI.SYS is ESC,[,2,J. Sending these four characters (decimal values 27,91,50,74) would clear and home. The sequence is more verbose than the corresponding ADM-3A sequence, and is slower in execution than the 10H interrupt calls (which are not disabled by ANSI.SYS), and is perhaps less portable than the interrupt method as some machines may not have ANSI.SYS. For that reason, we have not chosen to go this route. If you are using an IBM-PC or clone, but use another compiler rather than De Smet C, you will almost certainly have routines in your library that perform functions similar to those in the De Smet library. It is for you that we listed these routines and the locations of the calls to them.

The configuration file is necessary even for MS-DOS machines, because it contains configuration information about your printer. The defaults implemented currently are for a NEC- 8023A or C. Itoh 8510 on the parallel port and a Smith-Corona TP- 1 on the serial port. You will only have to change these defaults once, if you permit the configuration file to be saved by the program. You generally should skip the second half of the configuration stage, the terminal (no pun intended) configuration, if you are using the PC clone version. However, if you don't have something similar to PCIO.A but do have ANSI.SYS, you might want to implement the typewriter for your machine through the use of escape sequences to the video section. Write me if you have specific questions regarding bringing the typewriter up on your machine.

Feature Selection For NEC 8023a Printer

This simple code merely illustrates how to send control codes and use the usual C subroutines to talk to devices such as the console (keyboard and screen). If you are unfamiliar with the use of the switch statement, this should show you how its done.

Feature Selection For The Hp Laserjet Printer

This program may be viewed as an extended version of the printer setup program for the dot-matrix printers discussed above. Aside from a more extensive list of features to set, and the presence of defaults, the one feature of interest is the use of the fgets() function to input a line of text from the console. This function is used by functions rds() and rdf() to input strings and floating point numbers, respectively. The value pointed to by the argument of these functions is the value of the number read in (if any), while the function itself returns a 0 if the user merely typed in a carriage return to signify that he wished to use the default value. If the user does not want the default, the function returns 1 in the case of rdf() and the string length in the case of rds(). The default font for the LaserJet is Courier. If a typestyle cartridge is inserted, its primary font becomes the default. Although the program assumes that the cartridge inserted is the Prestige Elite font, as stated in the message, Letter Gothic or other cartridges are generally invoked if the codes for Prestige Elite are invoked, since the LaserJet selects the "closest" font to the one specified and the others are generally closer to Prestige Elite than Courier is. Boldface is the default, as it looks better than the ordinary elite in my opinion. Margins are specified in inches as floating point values. The lower margin defaults to the same value as the top margin. The top and left margins default to 1" and the right margin to 0". These default values are embedded in the code as they appear to be standard numbers. If your system has many different users, you might wish to have these numbers in a configuration file and use a procedure similar to that for the typewriter program to use that file to supply the default values.

Program Listing

(Begins next page.) There is no test problem output.

```
/* typewriter program
from More C Tools for Scientists and Engineers by L. Baker*/
/* select ONE OF THE FOLLOWING:*/
#define TURBOC 1
/*
#define DESMET
#define MICROC
#define CPM
*/

#ifdef TURBOC
#include <conio.h>
#include <dos.h>
#include <stdio.h>
#include <string.h>
#include <io.h>
#define write( stream, string, count) fwrite( string ,1, count , stream)
#define index( string, chr) strchr(string,chr)
#endif

#define NULL 0
#define EOF -1
#define O_RDWR 2
#define O_RDONLY 0
#define O_WRONLY 3


#define ESC 27
#define SPACE ' '
#define BACKSP '\10'
#define BELL 7
#define KONFIG 30
#define KONFM  KONFIG-1
/* OCTAL 10 = DECIMAL 8 */
#define isascii(x)  (x<127 && x>31)
/*#define put(x) bdos(6,x)*/
/* us unbuffered i/o terminal input, device output. buffered i/o files*/
int cnfig[KONFM],length;
```

```
int flagi=0,flagt=0,flags=0,flagho=0,flagin=0,flagot=0,coln;/*globals*/
int lmargin=1,rmargin=72,flaga=0;
#ifdef TURBOC
FILE *fi,*fo,*diskin,*diskout,*config;
#endif
#ifdef DESMET
int *fi,*fo,*diskin,*diskout,*config;
#endif
char filei[40],fileo[40],*chrr;
char line[80],tline[80],*newl,*newlp,*newls,newlc[6];
int bufsize,n_rw;
/* flags
   i  1 if incremental
   s  1 if serial i/o
   ho 1 if add h.o. bit
   in 1 if file input
   ot 1 if file output  */


confg(){
int i,yesno;

config=fopen("CONFTW.DAT","r+");
if(config){printf(" type D for disk config., other for current\n");
    yesno=get();
  if(yesno==68||yesno||100)
  {for(i=0;i<KONFIG;i++) fscanf(config,"%d",&(cnfig[i]));};}
  else
  { cnfig[0]=26;cnfig[1]=0;/*defaults-clear*/
    cnfig[2]=ESC;cnfig[3]=61;cnfig[4]=32;cnfig[5]=32;/*cursor*/
    cnfig[7]=10;cnfig[8]=13;cnfig[9]=0;/*parallel cr/lf*/
   cnfig[10]=13;cnfig[11]=0;cnfig[12]=0;/* serial cr/lf*/
  cnfig[13]=ESC;cnfig[14]=91;cnfig[15]=0;cnfig[16]=0;
  cnfig[17]=ESC;cnfig[18]=93;cnfig[19]=0;cnfig[20]=0;
   for(i=21;i<KONFIG;i++)cnfig[i]=0;
  }

printf(" do you want to (re)config terminal? Y or N\n");
```

```
    yesno=get();
 if(yesno==89||yesno==121) confgt();
 printf(" do you want to (re)config parallel printer? Y or N\n");
    yesno=get();
 if(yesno==89||yesno==121) confgp(0);
 printf(" do you want to (re)config serial printer? Y or N\n");
    yesno=get();
 if(yesno==89||yesno==121) confgp(1);
 printf(" do you want these changes made permanent?Y or N\n");
    yesno=get();
 if(yesno!=89&&yesno!=121)return;
 config=fopen("CONFTW.DAT","w+");/* this takes place of rewind*/
 for(i=0;i<KONFIG;i++)fprintf(config,"%d ",cnfig[i]);
 fprintf(config,"%d %d %d %d %d %d %d\n",
 flagi,flagt,flags,flagho,flagin,flagot,flaga);
 fclose(config);
 clearh();
 margin();
 menu();
 colno();
 return;
 }


 main(argc,argv)
 int argc;
 char *argv[];
 {
 char *chr,ch;
 int chri,chro,tab=8,pos,tabs=8,printer;
 register int i;
 /* screen codes- hex
    adm 3a conventions-default-
    7   beep
    C   cursor rt
    D   return
       17    clear to end of scr
       18    clear to end of line(24 decimal)
       1E    home
```

```
     1A    clear and home (26 decimal)
esc  =          row+20H,col+20H position
esc  E    insert line
esc  R    delete line
esc  A    display lower case as lower case,i.e. cancel esc-G
esc  G    lower case as Greek */
/* initialize*/
#ifdef DESMET
scr_setup();
#endif
  config=fopen("CONFTW.DAT","r+");if(config==0)confg();
    else
      {for(i=0;i<KONFIG;i++)
      fscanf(config,"%d",&(cnfig[i]))   ;
      fscanf(config,"%d %d %d %d %d %d %d",
      &flagi,&flagt,&flags,&flagho,&flagin,&flagot,&flaga);}
  fclose(config);

  fo=fopen("lst:","w");
  fi=open("con:",O_RDWR);
  strcpy(tline,
"1...5....0....5....0....5....0....5....0....5....0....5....0....5....0....5...."
);
  margin();
  newlp=newlc; newls=&(newlc[3]);
  newl=newlp;

  fo=fopen("LST:","w");/* default to LPT, CON:=CRT: */
  if(fo==NULL)fo=fopen("LPT:","w");
  if(fo==NULL) {printf(" trouble opening LST\n");}
  clearh();
  cursor(1,coln);
/*process  parameters */
  for(i=1;i<argc;i++){
    chrr=argv[i];
/*   ch=argv[i][1]; printf(" parameter=%s,%c%c\n",argv[i],ch,*chrr);*/
    if( *chrr=='-'){
    for(chrr++;*chrr!='\0';chrr++){
```

```
      switch(*chrr){
      case 'I':
        flagi=1;
        incr();
        break;
      case 'S':
        flags=1;
        fo=fopen("com1:","w");
        newl=newls;
        break;
      case 'P':
        ;
        break;
      case 'C':
        confg();
        break;
      default:
        argc=0;
        printf(" illegal option %c\n",*chr);
        break;
      }/*END SWITCH*/
    }/*END FOR*/
  } /* end if */
  }/*END WHILE*/
    for(i=0;i<3;i++) newlc[i]=cnfig[7+i];
    menu();
    colno();
/* configure for serial printer*/
  if(flags) newl=newls;
/* now process input*/
/* reserved control inputs:
   ^] screendump, if implemented-never gets here
   ^A add ho bit toggle- initially off
   ^B accept filename to output to
   ^F accept filename to obtain input from
   ^E incremental mode toggle-initially off
   ^D ^Zexit code (warm boot)
   del,backspace= eliminate chr if not incremental mode
```

```
^G clear line
^I tab (default=8 spaces)
^H BACKSPACE
^J R.C.
^T TOGGLE TAB AT COL. AND SET TAB MODE TO <COL.
^P RESET DEFAULT TAB TO INPUT SPACES
^O overstrike- caveat: can mess up coln.
^S toggle serial/parallel
^R set right margin- merely rings bell when equalled or exceeded
^L set left margin
^K reconfigure terminal/ports
*/


cursor(3,1);
while ( (chri=get()) != 04){/* ^D=04*/
if(isascii(chri))putchar(chri);/* display on screen, if appropriate*/
if(coln>=rmargin) putchar(BELL);
switch (chri){
case 1:
   flagho=  flagho ? 0 : 1 ;
   break;
case 2: /*readin filename,open as fo,write to it*/
   flagot=  flagot ? 0 : 1 ;
   if(flagot){filen(fileo);/* unbuffered i/o bad for files*/
       diskout= fopen(fileo ,"w");
     if(diskout==NULL)printf(" open error,file=%s",fileo);
          }
   else {i=fclose(diskout);printf(" close %d",i);}
   break;
case 6:/* readin filename, open as fi. on eof (^z or -1)
     return to stream input */
   flagin=  flagin ? 0 : 1 ;
   if(flagin)filen(filei);
   diskin= fopen(filei,"r");
   if(diskin==NULL)printf(" open error");
   break;
case 5:
   /*send incremental toggle*/
```

```
    /*tp1 on serial needs none*/
    flagi= flagi ? 0 : 1 ;
    incr();
    break;
case 11:
    confg();
    break;

case 10:
case 13:
    /* flush buffer output linefeed, cr */
    if(!flagi)
    { strncpy( &(line[coln-1]),newl,3);coln++;
/*    line[coln-1]=10;line[coln]=13;line[++coln]='\0';*/
      if(flagot){/* write to disk file*/
        cursor(16,1);printf("%s",line);
        fprintf(diskout,"%s",line);
          }
      else
        {/* write to line printer*/
        writelb(fo,line,coln-1);

        };
    }/* end non-incremental */
    else   {if(!flagot){length=strlen(newl);
        writelb(fo,newl,length);}
      else{
        i=fputs(newl ,diskout);
        if(i==EOF){printf(" fputs error");exit(0);}
          }
        }
      /*fall thru */
case 7:/* clear line*/
    clearh();/* clear and home*/
    menu();
    margin();
    colno();
    break;
```

```
case -1:
case 26:
  if(coln>1)writelb(fo,line,coln);/*GET INPUT CONSOLE*/
  if(flagin){ flagin=0;fo=open("con:",O_RDONLY);break;}
  else
  { /*^z taken to mean end of input */
    break;}
case 127:
case 8 :
  if(coln>1)coln--;
  cursor(3,coln);
  colno();
  break;
case 19: /* serial parallel */
  flags= flags ? 0 : 1 ;
  if(flags)fo=fopen("com1:","w");
    else fo=fopen("lst","w");
  newl= flags ? newls : newlp ;
  break;
case 15: /* overstrike, i.e., backspace */
  outpt(BACKSP);
  coln--;cursor(3,coln);colno();
  break;
case 16: /* set tab value in spaces*/
  cursor(20,1);
  printf("expand tab (spaces)=");
  fscanf(fi,"%d",&(tabs));
  cursor(3,coln);
  break;
case 12:/*set lmargin*/
  lmargin=coln;
  break;
case 18:rmargin=coln;
  break;
case 9: /*tab*/
  if(flagt) {/* jump to next tab stop*/
      chr=&( tline[coln]);
      chrr=index(chr,'T');
```

```
              if(!chrr)break;
              tab= chrr - chr+1;
              }
        else tab=tabs;
          for(i=0;i<tab;i++) outpt(SPACE);                    break;
      case 20: /* set tab*/
        pos=coln-1;
        if(tline[pos]!='T') /* set tab if not there*/
        { flagt=1; tline[pos]='T';/* set tab*/break;}
        else{/* clear tab*/
          tline[pos]='.'; i=coln % 5 ;
          if(!i)
          {
          i= coln % 10;
          tline[pos]= i ? '5' : '0' ;
          }/* end if*/
        /*unset flagt?*/ flagt=0;
          for(i=0;i<80;i++)
             flagt=(tline[i]=='T')? 1 :flagt  ;
          break;}/*end else*/

    default:
      if(flagho)chri=chri+128;
      outpt(chri);
      break;
    }   /*end Switch*/
  }/*end while*/

if(flagot){/* buffered i/o*/
    cursor(0,1); printf(" closing %s",fileo);
    /*debug*/ fprintf(diskout," typewriter I baker");
    i= fclose(diskout);
    printf(" close file=%s,%d",fileo,i);
    }
clearh();
exit(0);
}/* end MAIN*/
```

```
outpt(chr)int chr;
{int err;
char chrr[3]={'\000','\000','\000'};

/* output if immediate, else put in buffer */
if(flagi){/* incremental output*/
    if(flagot)err= putc(chr,fo);
    else   {err=putc(chr,fo);}
  coln++;
  if(err==-1)printf(" error on incr. output\n");
   }
else
  {/*place in buffer first column */
  line[coln-1]=chr;coln++;
  if(coln>80) {puts(" line buffer overflow");return;}
  }
colno();return;
}


colno(){
/* output column number on screen*/
char info[80]; int length;
info[0]='\0';
cursor( 0,1);
length=strlen(info);
if(flagi) {sprintf(&(info[length])," incremental");length=strlen(info);}
if(flagho){sprintf(&(info[length])," ho bit");length=strlen(info);}
if(flagin){sprintf(&(info[length])," input from %s",filei);length=strlen(info);}
if(flagot){sprintf(&(info[length])," output to %s",fileo);length=strlen(info);}
if(flagt){sprintf(&(info[length])," tabset");length=strlen(info);}

  else
  {if(flags&&(!flagot))sprintf(&(info[length])," serial     ");
  else
    if(!flagot) sprintf(&(info[length])," parallel ");};
printf(" column=%d %s lmargin=%d",coln,info,lmargin);
cursor(3,coln);
return;
```

```
}

filen(buffer)
char *buffer;
{
cursor( 20,1);
printf(" filename=");
fscanf(fi,"%s",buffer);
cursor(3,coln);
return;
}


incr(){   /* toggle increm. mode command to printer if
        its nec8023A  on  parallel*/
char strng[4];int nwrite,length,index;
if(flagot)return;/*ignore if file output*/
/*serial if flags=1, parallel if zero*/
index= (flags? 21:13) + (flagi? 0:4);
for(length=0;length<4;length++){strng[length]=cnfig[index+length];
        if(!strng[length])break;}
if(length>0){nwrite=writelb(fo,strng,length);
        cursor(22,1);
printf(" incremental print toggled\n");
        }
margin();
return;
}


menu(){
cursor(10,1);
/*PUTS SEEMS TO DO NEWLINE*/
puts(" menu: contrl-");
puts(" A- ho bit toggle, B outfile F infile E incr. toggle");
puts(" D end G line clear T toggle tab mode P tab space ct ");
puts(" S serial/parallel toggle O overstrike prev. Z endfile");
puts(" K reconfigure L leftmargin R rightmargin set");
puts(" typewriter copyright 1984 Louis Baker");
cursor(2,1);
```

```
puts(tline);
return;
}

margin(){
int j;
register i;
coln=1;
if(lmargin==1)return;
/*clear to cursor,output */
for (i=0;i<(lmargin-1);i++) {
    line[i]=SPACE;
    outpt(SPACE);/* nb- outpt incr. coln*/
    }
colno();return;
}


confgt(){
int yesno;
/*------terminal control codes-------
0-1 clear(&home code for screen) 1 is 0 if 1 chr code
cursor positioning-
2 typically ESC=27
3  = 61 for ADM3A
4 line+  (32)
5 coln+  (32)  NB- CAVEAT purdum gives -1,31 instead!
*/
/*CAVEAT- CONFIGURATIONS 2,3 UNTESTED- NO GUARANTEES,
   ESPECIALLY FOR CURSOR POSITIONING! BASED ON
   TABLE P.110 PURDUMS BOOK WHICH IS ERRONEOUS FOR
   ADM3A (=ADM3?). ASSUME his col,row numbers start
   from 1 (mine start from 0, so adders are 1 more than his*/
printf(" select printer number from menu\n");
printf(" 0=not in menu,setup by hand\n");
printf(" 1=KAYPRO,ADM3A\n");
printf(" 2= Heath,Zenith\n");
printf(" 3=SOROC,Televideo\n");
```

```
printf(" 4=IBM PC, BIOS CALLS\n");
printf(" 5=ANSI.SYS");
/* for IBM PC, rewrite routines clearh and cursor
to do BIOS 10H interrupt; see, e.g., Abel's book
Assembler for the IBM PC,Reston Publ.,p.101 */
fscanf(fi,"%d",&yesno);
switch(yesno)
{
case 4:
case 1: return;
case 2: cnfig[0]=27;cnfig[1]=69;
  cnfig[3]=27;cnfig[4]=89;cnfig[5]=32;cnfig[6]=32;
  break;
case 3: cnfig[0]=27;cnfig[1]=42;
  cnfig[3]=27;cnfig[4]=61;cnfig[5]=32;cnfig[6]=32;
  break;
case 5:
  flaga=1;
  break;
case 0:
default:
printf(" input integer for screenclear\n");
  fscanf(fi,"%d",&(cnfig[0]));
printf(" enter 2nd code for screenclear or else 0\n");
  fscanf(fi,"%d",&(cnfig[1]));
printf("enter 2 integer cursor position seq\n");
  fscanf(fi,"%d%d",&(cnfig[2]),&(cnfig[3]));
printf("enter 2 digits added to row and col\n");
  fscanf(fi,"%d%d",&(cnfig[4]),&(cnfig[5]));
}
return;
}


confgp(printer) int printer;{/* printer=0 parallel, else 1 serial*/
int i,j,k,l,m;
/*--------printer control codes-----------
      parallel   serial
cr/lf,cr,lf/cr    7-9      10-12
```

incr toggle:

| | on | 13-16 | 21-24 |
| | off | 17-20 | 25-28 |

AGAIN, FIRST 0 IN STRINGS TERMINATES SEQUENCE*/

```
printf(" type integer cr/lf seq integer/line term. by 0\n");
for(i=0;i<3;i++){
    printf(" enter chr %d\n",i+1);
    fscanf(fi,"%d",&j);
    cnfig[i+7+printer*3]=j;
    if(!j)break;
    }/* end for to input cr/lf seq. */
printf(" end line send sq: %d %d %d\n",
cnfig[7+printer*3],cnfig[printer*3+8],cnfig[printer*3+9]);
for(i=0;i<3;i++) newlc[i]=cnfig[7+printer*3+i];
/* INCREMENTAL TOGGLE*/
for(m=0;m<2;m++){
    if(m==0)printf(" type incrm. on");
    else     printf(" type incrm. off seq.");
     for(i=0;i<4;i++)
     {fscanf(fi,"%d",&j);
     l=m?17:13;
     cnfig[printer*8+i+l]=j;
     if(j==0)break;
     }/*end for i on/off */
    }/* end for m to input cr/lf seq. */
return;
}
/*MACHINE DEPENDENT SECTION*/

putn(numb) int numb;
{
/* numb 0-99 assumed*/
int hi,lo;
hi=numb/10;
lo=numb % 10;
if(hi)putchar(hi+48);
putchar(lo+48);
```

```
}

cursor(row,co)
/*row,column*/
int row,co;
{
if(!flaga)
{
#ifdef DESMET
scr_rowcol(row,co);
#endif
#ifdef TURBOC
gotoxy(row,co);
#endif
#ifdef CPM
putchar(cnfig[2]);putchar(cnfig[3]);
putchar(cnfig[4]+row);putchar(cnfig[5]+co);
#endif
}
else
   {/* ansi cmd seq.*/
   putchar(ESC);putchar('[');putn(row);putchar(';');
   putn(co);putchar('H');/* f or H */
   }
return;
}

clearh(){
if(flaga)
   {
   putchar(ESC);putchar('[');putchar('2');putchar('J');
   cursor(1,1);
   }
else
   {
#ifdef DESMET
scr_clr();
#endif
```

```
#ifdef TURBOC
clrscr();
#endif
#ifdef CPM
putchar(cnfig[0]);putchar(cnfig[1]);
#endif
  }
return;
}

int get(){
int x;/* ff=255*/
#ifdef DESMET
while((x=scr_csts())==0){};
#endif
#ifdef TURBOC
x=getch();
#endif
/* bdos returns 0 if chr not input- we must do the polling*/
return(x);
}

writelb(stream,string,count)
int count; char *string;
FILE *stream;
{
if(stream)write(stream,string,count);

else
   fprintf(stdprn,"%s",string);
}
/*END MACHINE DEPENDENT SECTION*/
```

CHAPTER 14

LU Decomposition Revisited

Chapter Objectives

In this chapter we will:

– present a more efficient version of the lufact() program included in *C Tools* which is more suitable to the typical C implementation

Introduction

The version of lufact() in *C Tools* was based upon the LINPACK program. This program was adapted to the FORTRAN method of storing array elements, and used a number of subroutine calls to BLAS support routines, incurring the overhead of those calls. We present here a replacement for this routine, more suited to a C implementation.

There is no test problem given. Simply re-run the programs of Chapter 3 of *C Tools* with the new version of lufact().

Program Details

The Gaussian elimination in an LU decomposition can be viewed as three nested loops. As discussed in Dongarra, et al., there are many ways to order the indices of these loops. Depending upon machine architecture, whether arrays are stored by columns as in FORTRAN (the first index varying most rapidly, i.e., A(1,1) is followed by A(2,1) in storage) or by rows as in C (C[0][0] followed by C[0][1]), etc. it can be useful to re-arrange the ordering of the loops. In the LU decomposition, this is complicated somewhat by the need to pivot, i.e., exchange rows.

The version of lufact() presented here should be more suitable to implementation in C than the previous version, which was based upon a loop ordering suitable for FORTRAN. In addition, the overhead of the BLAS linear algebra subroutine calls has been elimnated. This version of lufact() should therefore be faster than the one present in *C Tools* . No changes are needed in any of the routines which are used with lufact().

Reference

J. J. Dongarra, F. G. Gustavson, and A. Karp, *SIAM Review*, **26**,91, 1984.

Program Listing

(Listing begins next page.)

```
#include "ftoc.h"

/*
routines for linear systems processing via LU factorization
(from "More C Tools for Scientists and Engineers" by L. Baker)
```

PURPOSE:

perform LU factorization

CONTENTS:

```
lufact(a,coln,n,pivot,info)
    Factor an n by n matrix contained in type float array a
    which is dimensioned a[m][coln]. pivot is an integer array
    of size n which will contain pivoting information to be used
    by later routines.  info is pointer to an integer which returns
    0 if all is well, otherwise the row in which problems occurred.
```

DEPENDENCIES:

requires header file ftoc.h and lus.c routines

Modified from LU.C for improved access of matrix values
*/

```
lufact (a,coln,n,pivot,info)
float *a;
int coln,n,*pivot,*info;
{
    int i,j,k,l,kp1,nm1,last,*piv,ip,kp;
    float t,q;
    *info=0;
    nm1=n-1;
    piv=pivot;
    DOFOR(k,n)*(piv++)=k;
    if (nm1>=1)
    {/*nontrivial pblm*/
```

```
DOFOR(k,nm1)
{
   kp1=k+1;
   /*partial pivoting ROW exchanges-search over column*/
   /* in FORTRAN, the increment would be 1 not n in ismax call*/
t=0.;
l=k;
for(i=kp1;i<n;i++)
   {
   q=abs( a INDEX(i ,k));
   if(q>t)
      {
      t=q;
      l=i;
      }
   }
   pivot [k]=l;
   if (a INDEX(l,k)!=0.)
   {/*nonsingular pivot found*/
      if(l!=k)
      {/*interchange needed*/
   for(i=k;i<n;i++)
      {
         t=a INDEX(l,i);
         a INDEX(l,i)=a INDEX(k,i);
         a INDEX(k,i)=t;
         }
      }
   /* elementary row op */
   q=1./a INDEX(k,k);
      for(i=kp1;i<n;i++)
   {
      t=   -q*a INDEX(i,k);
      a INDEX(i,k) = t;
   for(j=kp1;j<n;j++)/*column*/
      {
      a INDEX(i,j) += t * a INDEX(k,j);
      }
```

```
        }
     }
        else /*pivot singular*/
        { *info=k;}
    }/*main loop over k*/
}/*if nontrivial*/
    pivot [nm1]=nm1;
    if (a INDEX(nm1,nm1) ==0.0)*info=nm1;
    return;
}
```

CHAPTER 15

Roman Numerals

Chapter Objectives

In this chapter, we will:

– convert a natural number to its representation as a string as a Roman numeral

Program

As the final chapter to this book, I present a slightly less serious but none-theless useful program to determine the Roman numeral corresponding to a given natural number (integer greater than zero). The number, to be repre-sented in ASCII, must be less than 9000 as one would need an overscored character to represent $\overline{M}$, etc., otherwise. The reader might enjoy develop-ing a version which relaxes this restriction. An such extension would depend upon the capabilities of the printer and computer involved.

Program Listing And Test Problem Output

(Listing begins next page.)

```
/* print integer in Roman form

from More C Tools for Scientists and Engineers by L. Baker
*/

#define NULL '\000'

main()
{
int in;
char out[50];
while(1){
scanf("%d",&in);printf("echo %d\n",in);
roman(in,out);printf("roman: %s\n",out);
alpha(in,out);printf("alpha: %s\n",out);
}
}

char wh[7]="IVXLCDM";
/* no D-overbar, M-overbar*/
roman( in,out)
int in; char out[];
{
int num,i,j,div,k,l;
char *point,chr;
num=in;
point=out;
*point=NULL;
div=1000;
if(num>3999)
   {printf(" warn %d too big\n",num);
   num=num%4000;
   }
for(k=3;k>=0;k--)
   {
   i=num/div;   num=num%div;
    switch (i)
      {
```

```
        case 0 : break;
        case 5 : *point= wh[2*k+1];
             point++;
             break;
        case 9 : *point= wh[2*k];
             point++;
             *point=wh[2*k+2];
             point++;
             break;
        case 4 : *point=wh[2*k];point++;
              *point=wh[2*k+1];point++;
              break;
        default:
             if(i>5)
                {
                *point=wh[2*k+1];
                i-=5;point++;
                }
             for(l=0;l<i;l++){
                    *point=wh[2*k];point++;
                    }
          }
      div=div/10;
       }
    *point=NULL;
    }

    alpha(in,out)
    int in;char *out;
 A {
    char *pointer;
    int kt,i,j,div,l;
    pointer=out;
    i=in;
    if(i<27) ß *(pointer++)= i+64;   ß
    else
 C {
       j=i;div=1;
```

```
for(kt=0;(j/=26)>0;kt++)div*=26;
for(j=0;j<=kt;j++)
  {
    l=i/div;
    i%=div;
    *pointer= l+64;
    pointer++;
    div/=26;
    }
  }
*(pointer)=NULL;return;
}
```

```
roman
5
echo 5
roman: V
alpha: E
4
echo 4
roman: IV
alpha: D
6
echo 6
roman: VI
alpha: F
100
echo 100
roman: C
alpha: CV
99
echo 99
roman: XCIX
alpha: CU
101
echo 101
roman: CI
alpha: CW
^C

A:\>
```

Appendix

Required Header Files and Programs from *C Tools*

Complex.h

FtoC.h

vector.C

matrix.C

invm.C

backsub.C (use with lufact to solve linear systems)

lus.C (support routines for invm.c, backsub.c)

```
/* COMPLEX.H header file
 * use for complex arithmetic in C
 * see MULLER.C for support functions such as
   csqrt(),clog(),cexp(),argmt(),polarxy()

from Handbook of C tools for Scientists and Engineers by L. Baker

*/

double sqrt();

struct complex { double x;
     double y;} ;
static double TP,T2,T3;/* dummy static so no conflict with other modules*/

/* for below, X,Y are complex structures, and one is returned*/

#define CMULTR(X,Y) ((X).x*(Y).x-(X).y*(Y).y)
#define CMULTI(X,Y)  ((X).y*(Y).x+(X).x *(Y).y)
/*
#define CMLT(Z,X,Y) {TP=(X.x+Y.x)*(X.y+Y.y);T2=X.x*Y.x;T3=X.y*Y.y;Z.y=
*/
#define CDRN(X,Y)  ((X).x*(Y).x+(Y).y*(X).y)
#define CDIN(X,Y)  ((X).y*(Y).x-(X).x*(Y).y)
#define CNORM(X) ((X).x*(X).x+(X).y*(X).y)
/*#define CNRM(X) (X->x*X->x+X->y*X->y)
*/
#define CDIV(z,nu,de) {TP=CNORM(de);z.x=CDRN(nu,de)/TP;z.y=CDIN(nu,de)
#define CONJG(z,X) {(z).x=(X).x;(z).y=-(X).y;}
/*#define CONJ(X) {(X).y=-(X).y}
*/
#define CMULT(z,X,Y) {(z).x=CMULTR((X),(Y)); (z).y=CMULTI((X),(Y));}
#define CADD(z,X,Y) {(z).x=(X).x+(Y).x;(z).y=(X).y+(Y).y;}
#define CSUB(z,X,Y) {(z).x=(X).x-(Y).x;(z).y=(X).y-(Y).y;}
#define CLET(to,from) {(to).x=(from).x;(to).y=(from).y;}
#define cabs(X) sqrt((X).y*(X).y+(X).x*(X).x)
#define CMPLX(X,real,imag) {(X).x=(real);(X).y=(imag);}
#define CASSN(to,from) {to.x=from->x;to.y=from->y;}
```

```
#define CTREAL(z,X,real) {(z).x=(X).x*(real);(z).y=(X).y*(real);}
#define CSET(to,from) {to->x=(from).x;to->y=(from).y;}
```

```
/*

header file to aid in conversion of FORTRAN code to C
(from "C Tools for Scientists and Engineers" by L. Baker)

PURPOSE:

performs in-line a number of useful chores including loops,
array subscripting, and finding minimum,maximum, and absolute value.

DEPENDENCIES:

none

USAGE:

invoke with preprocessor directive:
#include "ftoc.h"
   or
#include <ftoc.h>
 near the beginning of your program

*/


/* in-line functions for use with 2D arrays: */

/* row major order as in C  indices run 0..n-1 as in C*/
#define INDEX(i,j)  [j+(i)*coln]

/*various loop constructors */
#define DOFOR(i,to) for(i=0;i<to;i++)
#define DFOR(i,from,to) for(i=from-1;i<to;i++)
#define DOBY(i,from,to,by) for(i=from-1;i<to;i+=by)
#define DOBYY(i,from,to,by) for(i=from;i<t;i+=by)
#define DOBYYY(i,from,to) for(i=from;i<to;i++)
#define DOV(i,to,by) for(i=0;i<to;i+=by)
/* row major order as in C  indices run 1..n */
```

```
/*#define INDEX1(i,j)  [j-1+(i-1)*n]
*/
/* column major order, as in fortran: */
#define INDEXC(i,j) [i-1+(j-1)*rown]

/* usage: if a(20,30) is matrix, then
a(i,j) in C will be a INDEX(i,j) if n=30. */

/* to index vectors starting with 1 */
#define VECTOR(i) [i-1]

#define min(a,b) (((a)<(b))? (a): (b))
#define max(a,b) (((a)<(b))? (b): (a))
#define abs(x)  ( ((x)>0.)?(x):-(x))
```

```
/* vector processing routines
often simplified versions of BLAS routines for vectors
with contiguous storage

(from "C Tools for  Scientists and Engineers" by L. Baker)

CONTENTS:

dot(a,b,n)
   returns double value of dot product of two vectors a,b
   of n elements
pv(v,n)
   prints vector of n elements
mv(a,x,y,m,n)
   y=ax where a is m x n matrix
normv(v,n)
   normalize a vector (scale its length to one)
sqnor(v,n)
   square of the length of vector v of n elements
mvt(a,x,y,m,n)
   like mv except y=a^x a^ =transpose of a
resid(r,a,x,n)
   r=ax-x, a matrix all other vectors.
vs(v,s,n)
   scale vector by multiplying each element by s
vset(v,s,n)
   set vector v to scalar value s for each element
vcopy(x,y,n)
   y=x, vectors
vv(a,b,c,s,n)
   a=b+c*s, s scalar, a,b,c,vectors


DEPENDENCIES:
NONE
*/

#include "ftoc.h"
```

```
double dot(a,b,n) int n; float a[],b[];
{
int i;
double sum;
if(n<=0)return(0.);
sum=0.;
DOFOR(i,n)sum+=a[i]*b[i];
return(sum);
}

pv(v,n) int n;float v[];
{
int btm,top,i,ncol=4;
btm=0;
top=0;
while (btm<n)
    {
    top=min(btm+ncol,n);
    printf(" printing vector from %d to %d\n",btm,(top-1));
    for(i=btm;i<top;i++)printf(" %e",v[i]);
    printf("\n");
    btm+=ncol;
    }
return;
}


mv(a,x,y,m,coln) int coln,m;
float x[],y[],a[];
/* y=ax a(m,n) m rows n columns [row of length n]*/
{
int i,j,k;
float sum;
DOFOR(i,m)
   {
   sum=0.;
   DOFOR(j,coln) sum+= x[j]*a INDEX(i,j);
   y[i]=sum;
   }
```

```
return;
}

normv(v,n) int n; float v[];
{
double x,sqrt(),sqnor();
x=sqnor(v,n);
if(x!=0.)x=1./sqrt(x);
vs(v,x,n);
return;
}

double sqnor(x,n) float x[]; int n;
{
int i;
double ans;
ans=0.;
if(n<=0)return(ans);
DOFOR(i,n)ans+= x[i]*x[i];
return(ans);
}

mvt(a,x,y,m,coln) int coln,m;
float a[],x[],y[];
{
/* y= a^x  a(m,n) a m rows n columns [n elements/row]
a^ n rows m columns*/
float sum;
int i,j;
DOFOR(i,coln)
   {
   sum=0.;
   DOFOR(j,m)sum+= x[j]*a INDEX(j,i);
   y[i]=sum;
   }
return;
}
```

```
resid(a,x,y,r,n) int n;
float a[],x[],y[],r[];
{
int i;
mv(a,x,r,n,n);
DOFOR(i,n)r[i]-=y[i];
return;
}


vs(v,s,n) int n; float v[],s;
{
int i;
DOFOR(i,n)v[i]*=s;
return;
}


vset(x,s,n) int n; float s,x[];
{
int i;
DOFOR(i,n)x[i]=s;
return;
}



vcopy(x,y,n) int n; float x[],y[];
{
int i;
DOFOR(i,n)y[i]=x[i];
return;
}


vv(a,b,c,s,n) int n; float a[],b[],c[],s;
{
int i;
DOFOR(i,n) a[i]=b[i]+s*c[i];
return;
}
```

```
/* matrix & vector processing routines
(from "C Tools for Scientists and Engineers" by L. Baker)
```

CONTENTS:
  vdif(a,b,dif,n)
    vector difference of two vectors a and b
  swaprow(a,from,to,coln)   swap rows from and to of matrix a
  swapcol(a,from,to,coln) swap columns coln=# of columns

The following two routines are similar to mv()and mvt()
  in VECTOR.C Here, we process the first n columns of a
  matrix of coln columns. Previously, it was assumed n=coln. Note
  that there is one additional argument, the last.

  mvc   multiply vector by matrix
  mvct   multipy vector by transpose of matrix
  mcopy(a,aa,coln,nrow,ncol)
    copy the upper left-hand portion of one matrix, a,to another (aa).
    nrow rows and ncol columns are copied.It is assumed that
    both a and aa are dimensioned to have coln columns.

DEPENDENCIES:
ftoc.h
*/

```c
#include <ftoc.h>

vdif(a,b,dif,n) int n; float a[],b[],dif[];
{
int i;
DOFOR(i,n) dif[i]=a[i]-b[i];
return;
}

swaprow(a,from,to,coln) int from,to,coln; float a[];
{
int i;
float x;
```

```
DOFOR(i,coln)
   {
   x= a INDEX(from,i);
   a INDEX(from,i)= a INDEX(to,i);
   a INDEX(to,i)=x;
   }
return;
}

swapcol(a,from,to,coln) int from,to,coln; float a[];
{/*matrix assumed to be square=>number of rows=coln*/
int i;
float x;
DOFOR(i,coln)
   {
   x= a INDEX(i,from);
   a INDEX(i,from)= a INDEX(i,to);
   a INDEX(i,to)=x;
   }
return;
}


mvc(a,x,y,n,m,coln) int n,coln,m;
float x[],y[],a[];
/* y=ax a(m,n) */
{
int i,j,k;
float sum;
DOFOR(i,m)
   {
   sum=0.;
   DOFOR(j,n) sum+= x[j]*a INDEX(i,j);
   y[i]=sum;
   }
return;
}

mvtc(a,x,y,n,m,coln) int coln,n,m;
```

```
float a[],x[],y[];
{
/* y= a(T)x  a(n,m)*/
float sum;
int i,j;
DOFOR(i,m)
   {
   sum=0.;
   DOFOR(j,n)sum+= x[j]*a INDEX(j,i);
   y[i]=sum;
   }
return;
}


mcopy(a,aa,coln,nrow,ncol) float a[],aa[];
int coln,nrow,ncol;
/* copy upper left part of one matrix to another.
assumed matrices are float, and have same number of columns*/
{
int i,j;
DOFOR(i,nrow)
   {
   DOFOR(j,ncol) aa INDEX(i,j)=a INDEX(i,j);
   }
return;
}
```

#include "ftoc.h"

```
/*
routines for linear systems processing via LU factorization
(from "C Tools for Scientists and Engineers" by L. Baker)

PURPOSE:

invert a matrix given the LU factorization of that matrix

CONTENTS:

invm(a,coln,n,pivot,work)
     a contains LU factors of a matrix. a[m][coln], n is size of
     the actual matrix to be inverted. pivot has pivot information.
     work is a type float work array of size n.

DEPENDENCIES:

requires header ftoc.h and routines in LUS.C

*/

invm(a,coln,n,pivot,work)
int coln,n,*pivot;
float *a,*work;
{
    float t,ten;
    int i,j,k,l,kb,kp1,nm1;
    nm1=n-1;
/* no det calc.*/
/* inverse u*/
    DOFOR(k,n)
    {
      a INDEX(k,k)=t=1./ a INDEX(k,k);
      t= -t;
      sscal(k,t,&(a INDEX(0,k)),coln);
      kp1=k+1;
```

```
    if (nm1>=kp1)
    {
       DOBYYY(j,kp1,n)
       {
          t=a INDEX(k,j);
          a INDEX(k,j)=0.0;
          saxpy(k+1,t,&(a INDEX(0,k)),coln,&(a INDEX(0,j)), coln);
       }
    }

  }
/*inv(u)*inv(l)*/
    if (nm1>=1)
    {
       DOFOR(kb,nm1)
       {
          k=nm1-kb-1;
          kp1=k+1;
          DOBYYY(i,kp1,n)
          {
             work [i]=a INDEX(i,k);
             a INDEX(i,k)=0.0;
          }
          DOBYYY(j,kp1,n)
          {
             t=work [j];
             saxpy(n,t,&(a INDEX(0,j)),coln,&(a INDEX(0,k)),coln);
          }
          l=pivot [k];
          if(l!=k) sswap(n,&(a INDEX(0,k)),coln,&(a INDEX(0,l)),coln);
       }
    }
    return;
}
```

```
#include "ftoc.h"
```

```
/*
```
routines for linear systems processing via LU factorization
(from "C Tools for Scientists and Engineers" by L. Baker)

PURPOSE:

solve linear system given factorization of a matrix in a

CONTENTS:

backsub(a,coln,n,pivot,b)
   Solves system ax = b. Assumes a contains LU factors, pivot
   pivoting information. The matrix stored as a[m][coln] with the
   system to be solved n x n. Answer vector returned in b.

```
*/
```

```
backsub(a,coln,n,pivot,b)
int coln,n,*pivot;
float *a,*b;
{
    float t;
    int k,l,nm1;
    nm1=n-1;

    /* solve ly=b first*/
    DOFOR(k,nm1)
    {
        l=pivot[k];
        t=b[l];
        if(l!=k)
        {
            b [l]=b [k];
            b [k]= t;
        }
        saxpy( nm1-k,t, &(a INDEX(k+1,k)),coln,&(b[k+1]),1);
    }

    /* solve Ux=y*/
    DOFOR(l,n)
    {
        k=nm1-l;
        b [k]= b [k]/ a INDEX(k,k);
        t=-b [k];
        saxpy(k,t,&(a INDEX(0,k)),coln,b,1);
    }

    return;
}
```

```
#include "ftoc.h"
/*
```

routines for linear systems processing via LU factorization
(from "C Tools for Scientists and Engineers" by L. Baker)

PURPOSE:
support routines for LU factorization

CONTENTS:
isamax(n,sx,incx)
> Finds the location of the element of greatest absolute
> value in a vector sx of length n. Each incx-th element
> is examined (hence, if sx is a 2-D matrix, may be used
> to find largest elements in each row or column, depending
> upon whether incx is 1 or n.

saxpy(n,sa,sx,incx,sy,incy)
> Performs an elementary row operation sy= sy+sa sx where sx
> and sy are vectors and sa is a scalar. Used to subtract
> a scaled row sx from the sy row. incx,incy are as in isamax.
> Vectors of length n.

sdot(n,sx,incx,sy,incy)
> Takes the dot product of 2 vectors sx and sy, of length n.

sswap(n,sx,incx,sy,incy)
> Exchanges two vectors sx and sy. Used for row exchanges
> which occur during pivoting operation.

sscal(n,sa,sx,incx)
> Scale a vector sx= sa sx where a is a scalar and sx a vector.

sasum(n,sx,invx)
> Function type float which returns the sum of the absolute
> values of the elements of a vector.

(The above are all based upon BLAS routines.)
printm(a,coln,rown,col,row)
> Prints a 2-dimensional matrix a in readable form.

   The actual data of the form a(row,col) is stored
   within a matrix dimensioned a[rown][coln].
*/

```
int isamax(n,sx,incx)
int n,incx; float *sx;
{int maxi,ix,i;
   float temp,smax;
/*returns 1 less than corresponding FORTRAN version*/
   if (n<=0)return -1;
   if(n==1)return 0;
/* ix=0*/
   maxi=0;
   smax=abs(sx[0]);
   ix=incx;/*ix=ix+incx=incx*/
   DFOR(i,2,n)
   { temp=abs(sx[ix]);
     if (temp>smax)
     {smax=temp;
        maxi=i;
/* return ith element as max,NOT subscript a[ix] ix=i*incx*/
     }
       ix+=incx;
   }
   return maxi;
}


 saxpy (n,sa,sx,incx,sy,incy)
int n,incx,incy;
float sa,*sx,*sy;
{/*sy=sa*sx+sy*/
   int i,iy,ix;
   if(n<=0)return;
   if(sa==0.)return;

   iy=ix=0;
   if(incx<0) ix=incx*(1-n);
   if(incy<0) iy=incy*(1-n);
```

```
    DOFOR(i,n)
    {
        sy[iy]=sy[iy]+sa*sx[ix];
        iy+=incy;
        ix+=incx;
    }
    return;
}

float sdot(n,sx,incx,sy,incy)
int n,incx,incy;
float *sx,*sy;
{float stemp;
    int i,ix,iy;
    if(n<=0)return(0.);
    ix=iy=0;
    stemp=0.0;
    if(incx<0) ix=incx*(1-n);
    if(incy<0) iy=incy*(1-n);
    DOFOR(i,n)
    {
        stemp+=sy[iy]*sx[ix];
        iy+=incy;
        ix+=incx;
    }
    return stemp;
}

sswap(n,sx,incx,sy,incy)
int n,incx,incy;
float *sx,*sy;
{
    int ix,iy,i;
    float t;
    if(n<=0)return;
    ix=iy=0;
    if(incx<0) ix=incx*(1-n);
    if(incy<0) iy=incy*(1-n);
```

```
    DOFOR(i,n)
    {
        t=sx [ix];
        sx [ix]= sy [iy];
        sy [iy]=t;
        ix+=incx;
        iy+=incy;
    }
    return;
}

sscal(n,sa,sx,incx)
int n,incx; float sa,*sx;
{/*scale vector*/
    int i,nincx;

    if (n<=0) return;
    nincx=incx*n;
    DOV(i,nincx,incx)
    sx[i]=sx[i]*sa;
    return;
}

float sasum(n,sx,incx)
float *sx;
int incx,n;
{/* ssum abs values*/
    int i,nincx;
    double stemp;
    stemp=0.0;
    nincx=n*incx;
    if (n<=0)return 0.0;
    DOV(i,n,nincx) stemp=stemp+abs(sx[i]);
    return (stemp);
}
```

```
printm(a,coln,rown,col,row) int rown,row,col,coln; float a[];
{
    int i,j,btm,top,count;
    printf("\n");
    btm=top=0;
    while(btm<col)
    {
        top=min(col,(btm+8));
        printf(" printing matrix columns %d to %d\n",btm,(top-1));
        DOFOR(j,row)
        {
            for(i=btm;i<top;i++)
            {
                printf(" %e",a INDEX(j,i));
            }
            printf("\n");
        }
        btm+=8;
    }
    return;
}
```

Index